TWIN visions

TWIN TWIN visions

BORIS VALLEJO AND JULIE BELL

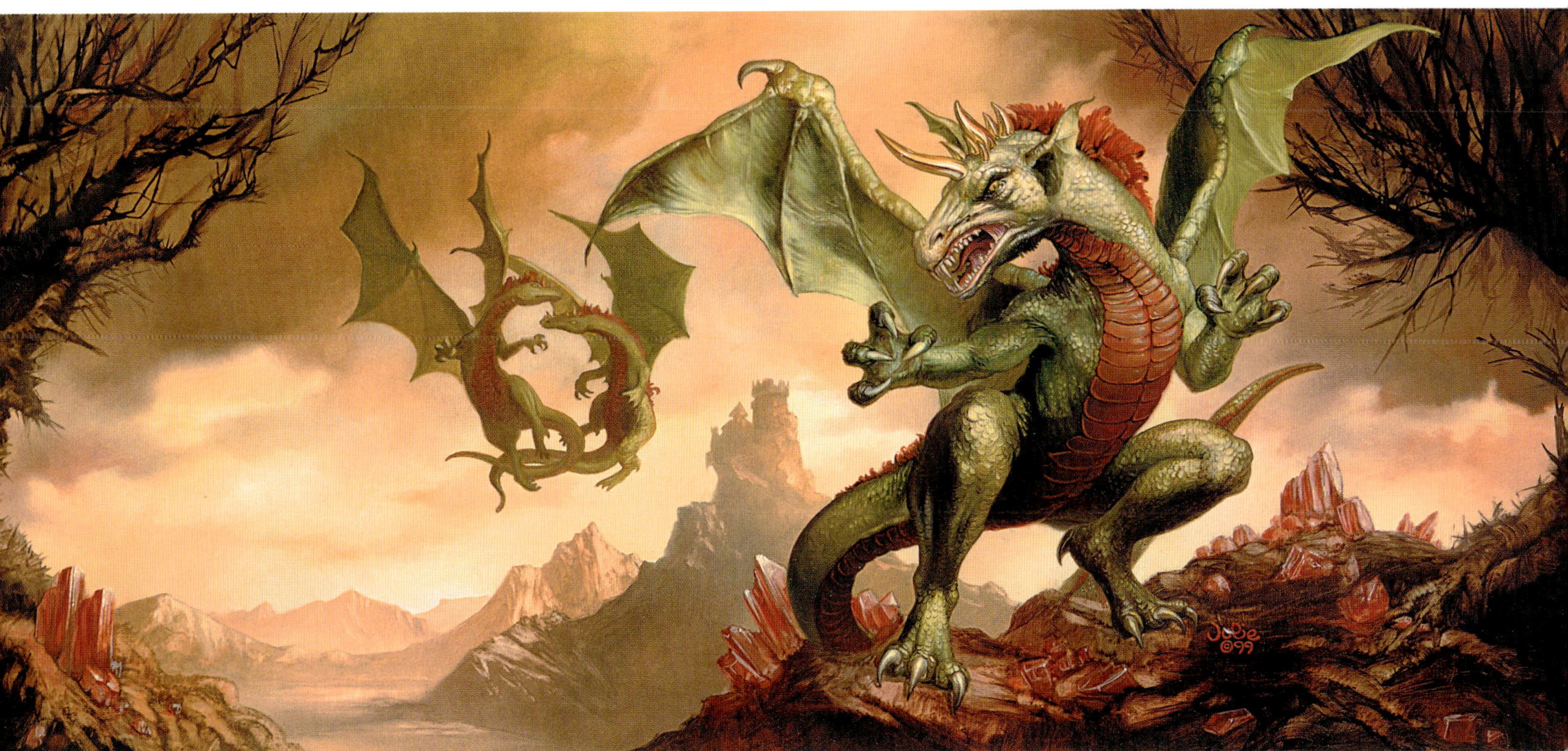

THUNDER'S MOUTH PRESS

NEW YORK

TWIN VISIONS: *The Magical Art of Boris Vallejo and Julie Bell*

Published in the United States by

Thunder's Mouth Press

An Imprint of Avalon Publishing Group Incorporated

161 William St., 16th Floor

New York, NY 10038

First published in Great Britain in 2002 by Paper Tiger

A member of **Chrysalis** Books plc

Library of Congress Cataloging-in-Publication Data

Twin visions: the magical art of Boris Vallejo and Julie Bell/by Boris Vallejo and Julie Bell.

p. cm.

ISBN 1-56025-379-7 (cloth)

1. Vallejo, Boris--Catalogs. 2. Bell, Julie--Catalogs. 3. Artist couples--United States--Catalogs.

4. Fantasy in art--Catalogs. I. Bell, Julie. II. Title.

ND237.V14 A42002

758'.98130876'074--dc21 2002018066

9 8 7 6 5 4 3 2 1

Distributed by Publishers Group West

Colour reproduction by: Classic Scan, Singapore

Printed and bound by Craft Print International Ltd, Singapore

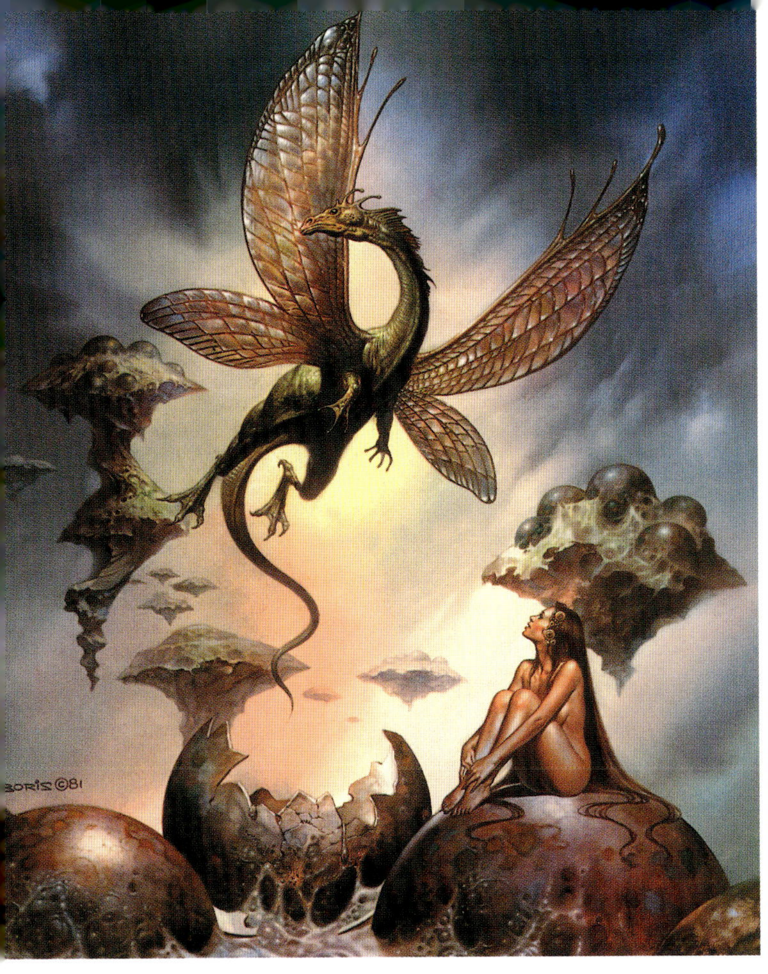

contents

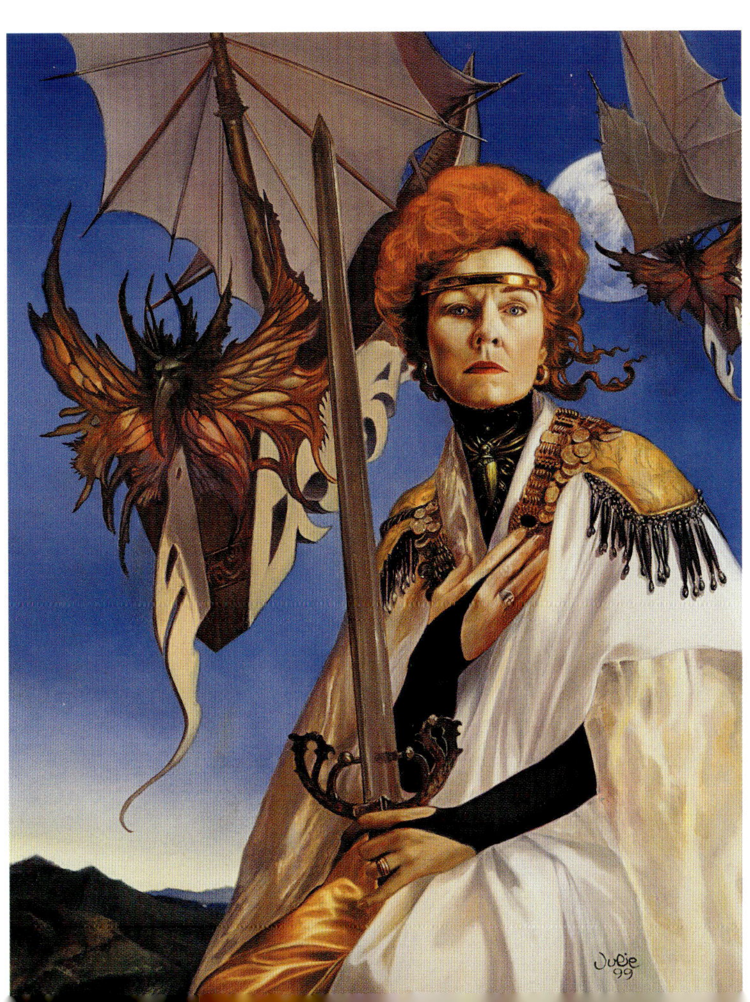

introduction

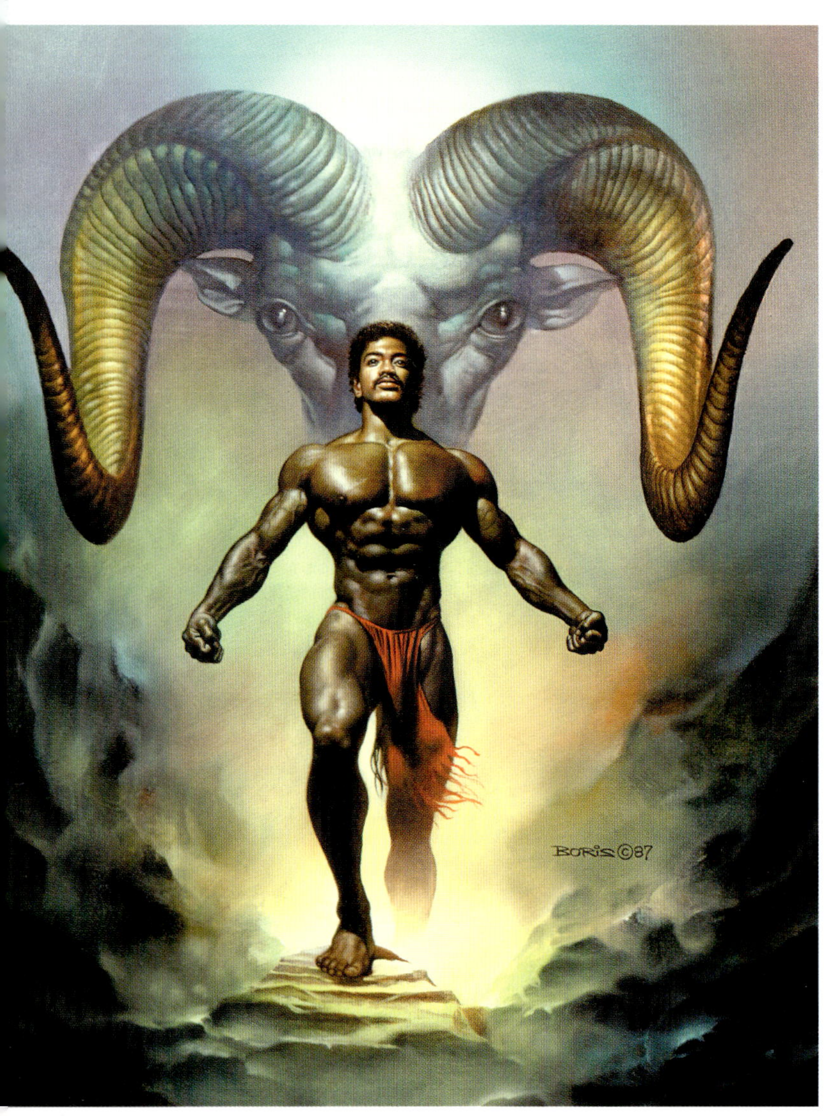

ARIES

1987, Boris *(above)*

One of a set of astrological paintings Boris produced for a calendar. He's not completely happy with it because he really wanted the picture to be half realistic and half graphic design with astrological symbols, but his publishers had their own ideas. Was he tempted to go back and change the painting later? 'No, I almost never rework paintings. I can't understand artists who do. For me once a picture is finished, that's it. I would rather move on and start a new painting.'

Boris Vallejo and Julie Bell make a rare husband and wife team, being so equally matched in their artistic talents that without a signature it is often impossible to tell which of them is responsible for a painting. They do have different tendencies. In arranging the pictures for this collection there were places where they tended to fall into separate piles, but not very often and there were always some pieces to fill the gaps. What seems to happen is that when one artist comes up with a new idea or slant, the other will soon try and match or surpass it. They have a competitive relationship, but competitive in the healthiest sense of always spurring each other on to greater efforts and new directions.

Much of the similarity comes from Julie having learned her craft from Boris, who gave her a crash course in techniques and attitudes he had carefully honed over many years as a professional. She had previously dreamed of being a professional artist but it seemed little more than a wishful dream. Time and circumstances conspired against it until she met Boris and a spark was kindled. The speed with which she absorbed his lessons was astonishing enough, but Julie is much more than a simple copyist. Armed with technique she soon proved just as capable as Boris of realizing her ideas.

Also they usually set up their easels side by side in the studio so they can discuss and comment on each other's work in progress; and they are rarely apart so they are subject to all the same influences in both life and art. They have only very rarely worked directly on a painting together, though.

The aim of this collection is to gather pictures that have not previously been published in anthology form. Well, one or two may have slipped through the net, but hopefully not. So even if you have all of Boris and Julie's other books, these pictures should be fresh to your eye. Most have appeared in some form or other – as calendars, book covers, posters and so on – because the artists usually work on commission, but only the most avid collectors of their work (of whom there are quite a few) will be familiar with much of this work.

Some artists find the thought of working to commission inhibiting but Boris and Julie are quite happy with it and usually find it possible to project something of themselves into the painting. Book jackets for example usually do have tight limits. The scene and characters are decided by the storyline and usually the publishers already have a strong idea of the overall impact they want the cover to make; but even within these limits there is usually a call for some personal touch in the figures or the setting. On the other hand with calendar illustrations they have almost a free hand. A general theme and approach will be agreed with the publisher beforehand but beyond that it is up to the artists' own imaginations.

One great advantage of working to commission is never knowing exactly what is coming along next and where it will lead. And then even the most strictly-controlled assignments often suggest new techniques or ideas that can later be explored in more personal work. These are the attitudes Boris and Julie take into their work and they perhaps explain why there is no glaring contrast between their purely commercial assignments and paintings for simple pleasure. They are as happy doing either and this pleasure in their work shines through. So step in and enjoy!

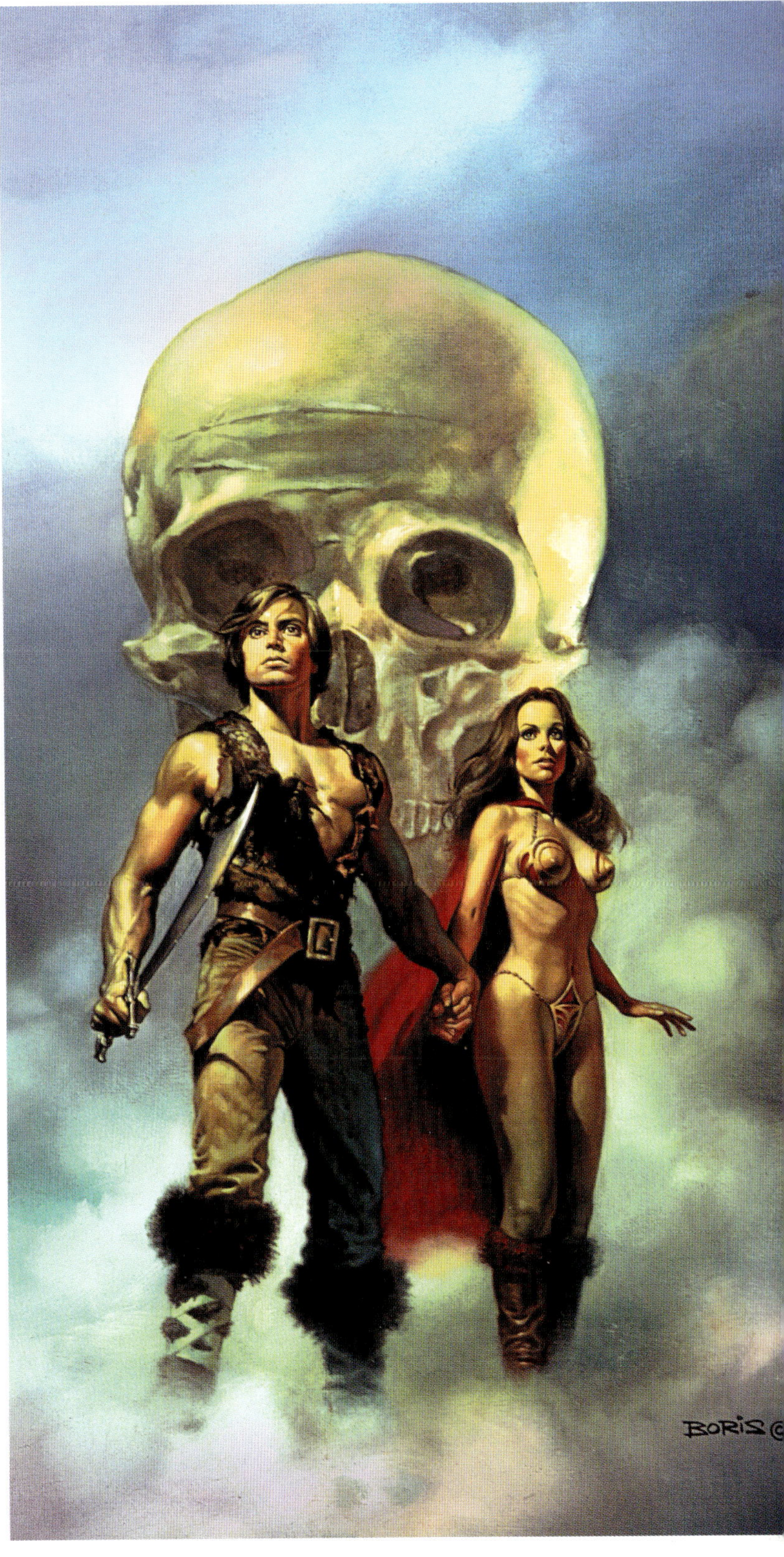

DEATH JOURNEY
1978, Boris

An example of how Boris's portrayal of women has changed. To his eye now the female on this book cover looks too timid and gentle, almost scared. She's dependent on the strong male for protection whereas now his females in a similar position are always equal partners.

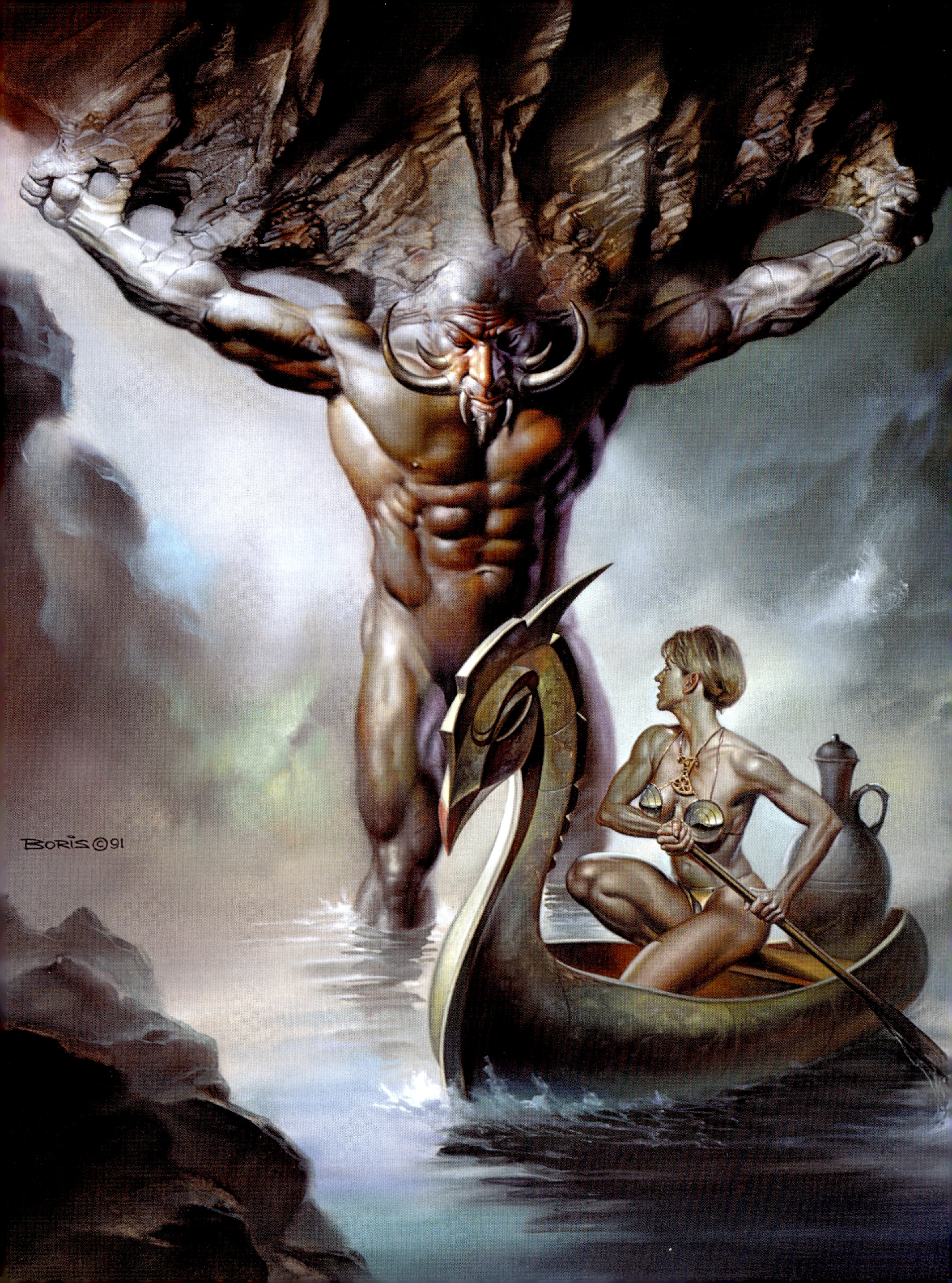
BORIS©91

chapter 1

BEAUTY AND THE BEAST

What might loosely be called 'Barbarian Fantasy' is the area in which Boris first became widely famous and it is one to which he still happily returns whenever the chance comes. He has other interests but this is a natural territory providing endless scope for exploring his favourite themes, not least of them the human form honed to perfection. Like the ancient Greek sculptors, Boris finds the perfected human form a source of endless inspiration as did William Blake, who constantly returned to the idea that the human form is the nub of everything, most famously in his *Songs of Innocence:*

> For Mercy has a human heart,
> Pity a human face,
> And Love, the human form divine,
> And Peace, the human dress.
>
> Then every man, of every clime,
> That prays in his distress,
> Prays to the human form divine,
> Love, Mercy, Pity, Peace.

Many people get uncomfortable when such comparisons are made with modern popular art such as Boris and Julie's, but this is perhaps a good place to remind them that Greek sculpture was intended to please the general people, not just an intellectual elite. Similarly with William Blake who set out to be a popular balladeer and illustrator rather than a Fine Artist. That he totally failed during his lifetime was his personal tragedy but he has been triumphantly vindicated since.

However, we're in danger of straying from the point so let's just say that in my view it is not pretentious at all to compare modern illustrators with the great figurative artists and illustrators of the past because that is often their inspiration and they are carrying the same torch, while Fine Art has taken off in a wholly different direction. Often very admirable in its own way, but something quite different.

PILLAR OF THE CAVE
1991, Boris
Boris once spent several years concentrating on mainly Greek and Roman myths till he felt he had exhausted their potential – not because he ran out of myths but because he felt he was beginning to repeat himself and it was time to move on. Also he received some flak for supposed liberties he took: 'Some people criticized the accuracy of my interpretations, but to me that is an oxymoron because how can myths be accurate? They're not history but imagination.'

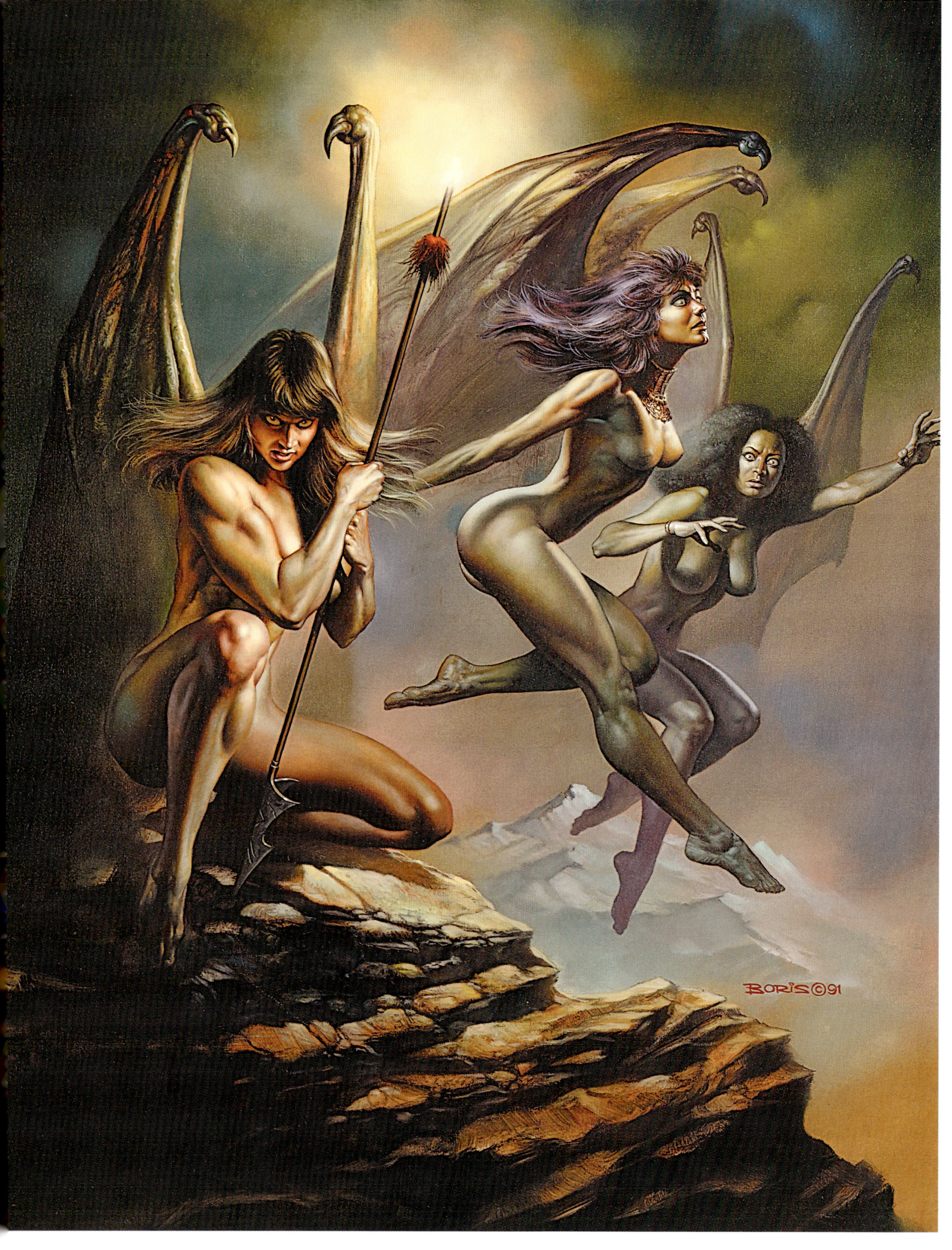
BORIS©91

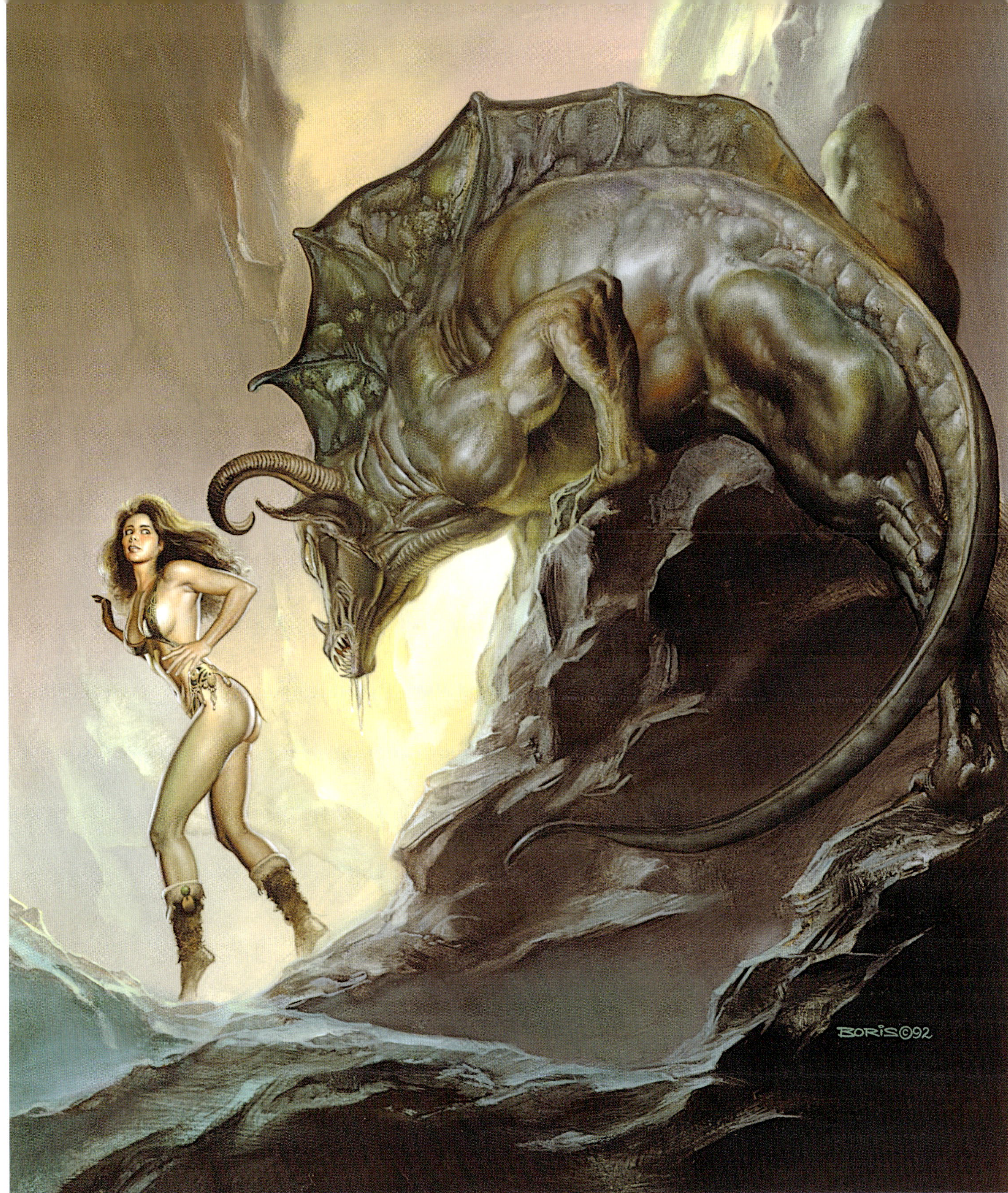

FURIES

1991, Boris *(left)*

Another picture from one of Boris's mythology calendars showing the famous revenging scourges from Greek legend. This is more how Boris likes to show women – full of power and aggression.

SUPRISE

1992, Boris *(above)*

Another variation of the Beauty and the Beast scenario. Boris mostly did this picture because he wanted to paint the model, who was a friend's secretary. Ironically this friend was himself a Playboy photographer who also tried to get her to pose for his camera, but she refused. Why she agreed to do it for Boris remains a slight but satisfying mystery.

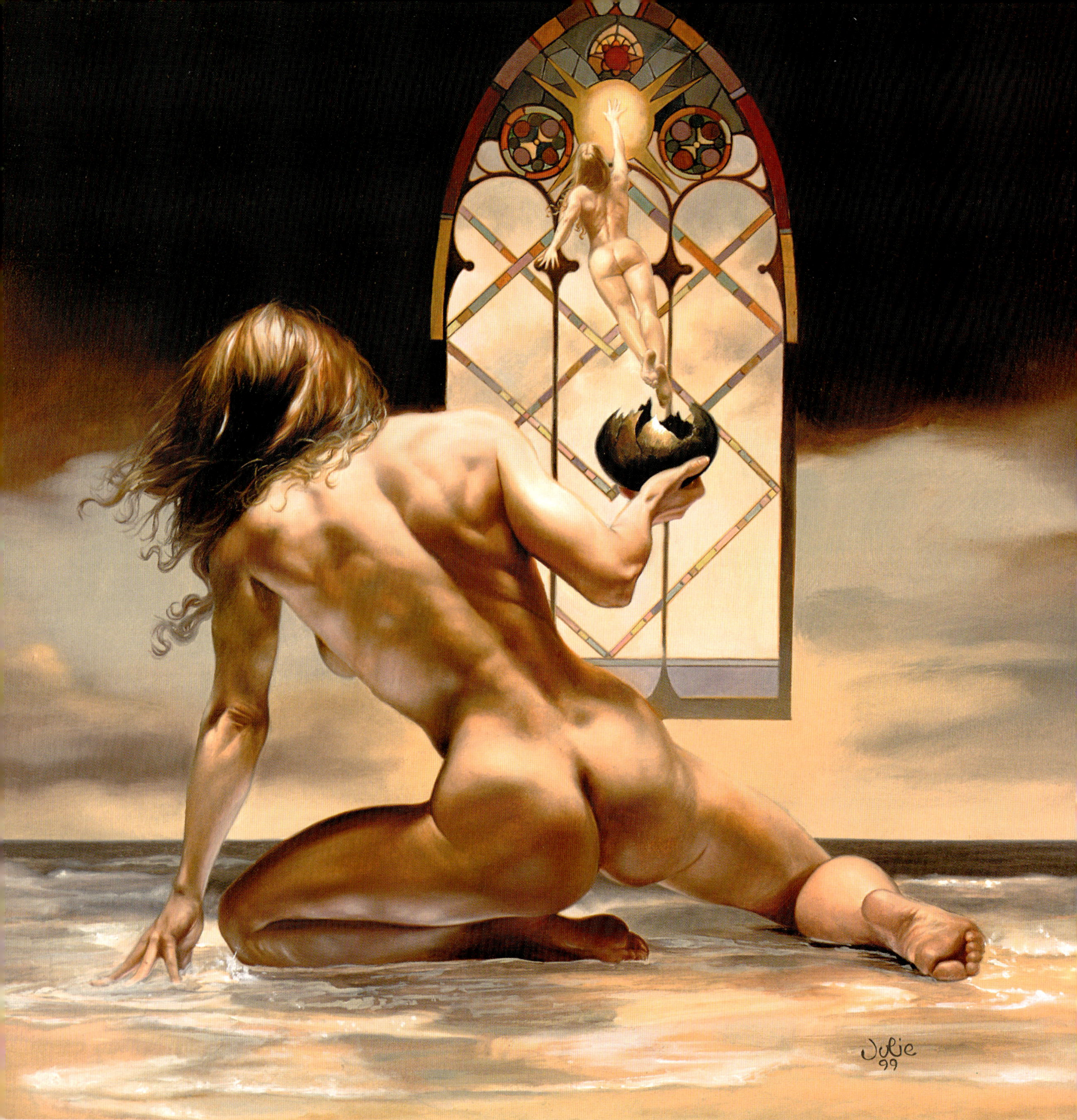

EL VITRAL

1999, Julie

A symbolic calendar painting which captures Julie's feeling that spirituality is as often to be found in untamed nature as in spiritual art, represented by the stained glass window (*el vitral* in Spanish).

THE RAINBOW

1988, Boris

Boris always enjoys painting people from different ethnic backgrounds because it adds to the whole feel of a painting. He finds though that there are strangely few female African Americans interested in modelling, so he and Julie make the most of the chances that come along, as here when these four subjects came along together. They all had beautiful physiques, perfect for this kind of painting. The rainbow suggested itself as a motif for racial harmony.

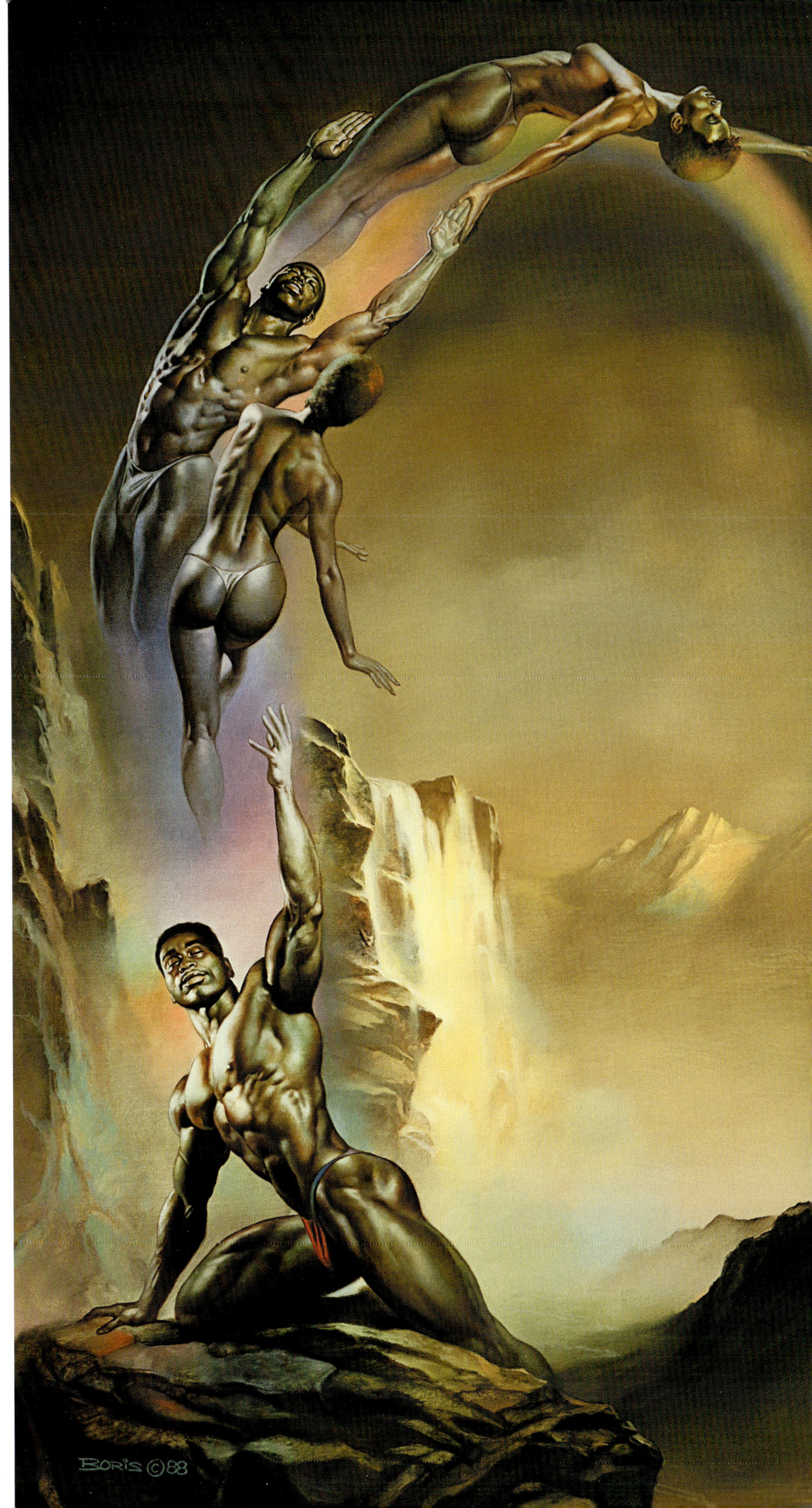

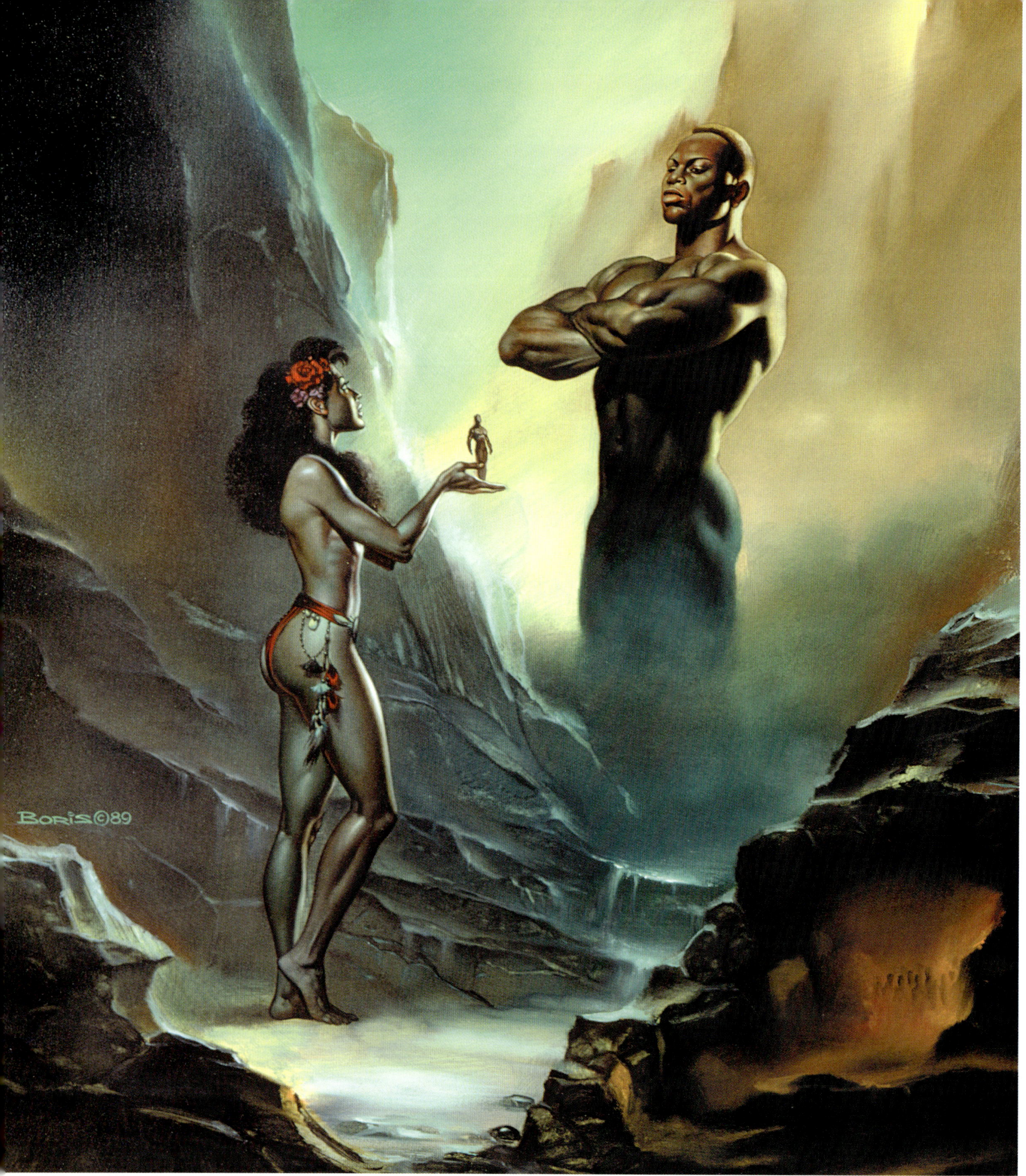

EBONY GOD

1989, Boris

An African scene from Boris's world mythology series, showing the creation of a human in the image of the gods. While doing this series Boris was impressed by the similar principles underlying the myths of all cultures.

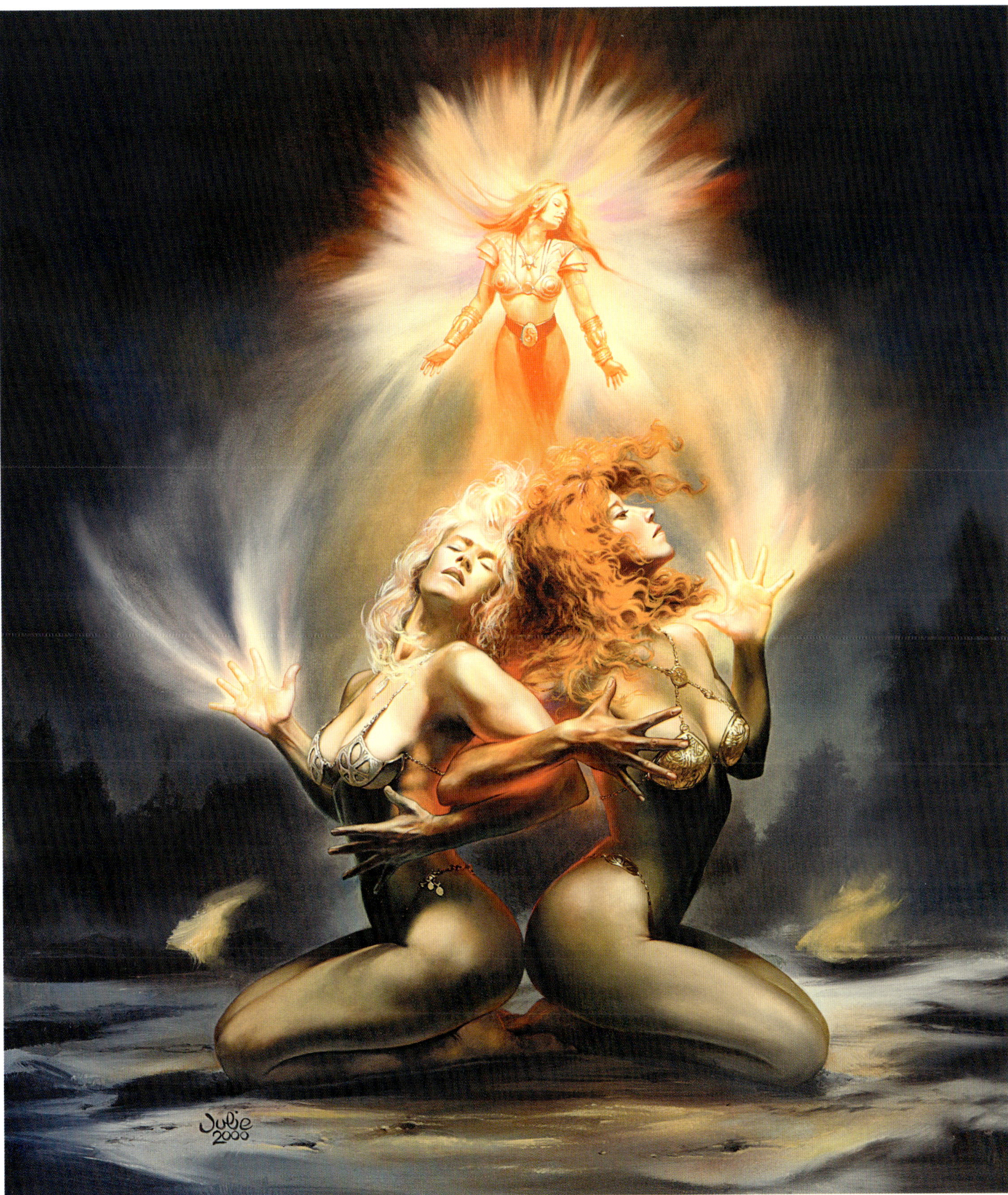

RITUAL

2000, Julie

This painting was inspired by a studio photograph of the two models who conjured this moving ritualistic dance pose suggesting some shamanistic ceremony. The hands in particular suggested the summoning of some force outside of themselves, so here in an atmospheric outdoor setting we see it taking the form of a third ethereal female somehow combining the energies of the other two. Some two years elapsed between the original photograph and the painting.

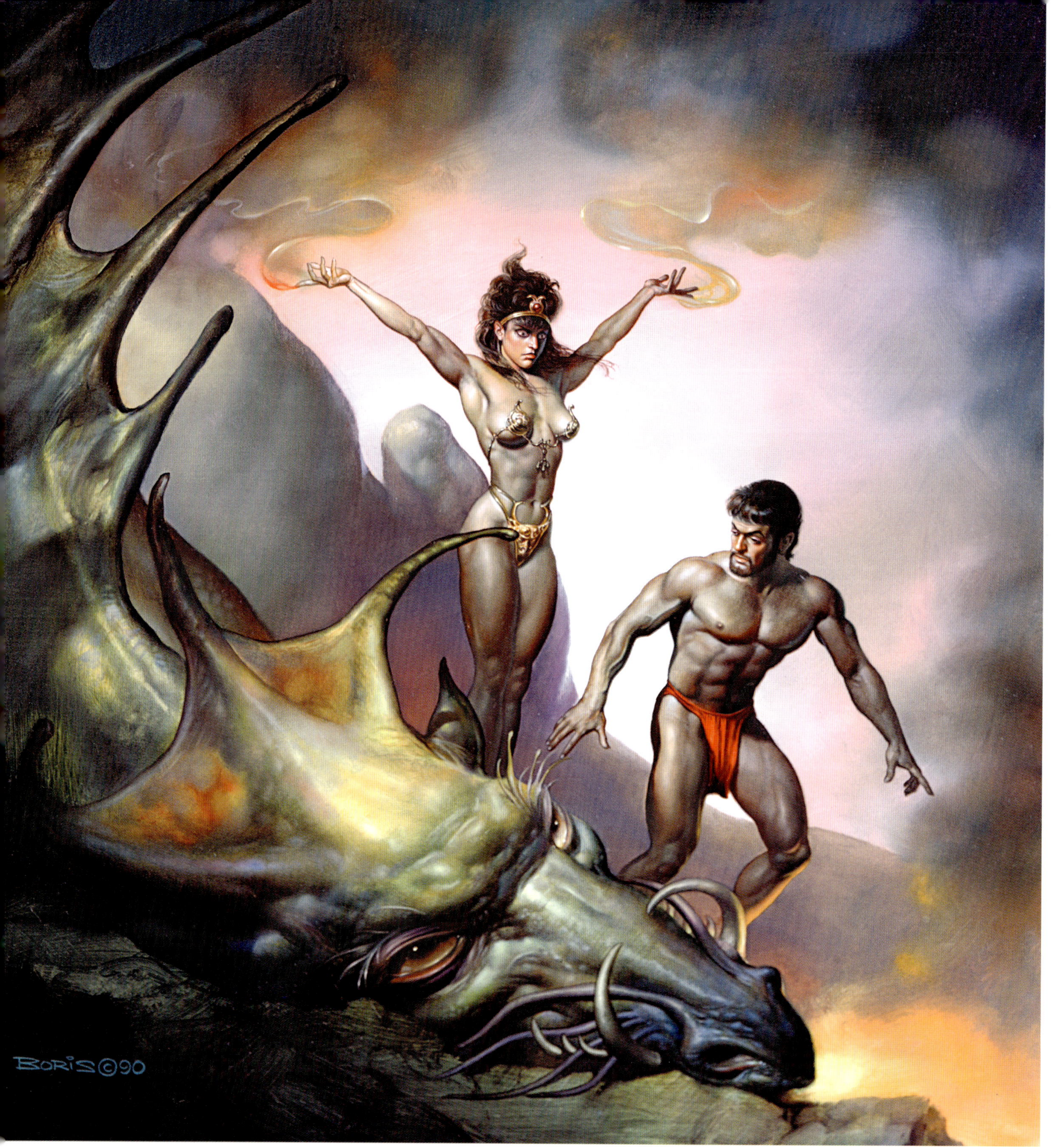

SLEEP OF THE DRAGON

1990, Boris

This shows the enchantress Medea from Greek mythology helping Jason the Argonaut sedate the dragon guarding the Golden Fleece. Some people might find his portrayal of Medea more muscular than they imagined, certainly this is not typically how she is shown, but Boris sees no reason why she should not be like this. He just likes to depict people at the height of physical fitness.

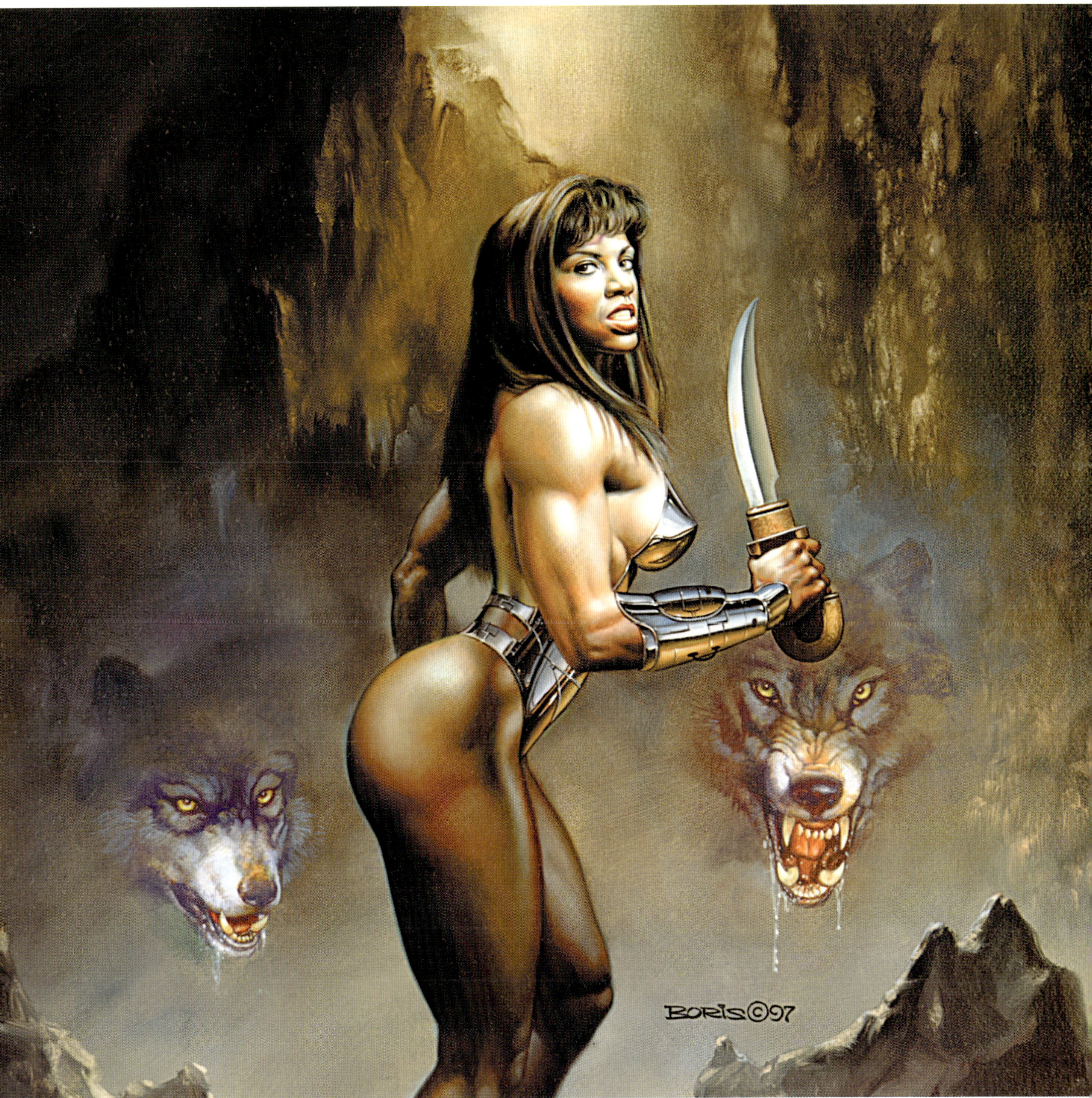

WOLF FANGS

1997, Boris

Most of Boris and Julie's calendars have no particular theme and offer the chance to paint just whatever comes to mind. This picture was inspired mainly by wanting to do justice to the model – a professional bodybuilder in the physical fitness field. Also by a love of painting animals. The attraction of wolves is that they have an ambivalent relationship with us, being known both for their occasional sweet friendliness and their ferocity. An otherworldly element is introduced here by having them materialize out of thin air, but like true wolves they have chosen a moment when their prey is looking the wrong way, despite being on the alert.

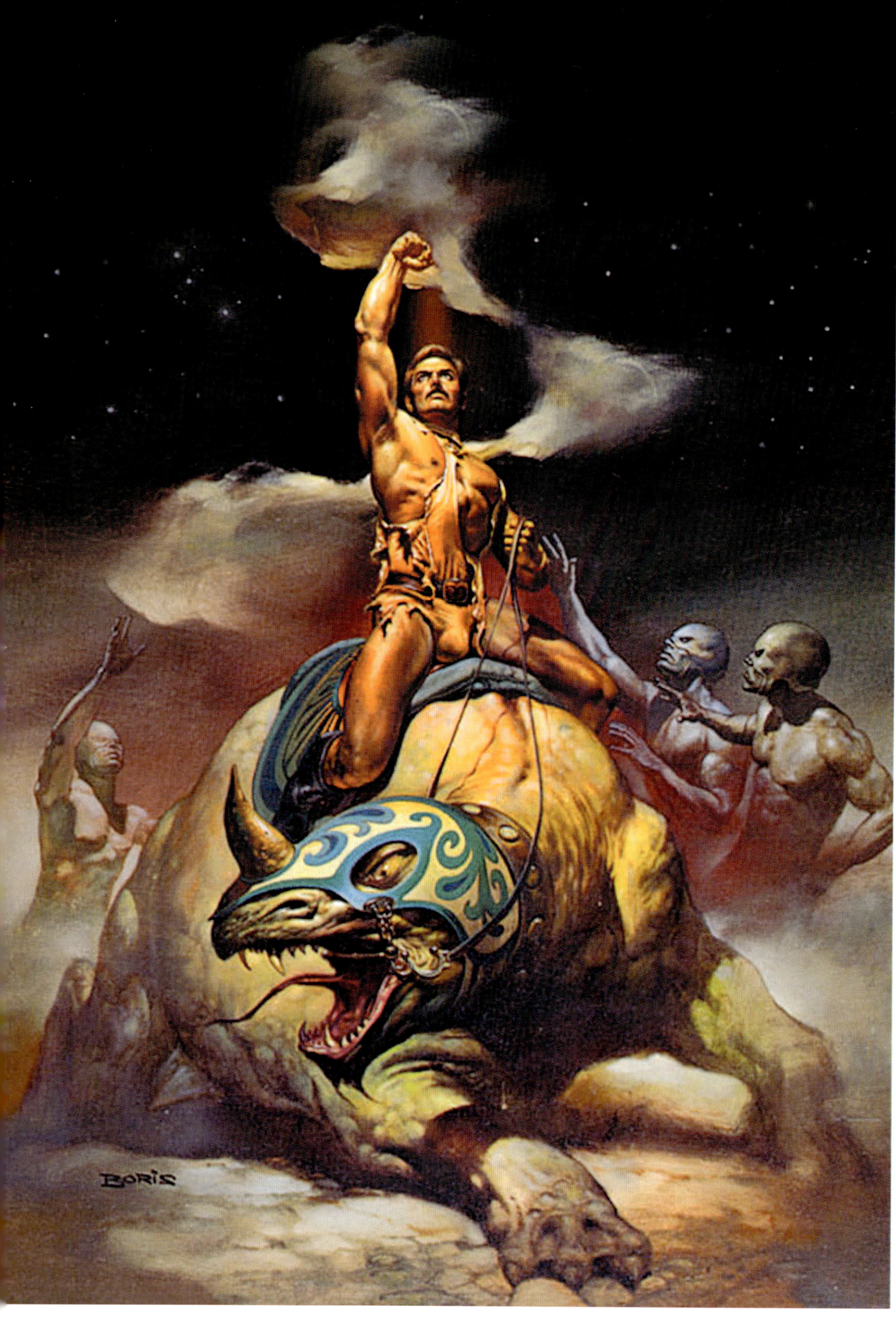
BORIS

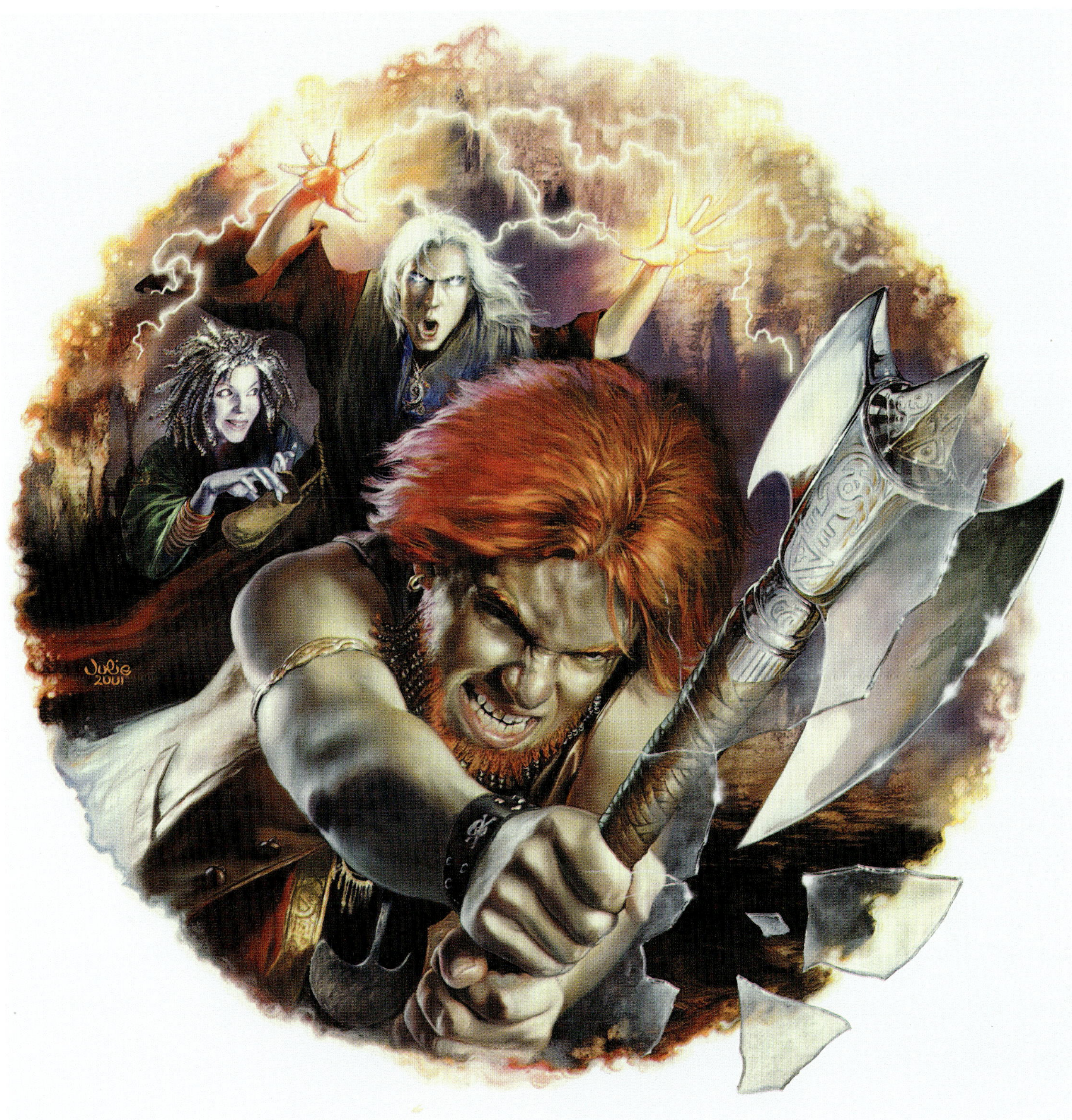

FIST OF POWER

1979, Boris *(left)*

A poster from the 1970s before Boris introduced his characteristic signature with copyright sign and date, so we've had to guess the date. A very popular and characteristic image of the period, helped maybe by the monster's exotic mask. The picture prompts the question: what exactly is going on here? But it is up to the viewer to supply an answer; the scene is not taken from any established story.

THE PORTAL

2001, Julie *(above)*

Cover for a Japanese computer game. The aim was to create an illusion of depth with the dwarf breaking out of the CD case into our plane of reality. The fey female is mischievously smiling, not something that happens often in Boris and Julie paintings. This is not because of any lack of humour on their part, quite the opposite, just that smiles are rarely called for in this area of fantasy. Julie's sons posed for the dwarf and wizard, after suitable transmogrification!

SIRENS

1988, Boris

Boris: 'This was really just an excuse to paint four great, lovely women! The trick with mermaids is to make their lower body fishlike enough while keeping a sensual human quality. To me in any case I enjoy painting mermaids from time to time – they're beautiful creatures and I love painting water.'

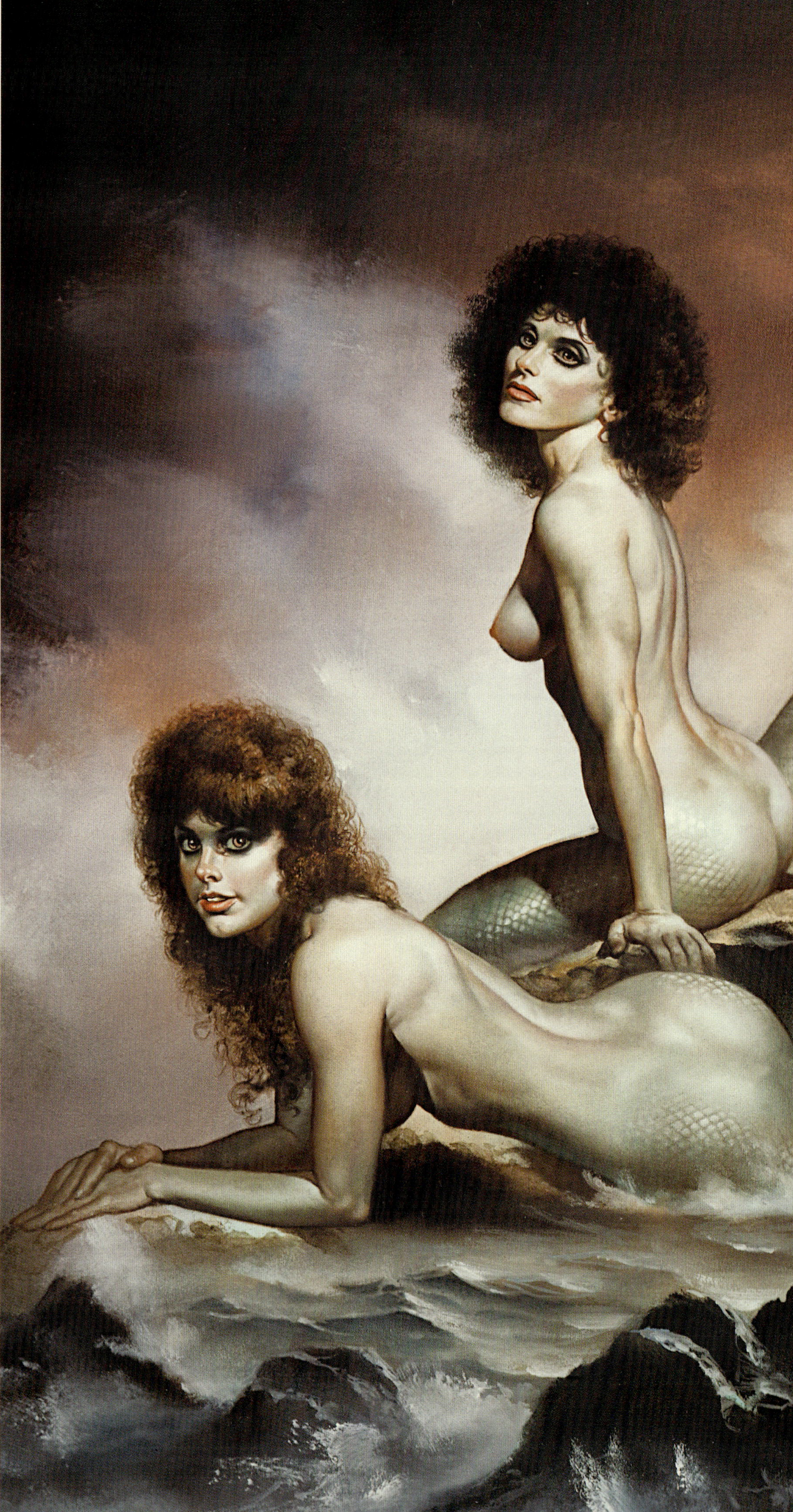

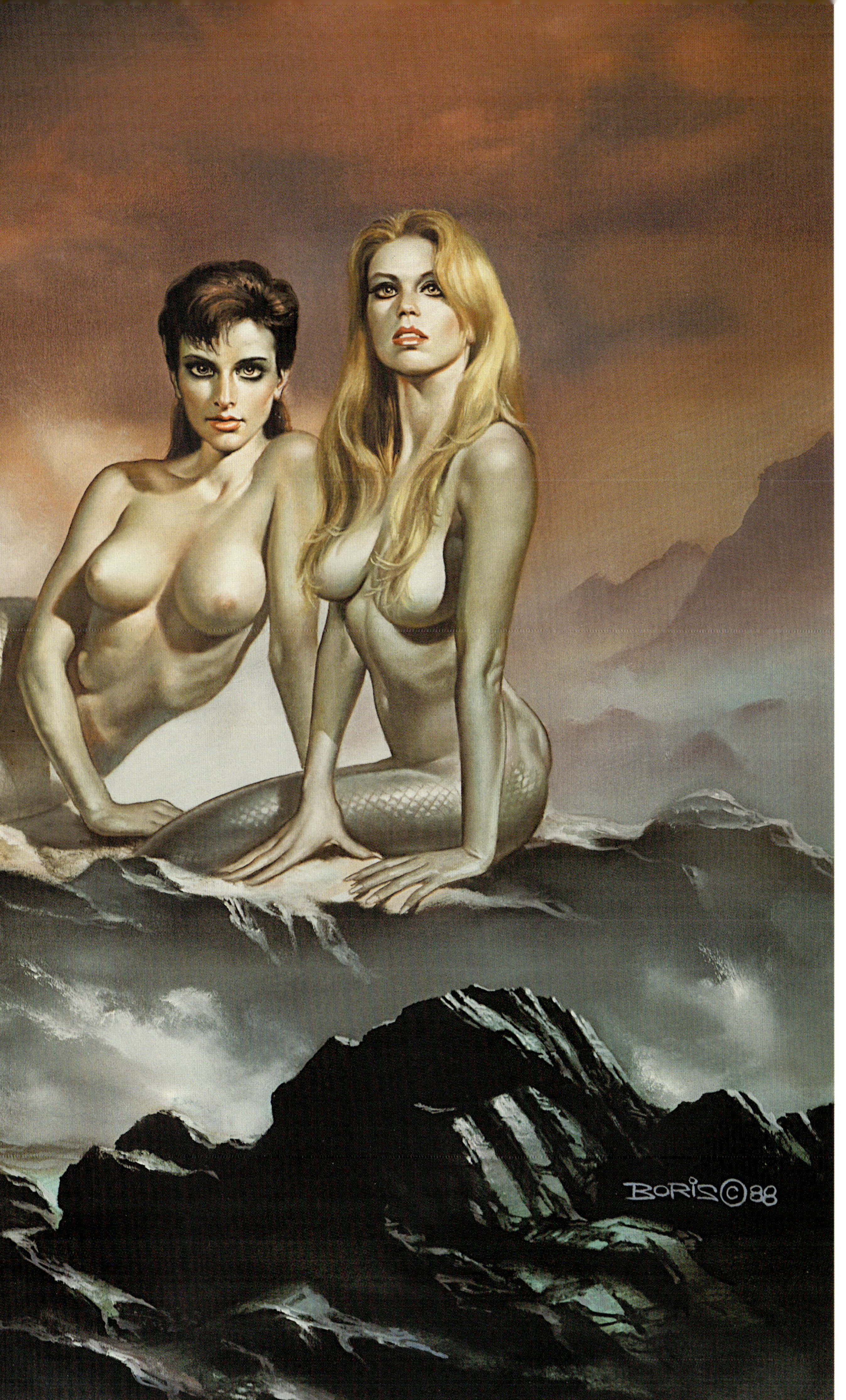
BORIS©88

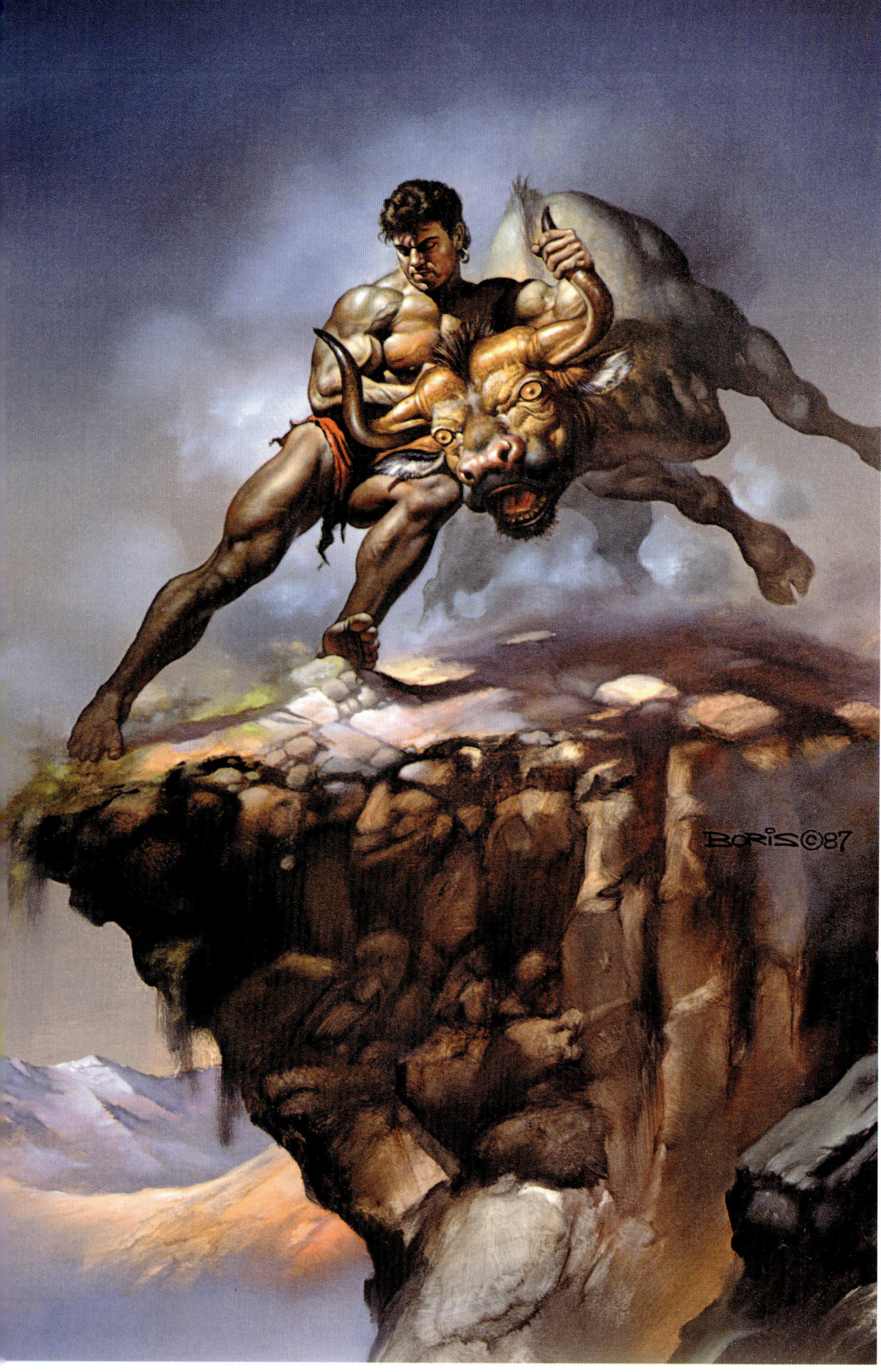

TAURUS

1987, Boris *(left)*

From Boris's zodiac series. Here he took the naturalism wanted by the publishers to an extreme by showing a purely dramatic scene and using a water-buffalo as the bull. A very untypical astrological picture but in a way it does capture the character of the sign very well.

SUSAN

2000, Julie *(right)*

A commissioned portrait by the joint owner of a New York art gallery who wanted to see herself in a fantasy setting. Often when illustrating, say, comic book characters the features of a model will be exaggerated as much as necessary to suit the fictional scenario; but in situations like this the aim is to get as good a likeness as possible with the main figure, then imagination is let loose on the magical setting.

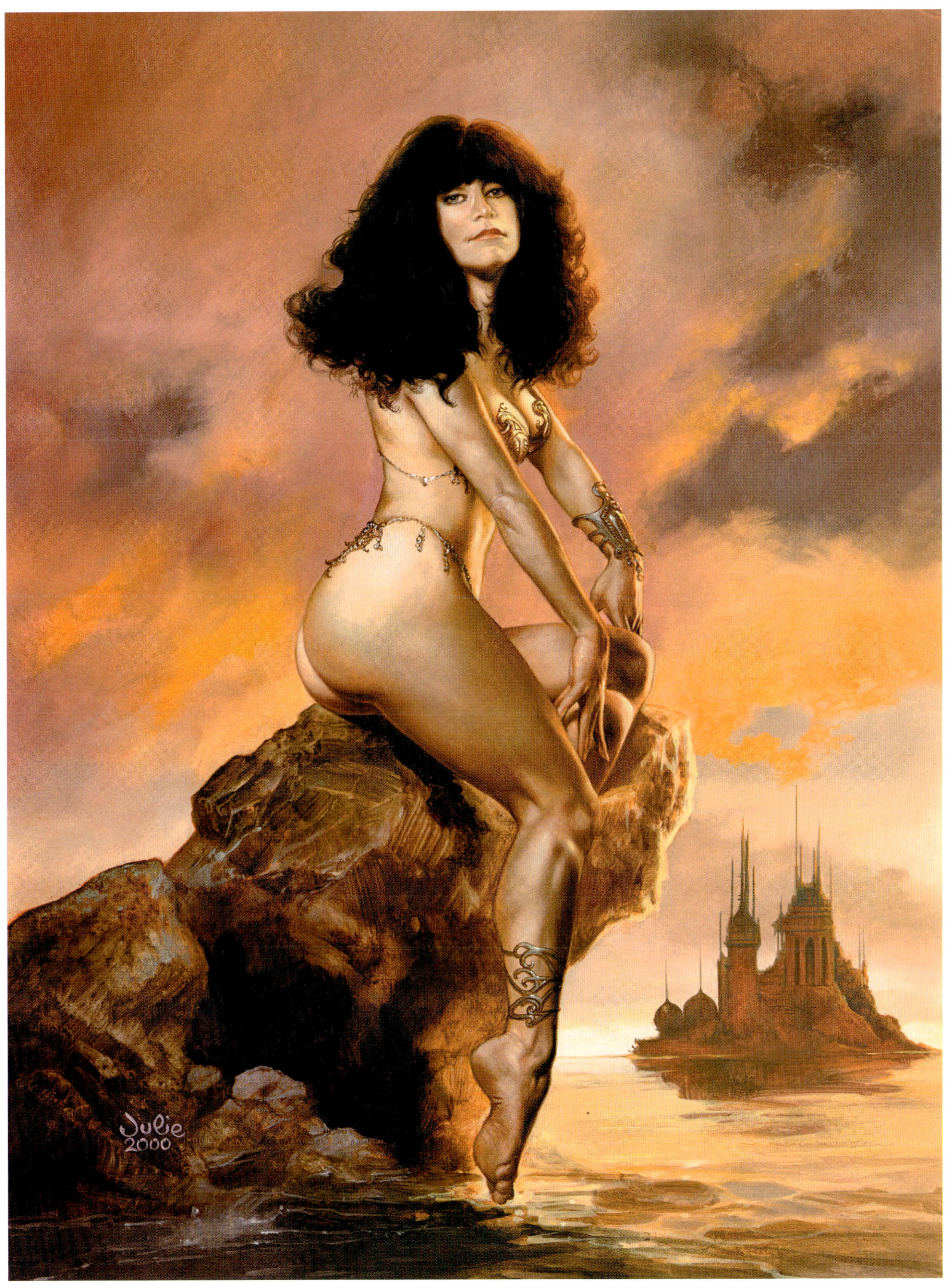
Julie
2000

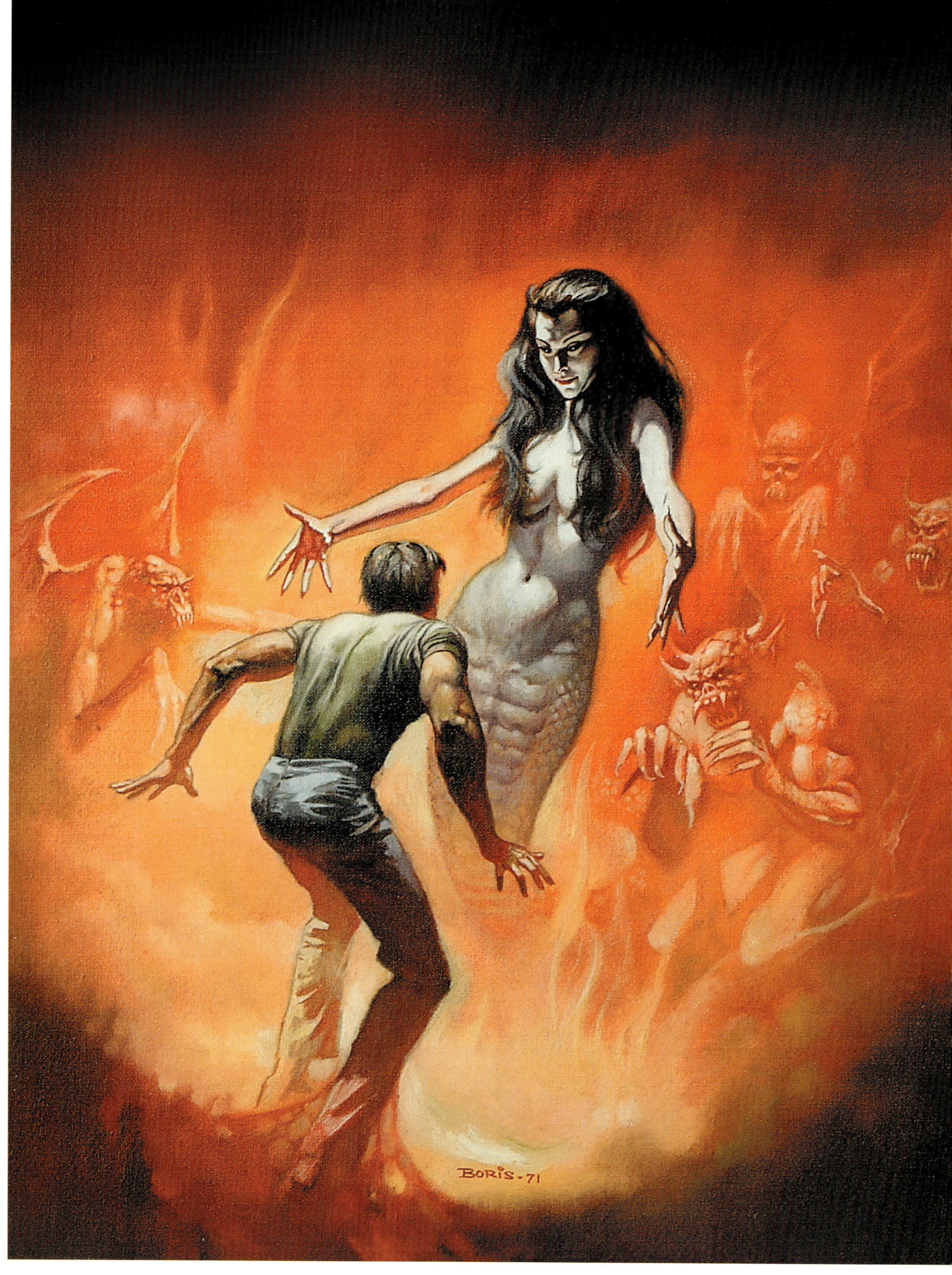
BORIS-71

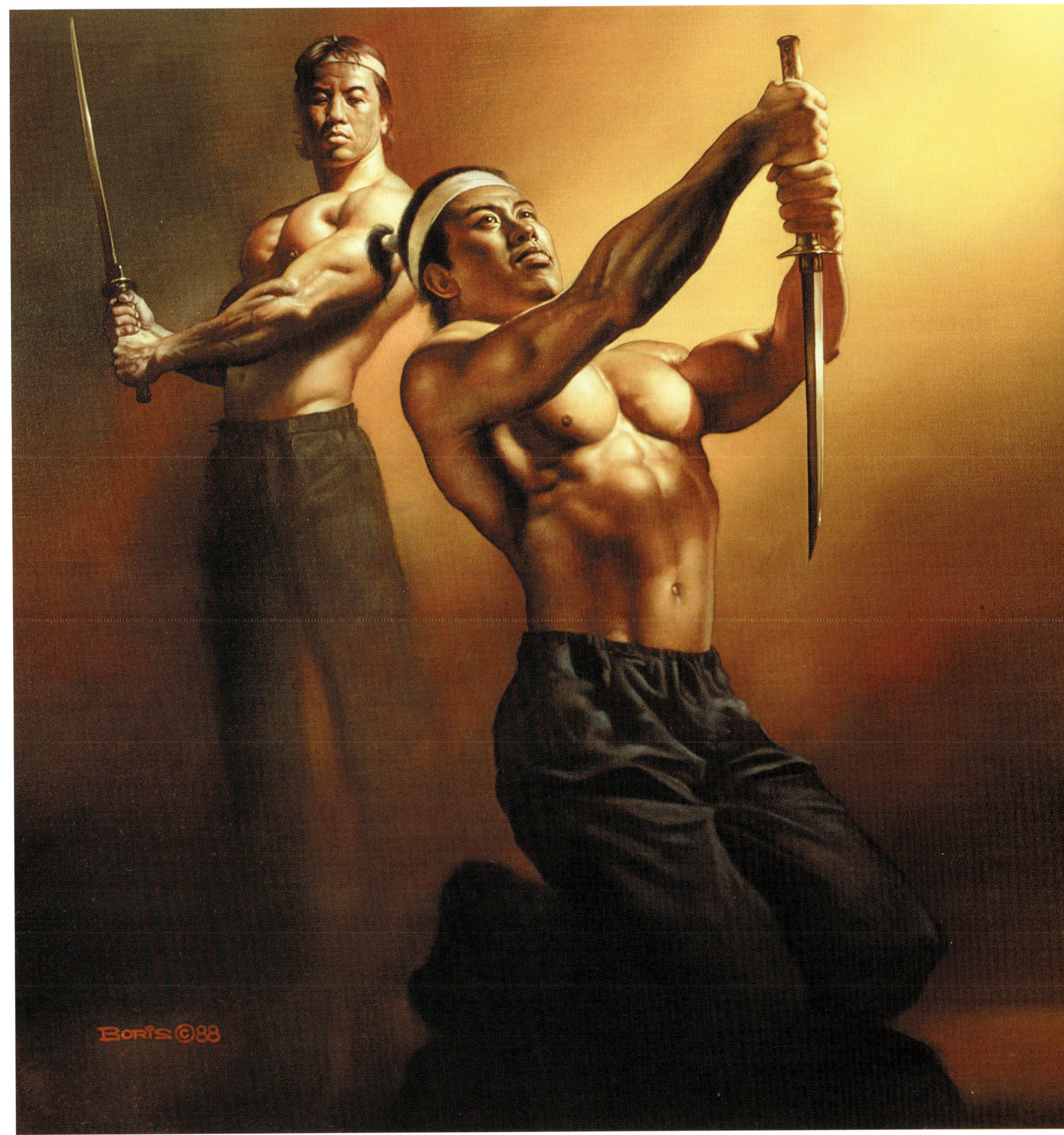

NIGHTMARE

1971, Boris *(left)*

A very early cover picture that was part of a set of four for *Nightmare* magazine. Here you can see Boris's style of painting really developing, though still somewhat crude and unpolished beside his later work. To him the composition now looks very contrived but it's included by way of contrast.

NO PLACE FOR DISGRACE

1988, Boris *(above)*

This was the cover for a music album of the same name.

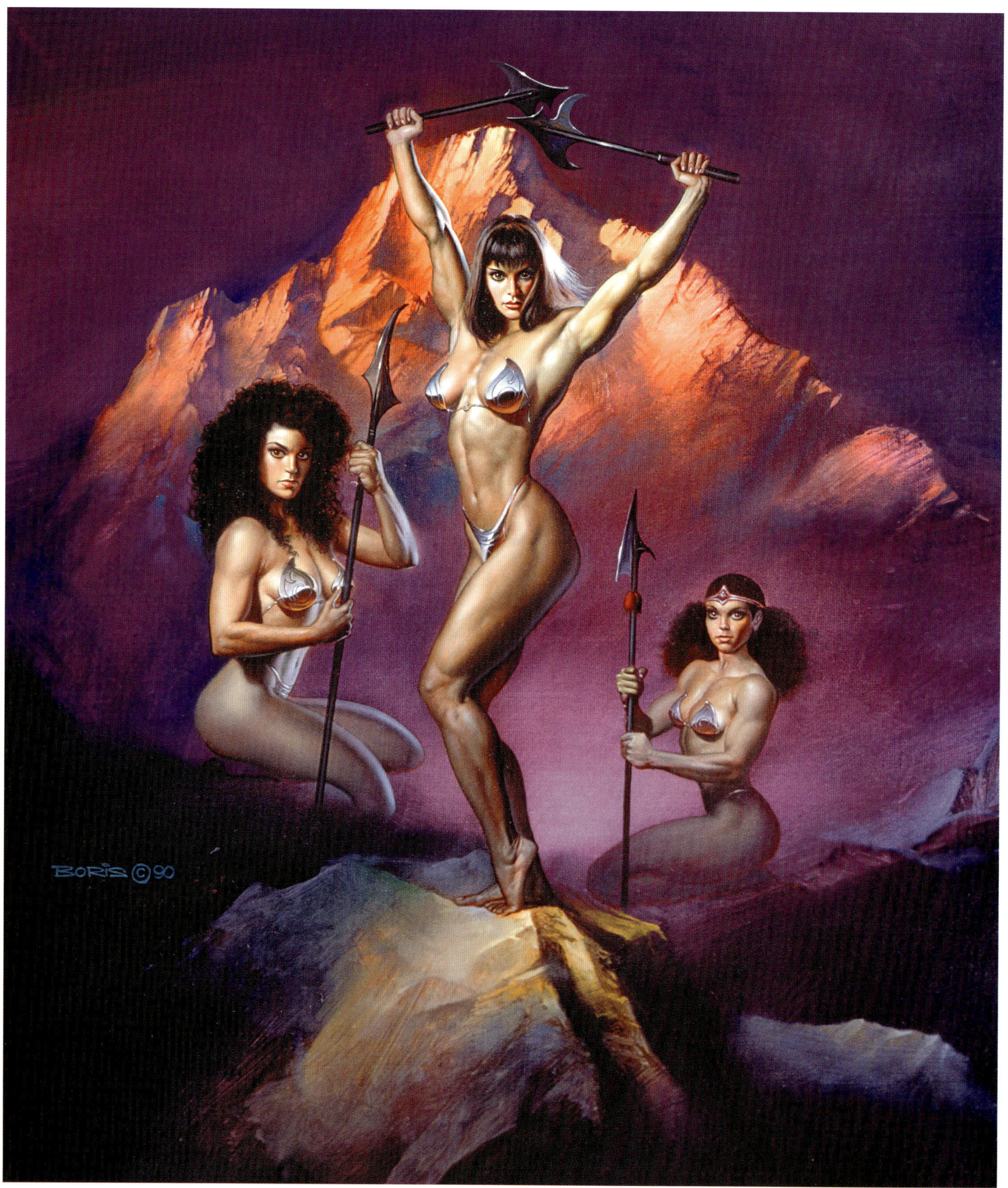

THE LASSAS

1990, Boris *(above)*

This is from the Greek myth series but, as Boris says, it could be any three powerful women in a fantastic setting. He loves to paint the outdoors and scenes like this that combine his three favourite subjects – mountains, rocks and women.

THE MINOTAUR

1991, Boris *(right)*

A distinctly contemporary woman in an classical setting.

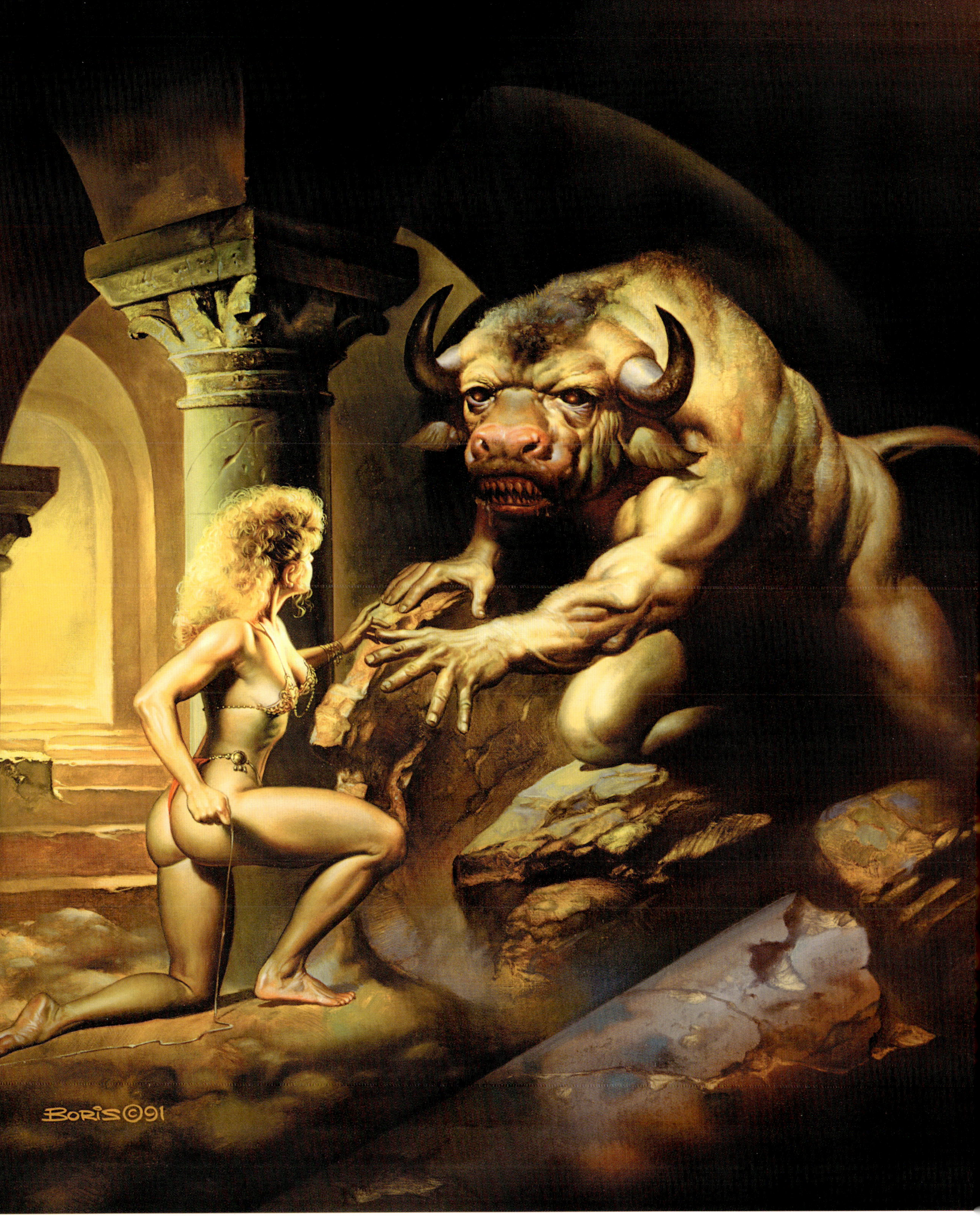
BORIS©91

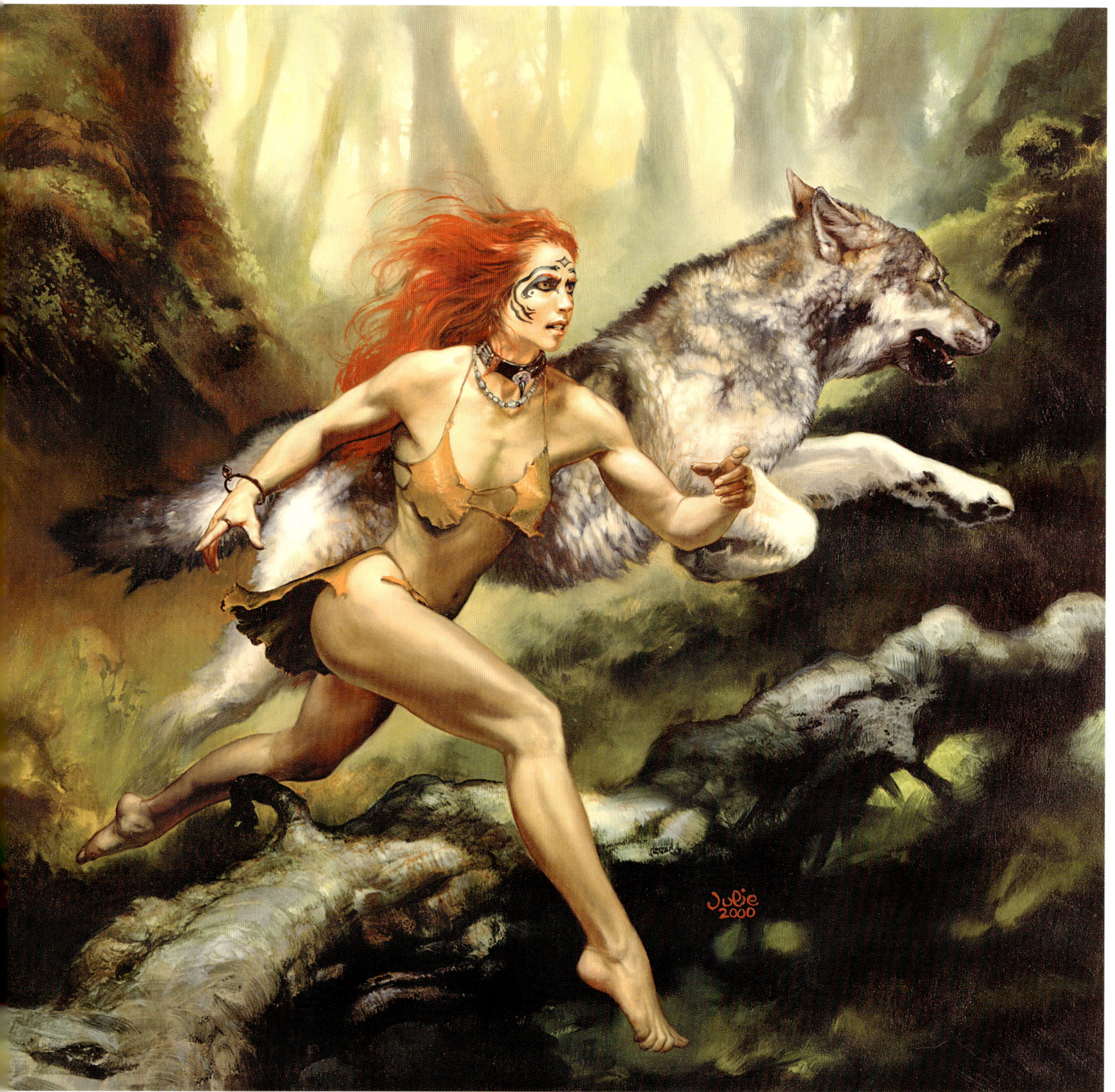

COMPETITION

2000, Julie *(above)*

Competition, Julie feels, too often gets a bad press. Yes, certainly destructive competition where a contestant is more concerned with undermining rivals than in excelling – that is a negative thing. But it has a more constructive aspect where two competing friends can inspire each other to push harder and further than either would alone. That is what she is showing here, and that is also how she and Boris operate. Neither ever seeks to undermine the other, but also neither wants to be left behind! Her feeling is that competition is great as long as there is respect on both sides. She loves the freedom of painting natural backgrounds like this. They start off 'really loose' and then one goes back to refine the details. She loves the woods anyway.

CONDORCHUQUI

1992, Boris *(right)*

Based on a Peruvian myth, though Boris doubts anyone out there has imagined it quite like this.

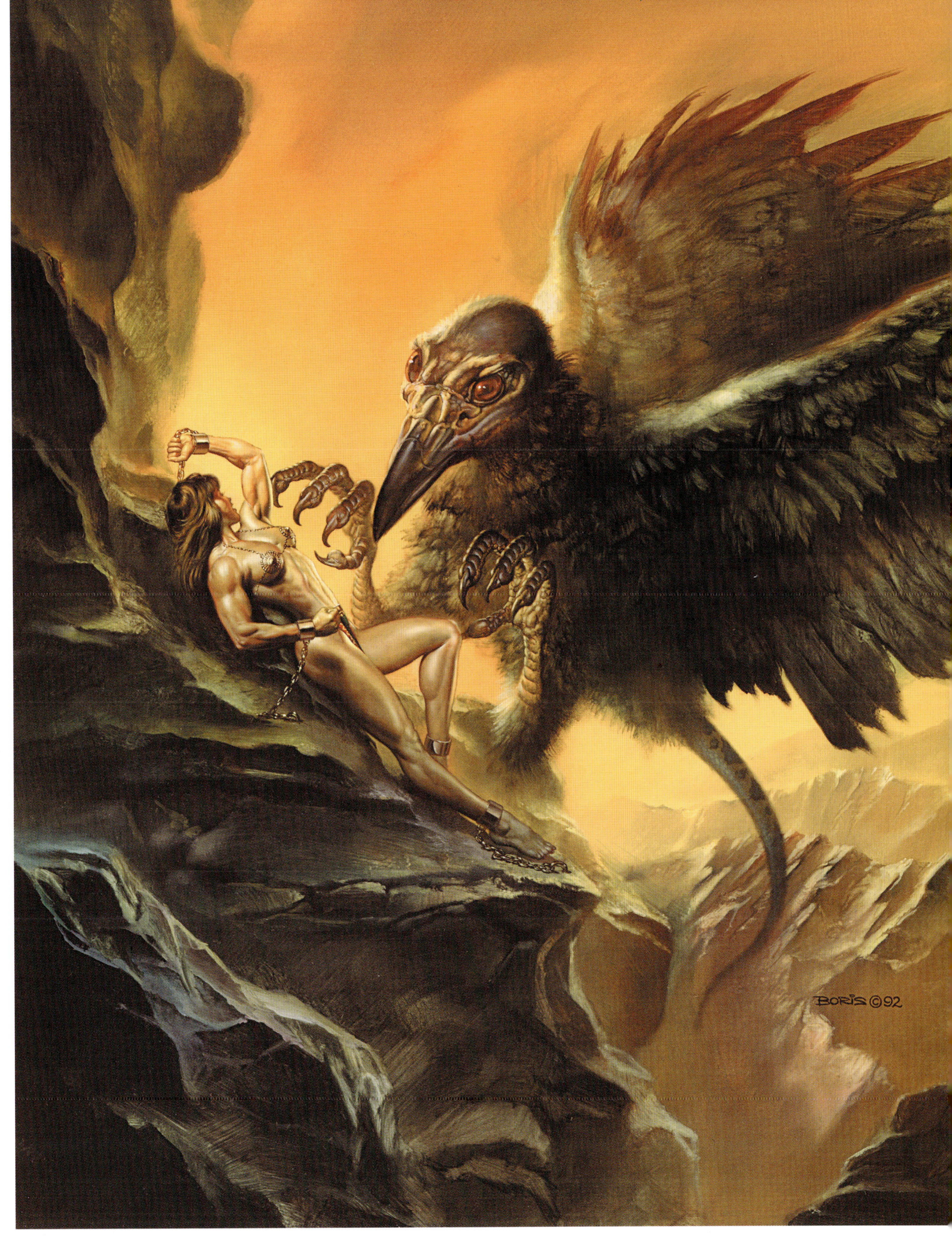
BORIS ©92

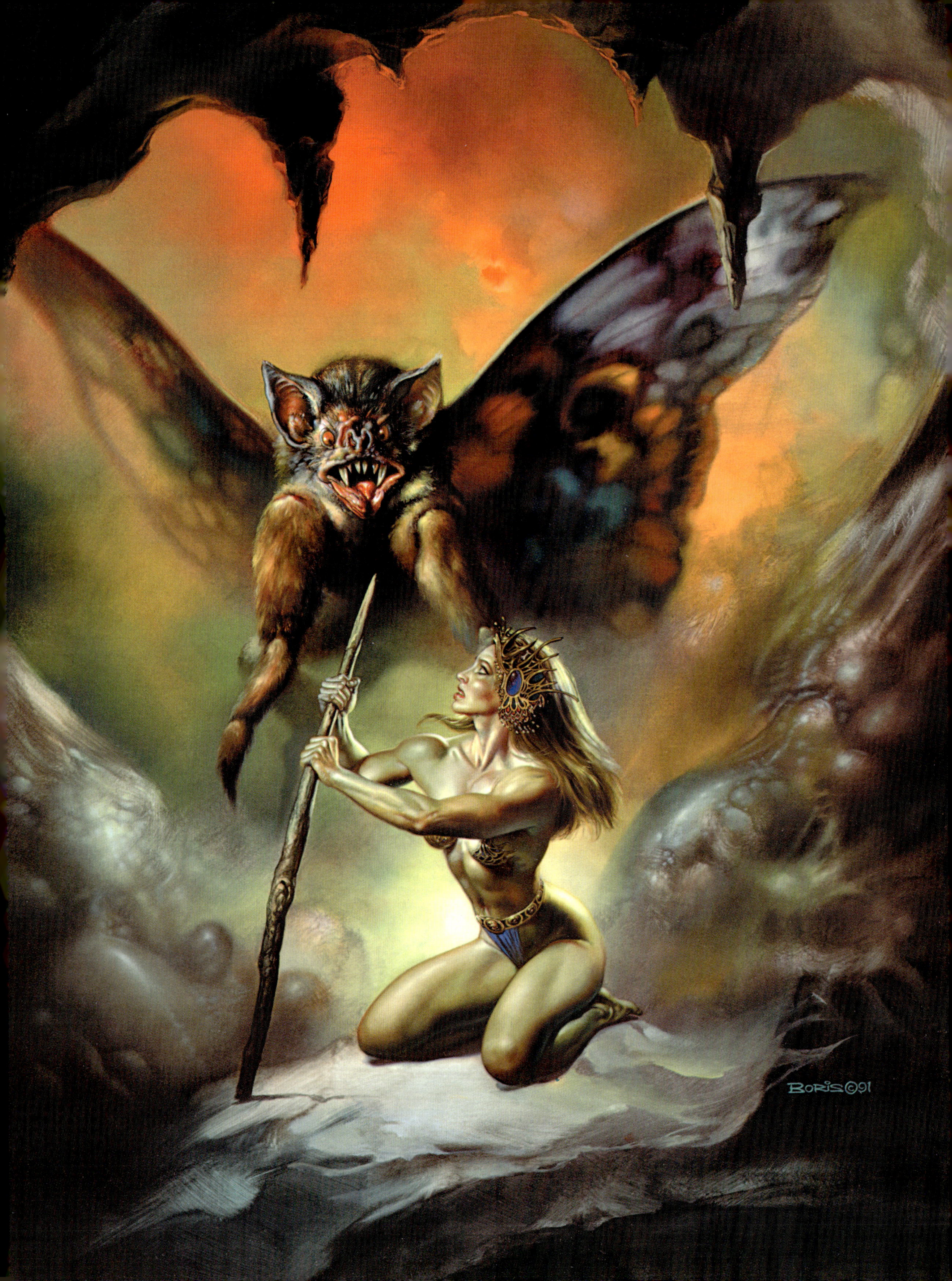
BORIS©91

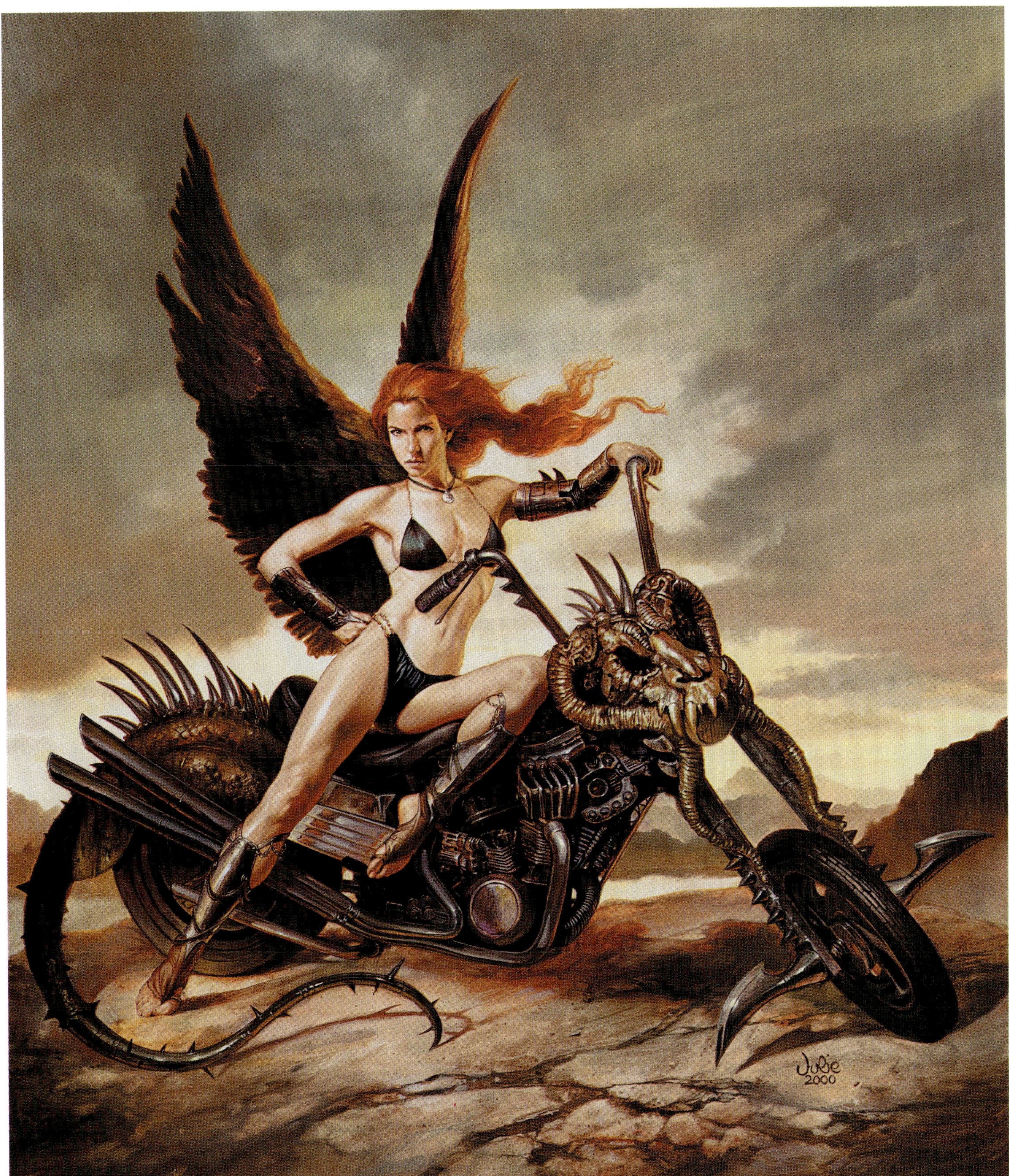

MOTH

1991, Boris *(left)*

Although most people seem to be put off by bugs, Boris enjoys the amazing body structures of insects and likes to use them in his work.

ANGEL RIDER

2000, Julie *(above)*

Based on a sculpture design for the Franklin Mint, one of four exotic motorcycles that have proved very popular. Julie was so happy with this whole project that she wanted to see how one of her original sketches would look as a painting as well as a sculpture.

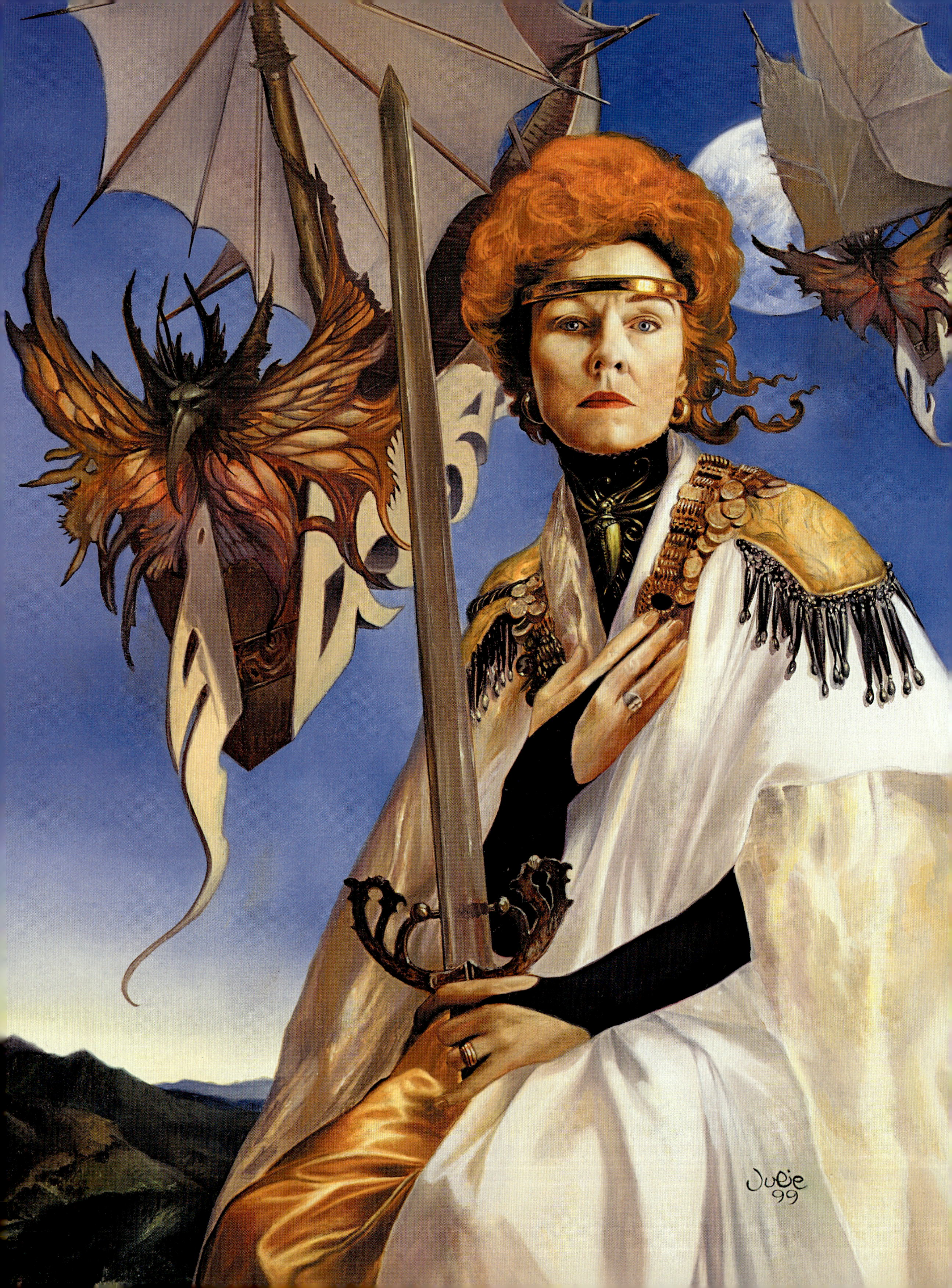
Julie
99

chapter 2

MAGICAL MYSTERY

The human figure honed to perfection is the focus of most of Boris and Julie's paintings. It helps that they are both regular bodybuilders, using the term in its broadest sense because it covers a wide spectrum. Some bodybuilders aim for size, building up their muscles as much as possible and often to the point that the Incredible Hulk begins to look a bit of a wimp. Others go more for general fitness and well-being, which is Boris and Julie's preference. To those of us who don't work out every day the distinction is quite relative, of course.

The great thing about being so involved in bodybuilding is that they meet a constant stream of people with great physiques who are usually only too happy to have them immortalized in a painting. Some champions even fly great distances for this honour, though most models are people they happen to meet. This is how Boris and Julie first met, when she came to sit for one of his paintings. Then they found they had more than an interest in bodybuilding in common . . .

Unless a commission calls for deliberate exaggeration, their paintings are usually quite faithful representations of subjects who have come to the studio for a photo-session. Unless the session is undertaken with a particular end in mind, the resulting photographs often sit around for years before they inspire an idea or happen to suit a commission that comes along. Although this photography is generally a hidden part of their art, the artists have through long practice become very professional at it and Boris has published a couple of books of his figure studies on camera – *Hindsight* and *Bodies*.

So human figures are the centre of attention in most of Boris and Julie's paintings and to them everything else is secondary, but there is often a lot else going on. Combining realism with pure fantasy is their trademark. Often it takes just a small touch, a tiny detail, to turn a straight representation into fantasy. But where necessary they are quite happy to create complete landscapes or worlds in which to set their figures.

PASSAGE
1999, Julie

A very untypical picture for Julie, whose subjects are rarely this elaborately dressed. She was aiming for a slightly Tarot-card feel to the picture and to express a sense of life's possibilities. The ships are the opportunities that come our way in life, periodically offering the chance of journeying to new territories if we choose to step aboard. The model was Julie's stepmother Hester.

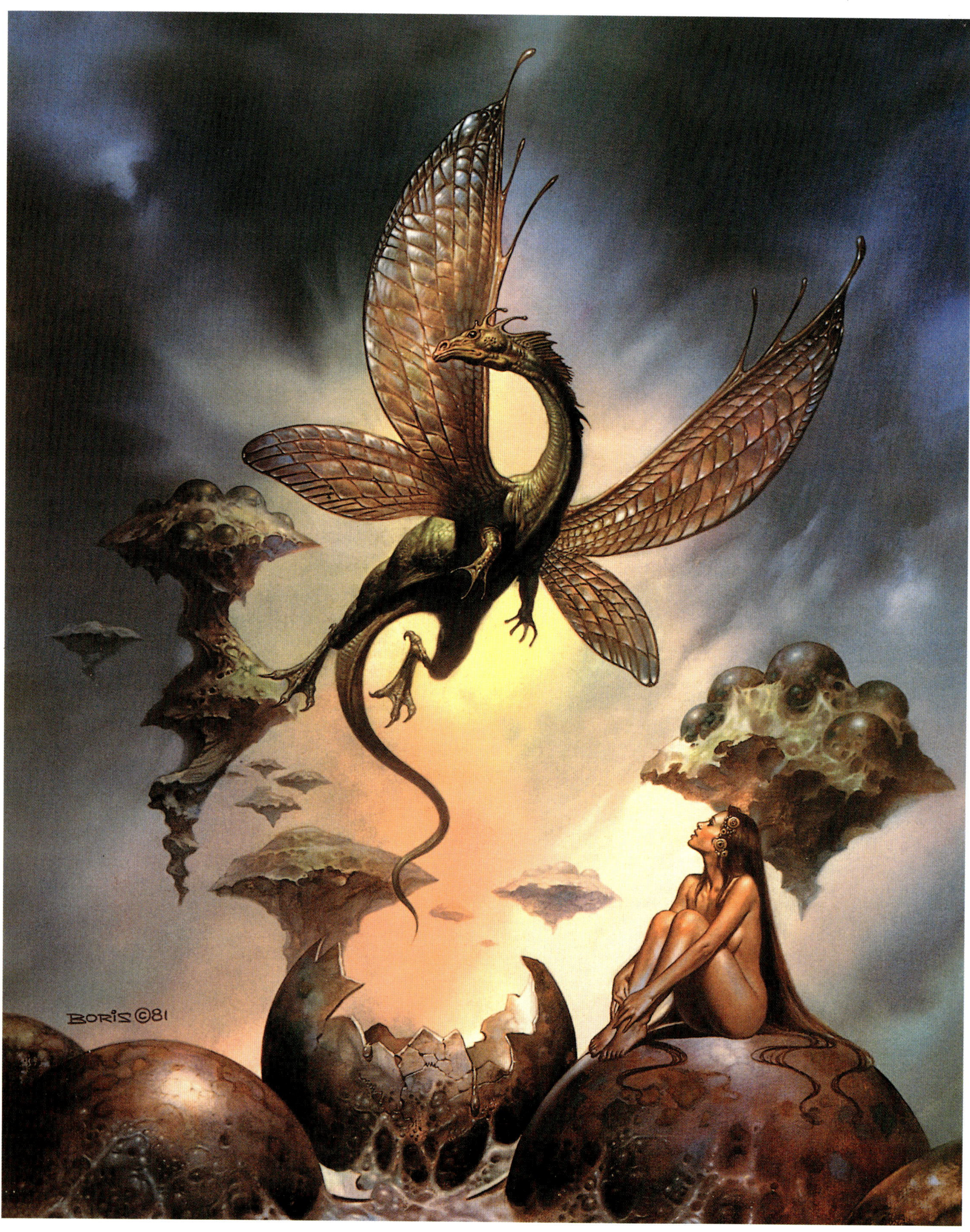
BORIS ©81

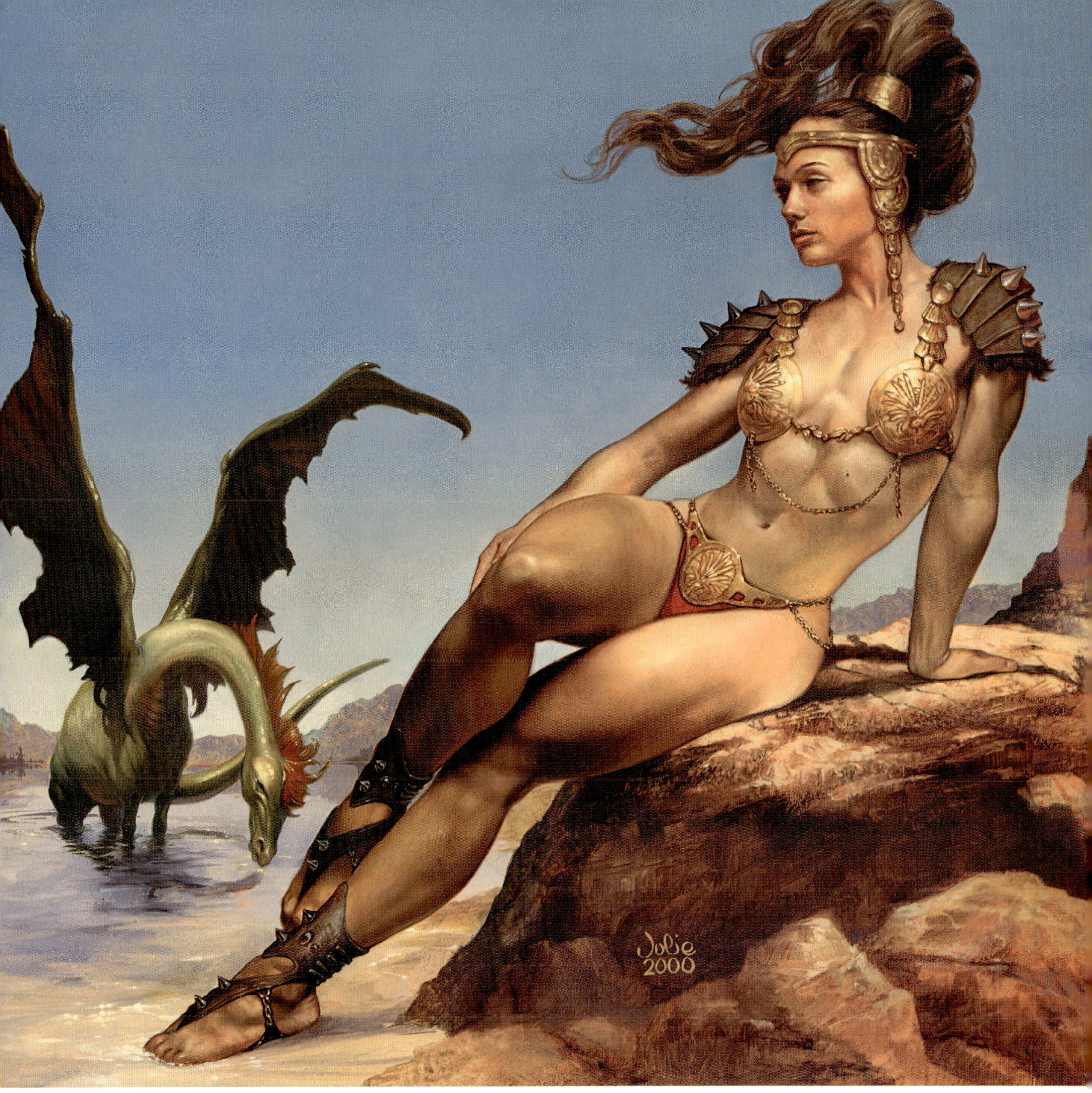

DRAGON'S BIRTH

1981, Boris *(left)*

One of Boris's favourite themes is that of Beauty and the Beast, though in this case the beast is neither monstrous nor threatening. It is just a beautiful, delicate dragon freshly hatched from its egg to the wonderment of its audience. Looking at the picture now, Boris can see how his portrayal of women has changed since this period. She's very sweet and gentle whereas his women now tend to be much stronger and more assertive. It was painted for the cover of a magazine called *Dragon.*

FARAWAY MEMORIES

2000, Julie *(above)*

These two seem as if they are maybe resting on a journey. The woman's faraway look conjures all kinds of possibilities that we can never know for sure. Is she thinking about where they have left or where they're going?

PYRAMIDS

1999, Boris & Julie

One of only three or four paintings the artists have worked on together and their first joint calendar picture. This is in fact only the background of what appeared because they added two metallic human figures by computer. These were painted separately mainly for the convenience of being able to work on them simultaneously – Julie doing the female and Boris the male. The background stands up well enough on its own though.

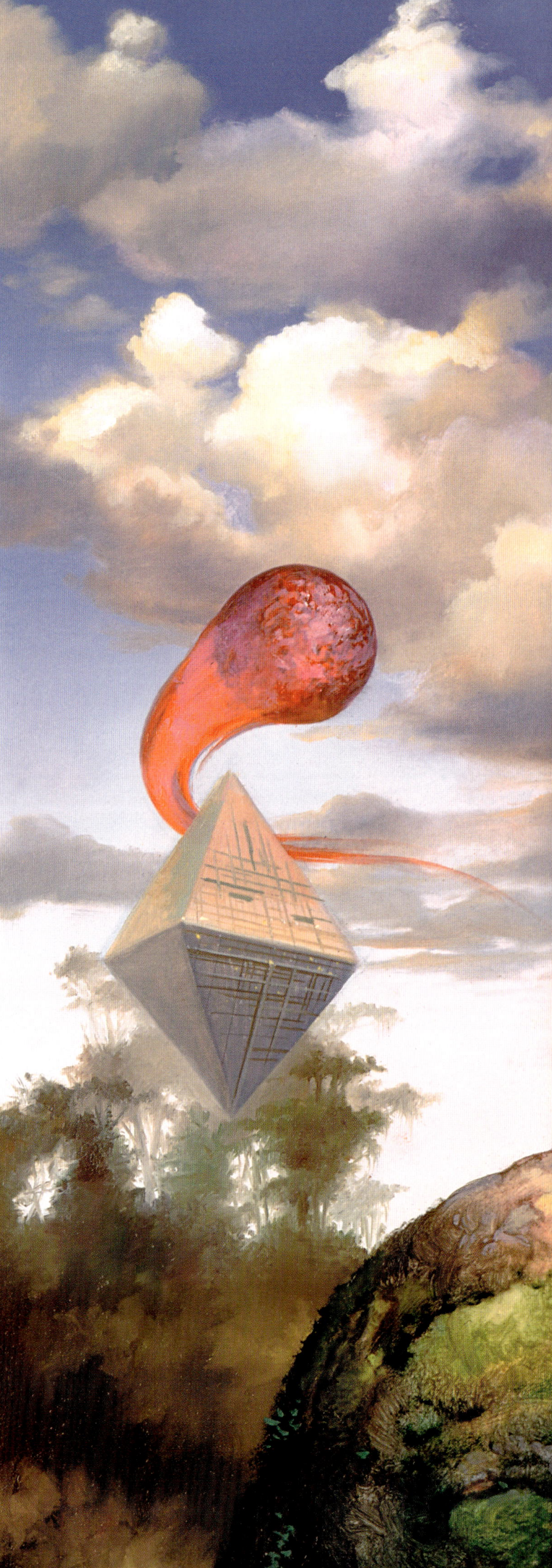

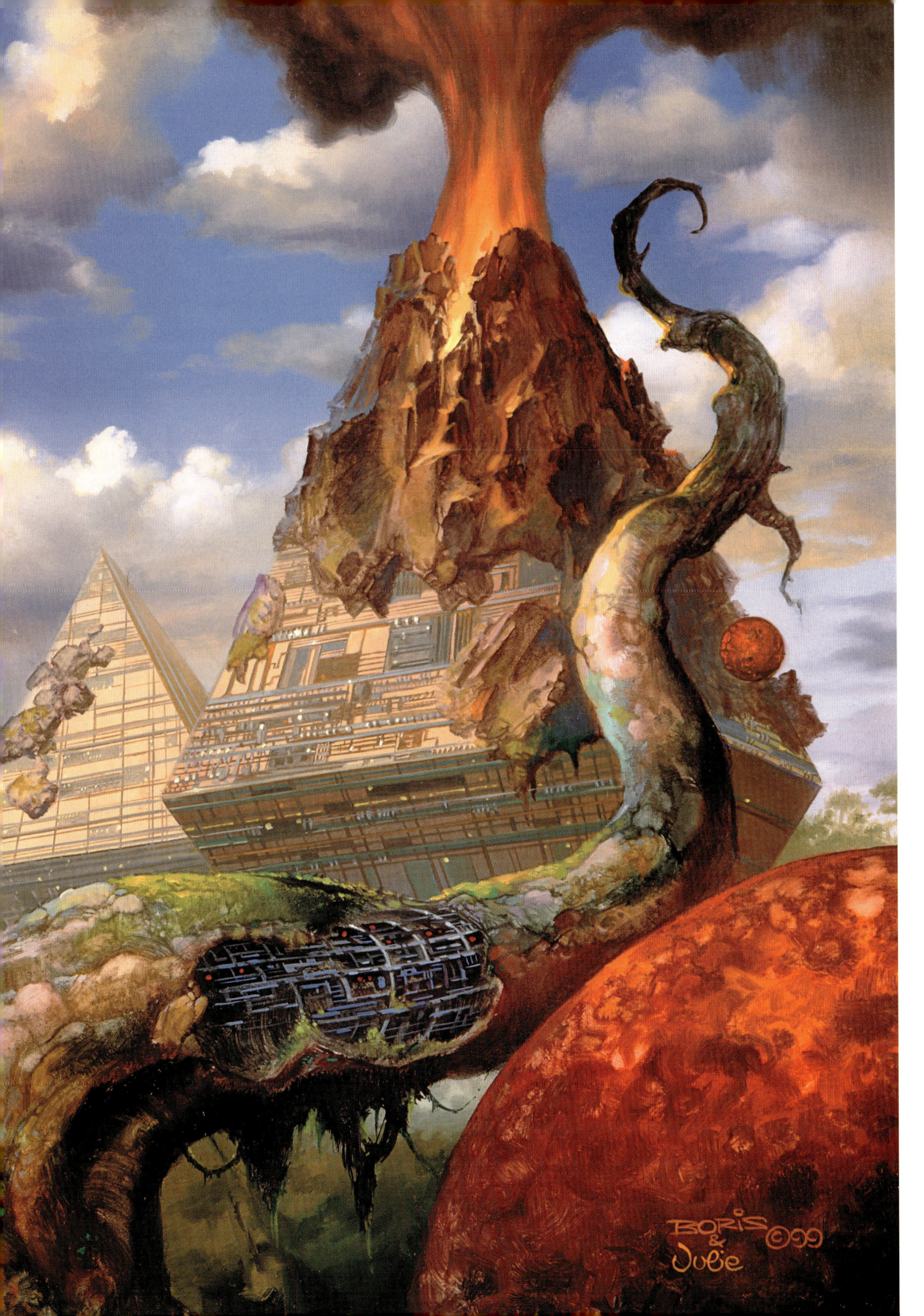
BORIS & Julie ©99

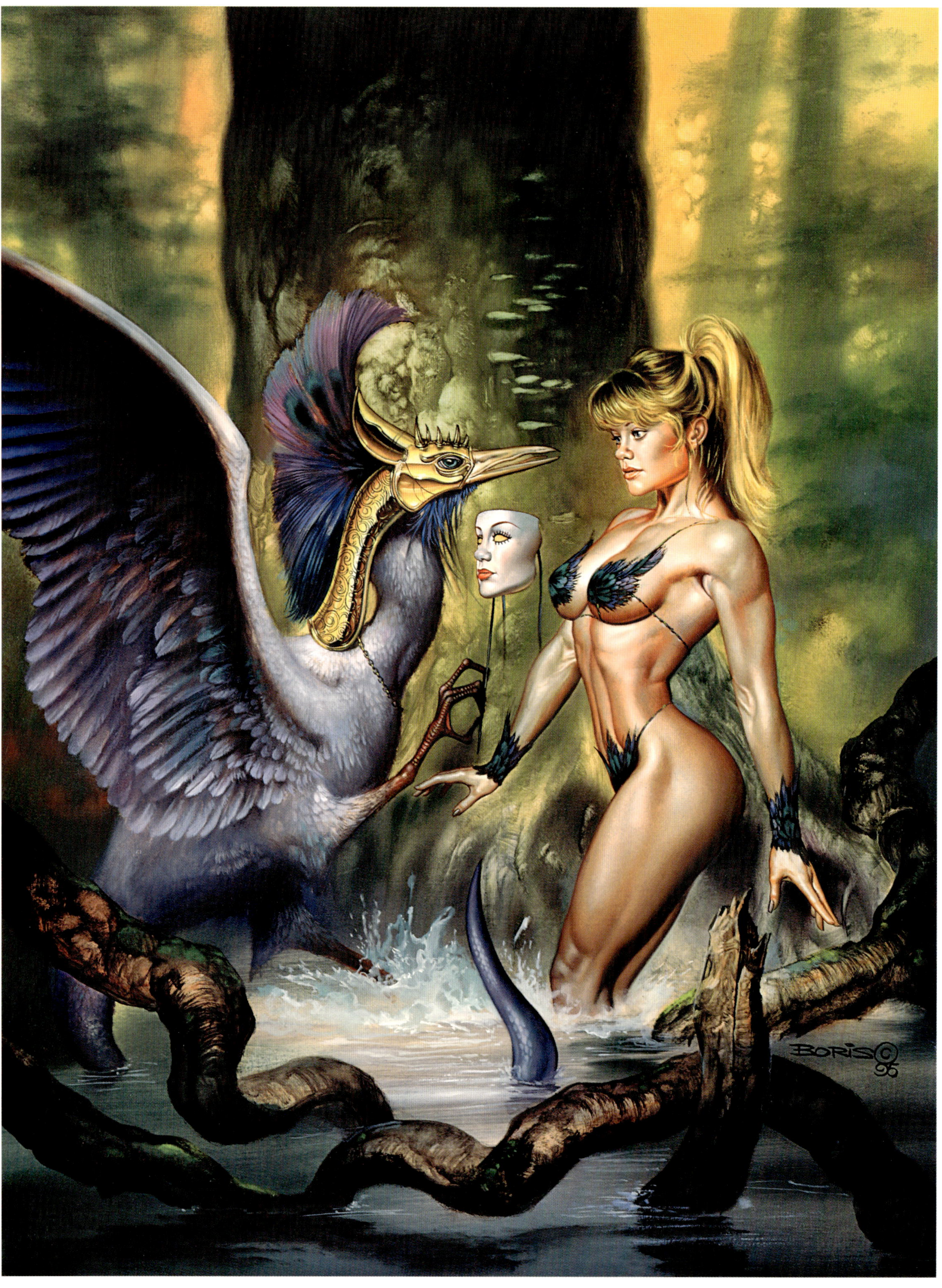
BORIS©
95

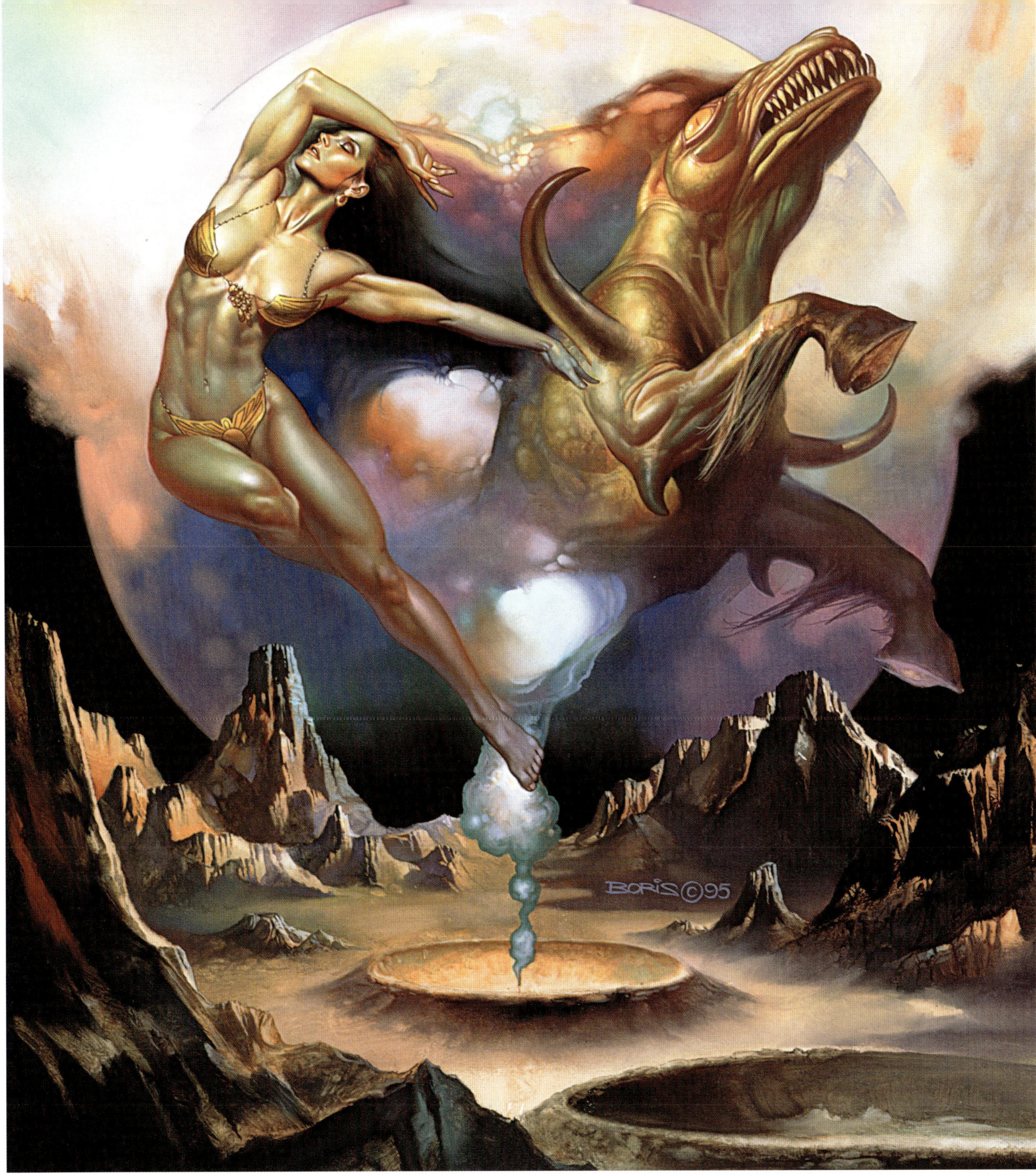

MASK

1995, Boris *(left)*

When the artists do these symbolic calendar paintings they hand them to a writer friend who supplies the captions. What he writes is as much a surprise to the artists as anyone else when the calendar appears. Boris especially enjoys leaving interpretation of his paintings up to the viewer. He does, of course, have his own concepts but doesn't like describing them since he believes the pictures should mean different things to different people. Julie is more willing to share her thoughts.

SYMBIOSIS

1995, Boris *(above)*

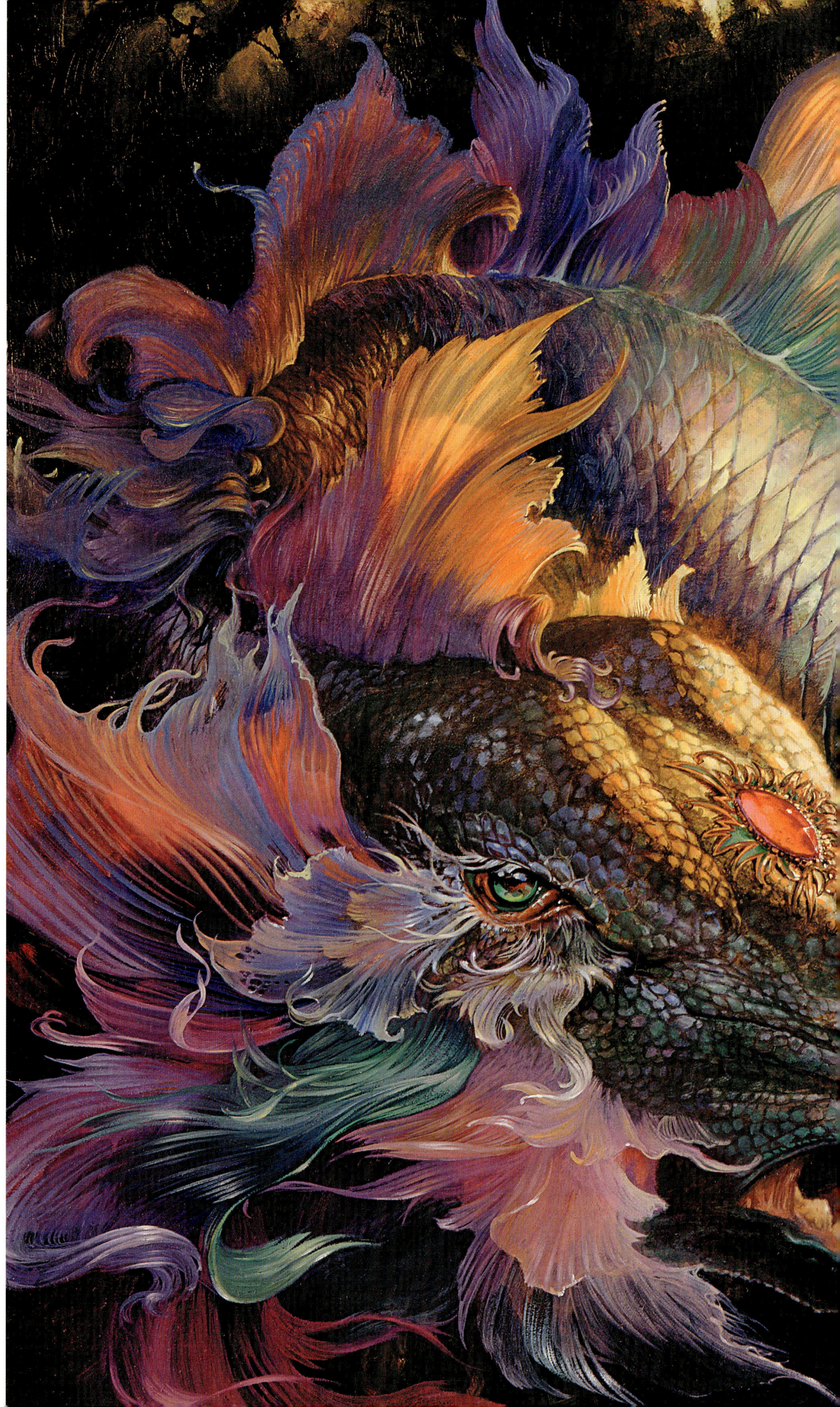

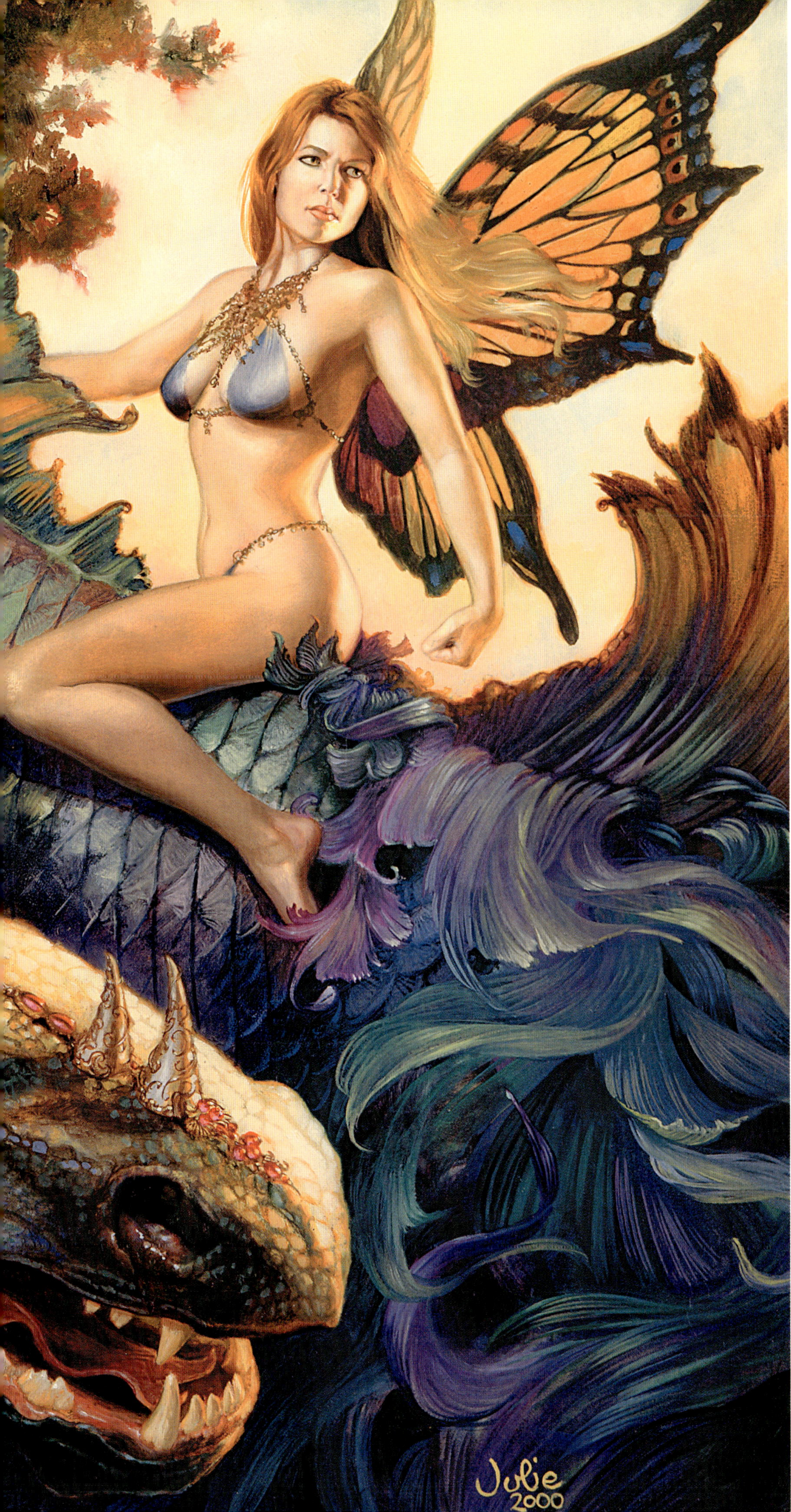

FAERIE SUZANNE

2000, Julie

Julie was playing here with the idea of making the large dragon merge into the background by means of lighting contrast, so the smaller fairy becomes the main figure. The dragon was inspired by Siamese Fighting Fish with their filmy fins while the fairy was modelled by Julie's sister.

WARRIOR GIRL
1999, Julie

BLOOMING
1994, Boris *(page 44)*
This picture had to be painted overnight to meet a calendar deadline but Boris was pleased enough with the result, which is not his usual type of picture. Such last minute panics used to happen every now and then but are rare these days.

ANGEL WINGS
1999, Julie *(page 45)*
Julie was inspired here by the pretty, innocent look of the model, and by the texture of the fabric she's holding. Between them these suggested the wings, which are not too sharply defined and fade off into light on the right as if perhaps they and the angel are just materializing out of it.

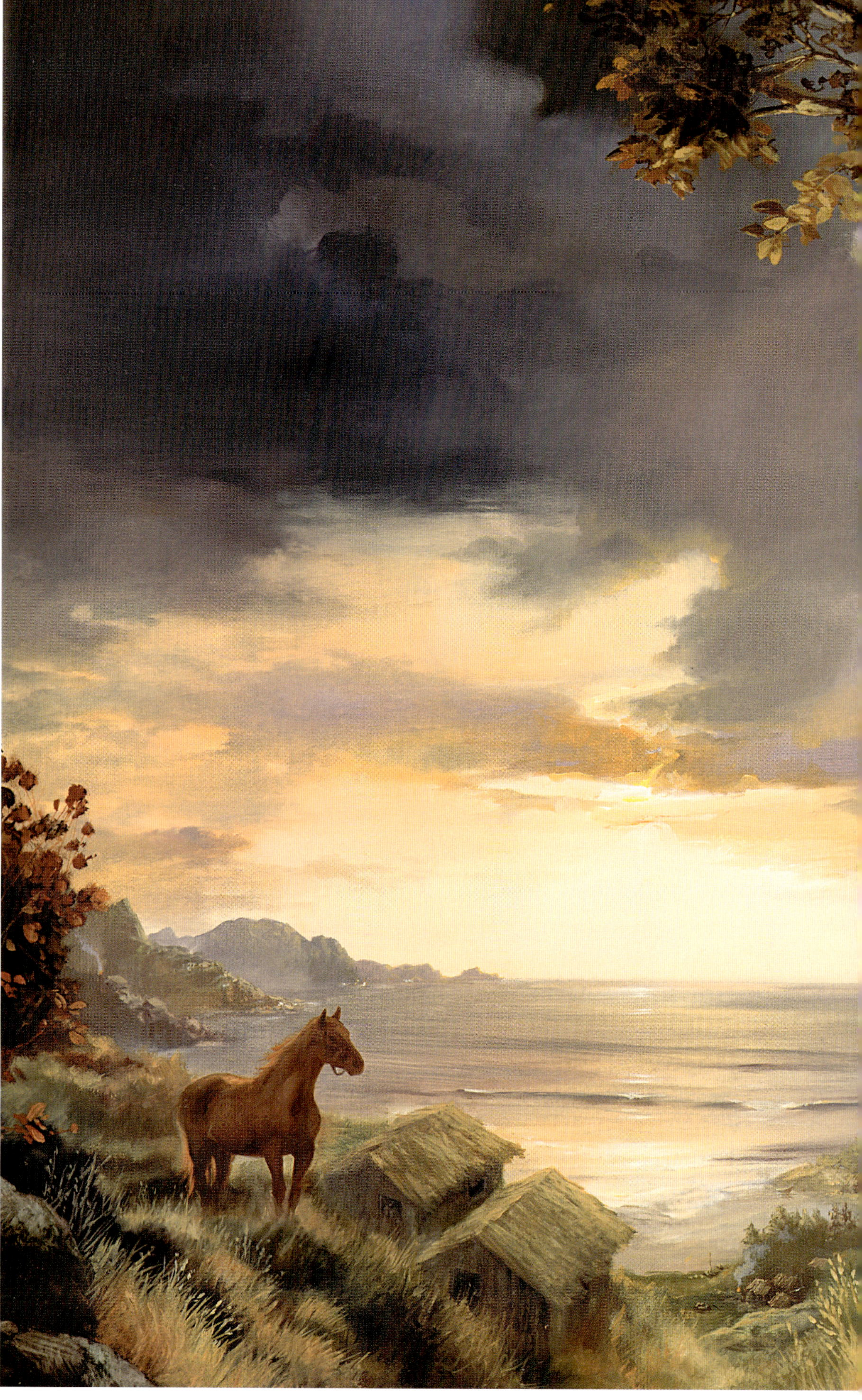

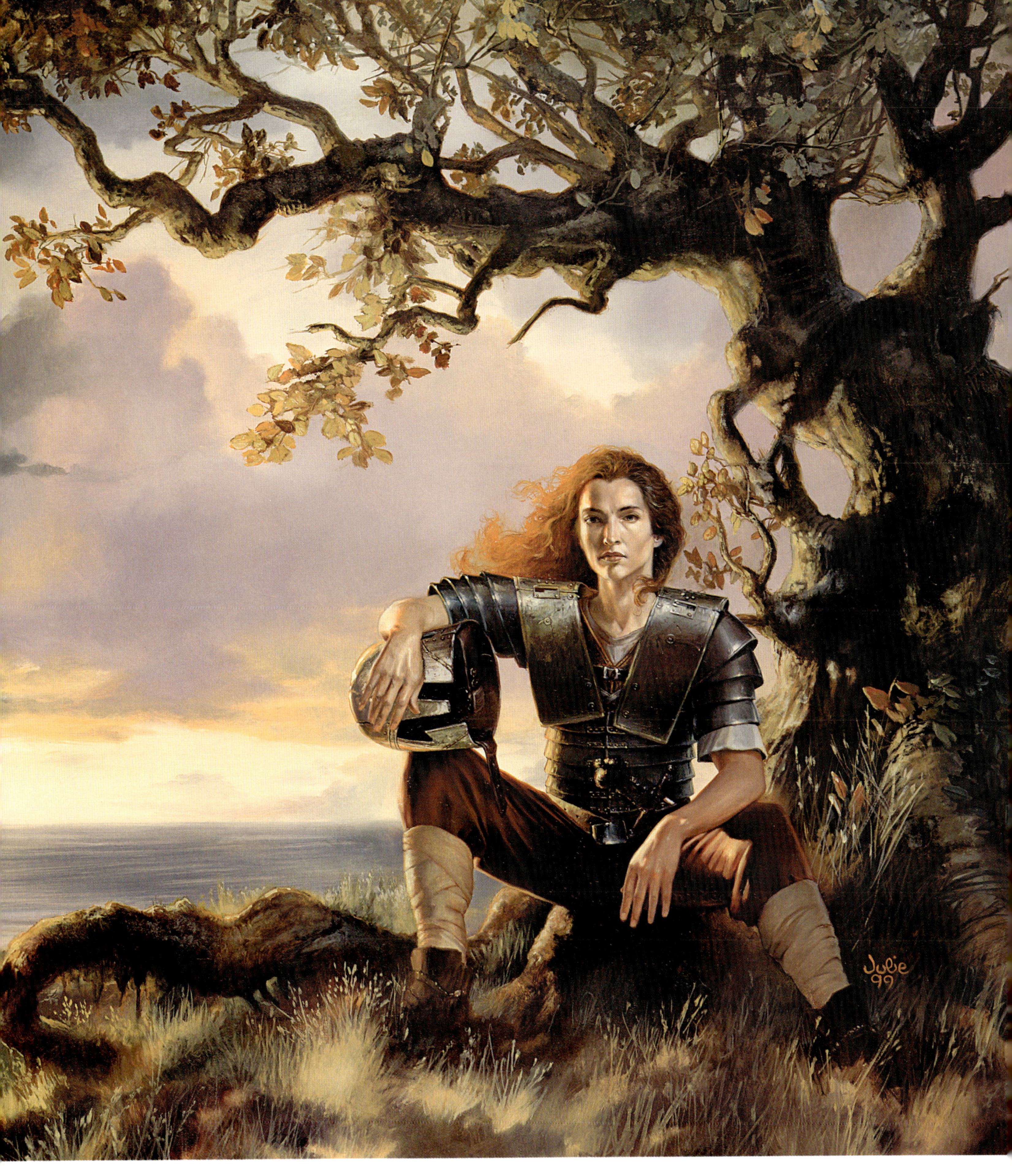
Julie
99

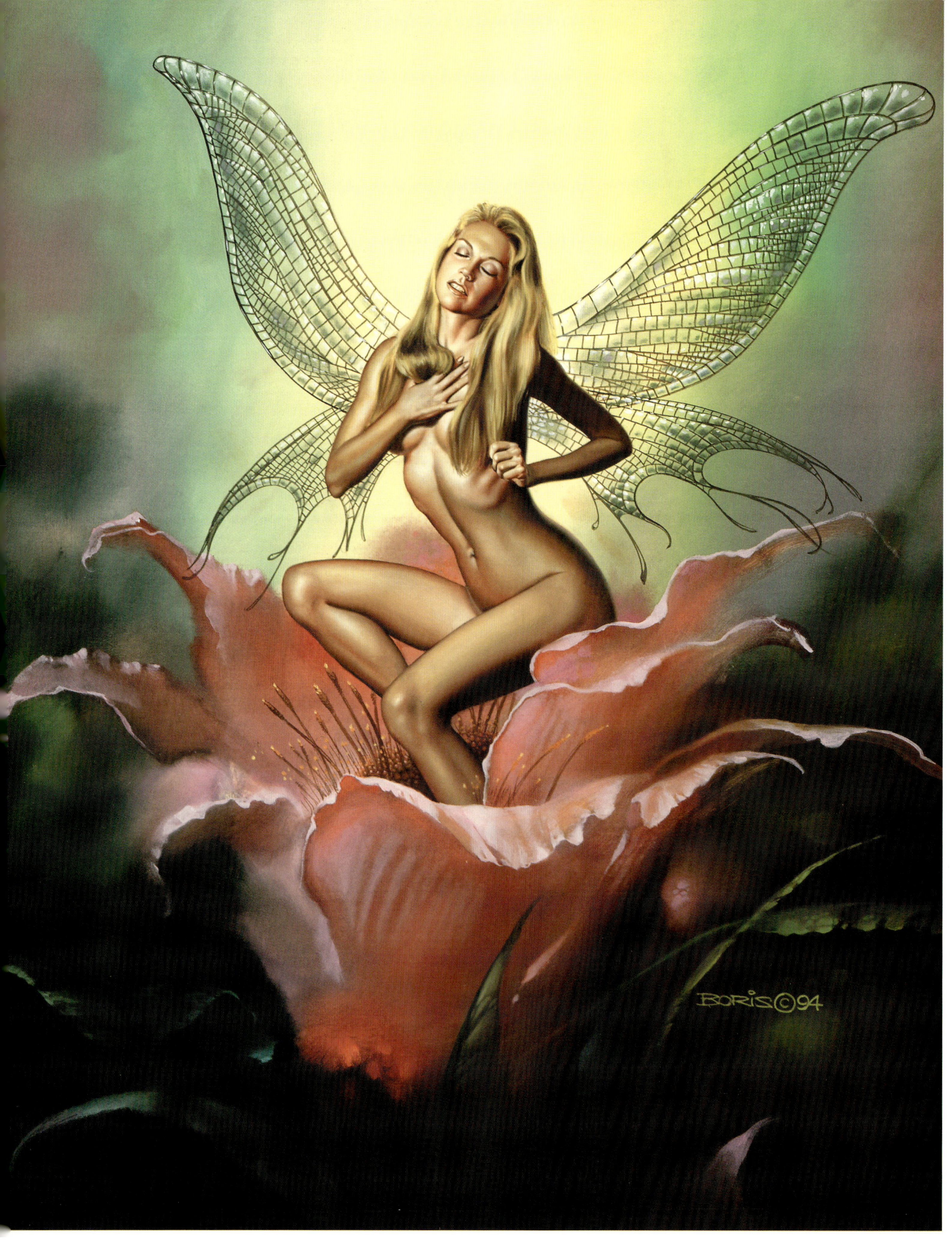
BORIS©94

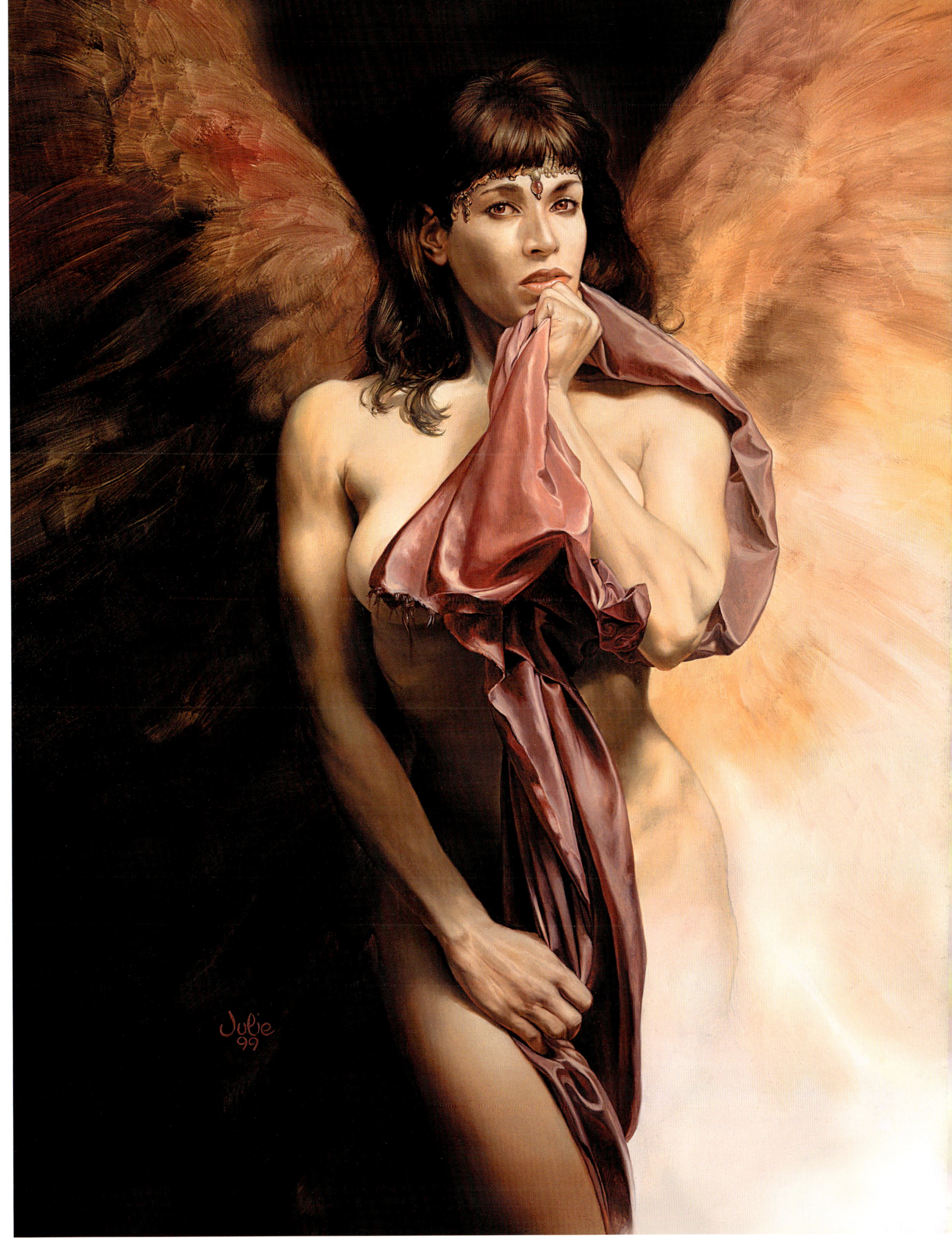
Julie
99

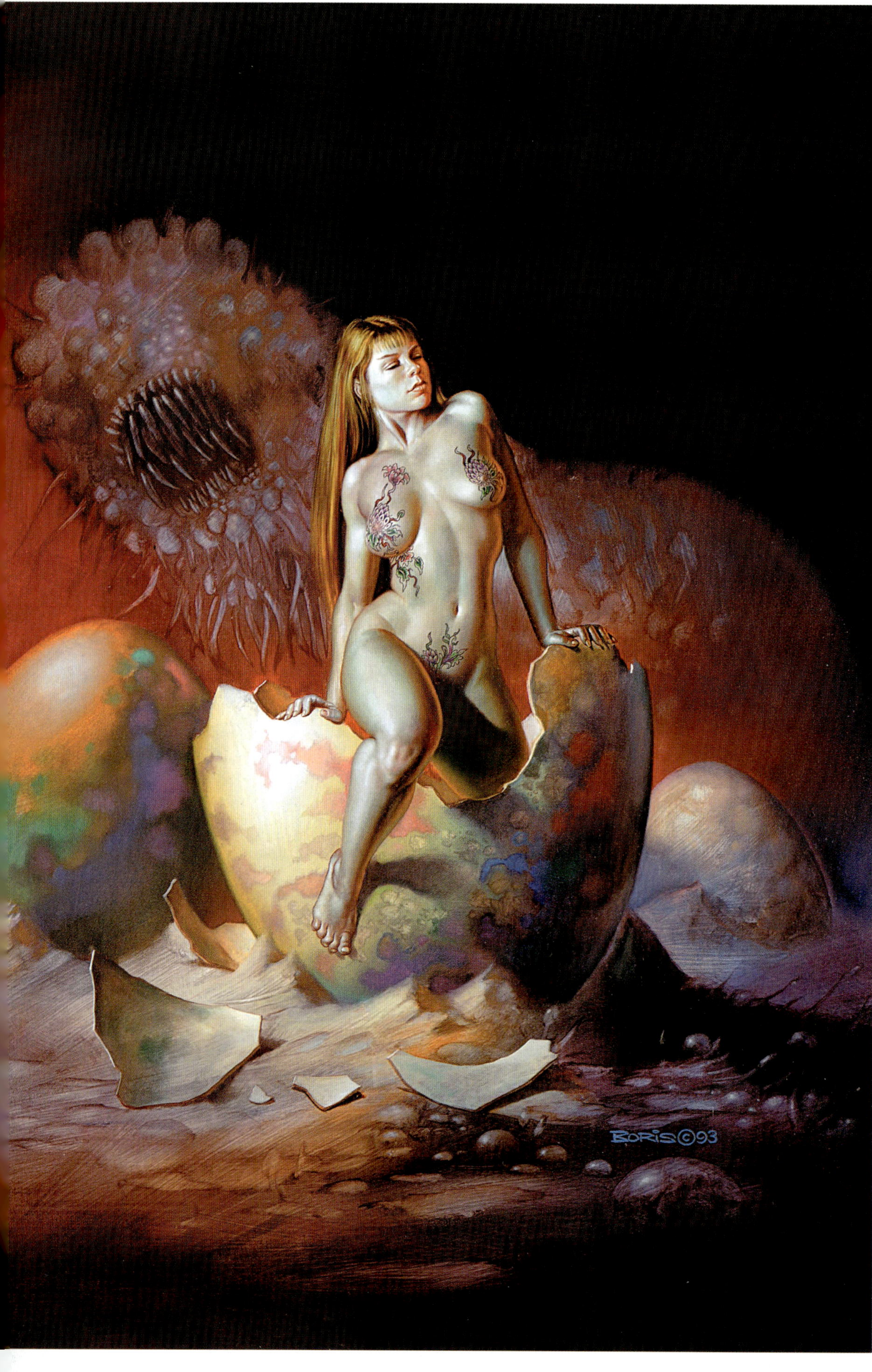

HATCHING

1993, Boris *(left)*

Showing creatures or people hatching from eggs is one of Boris's recurring themes and here he played with it again, using one of Julie's sisters as the model. The monster looming in the background is just a little joky twist to add contrast.

WHITE ANGEL

1987, Boris *(right)*

This was another overnight job for a book jacket.

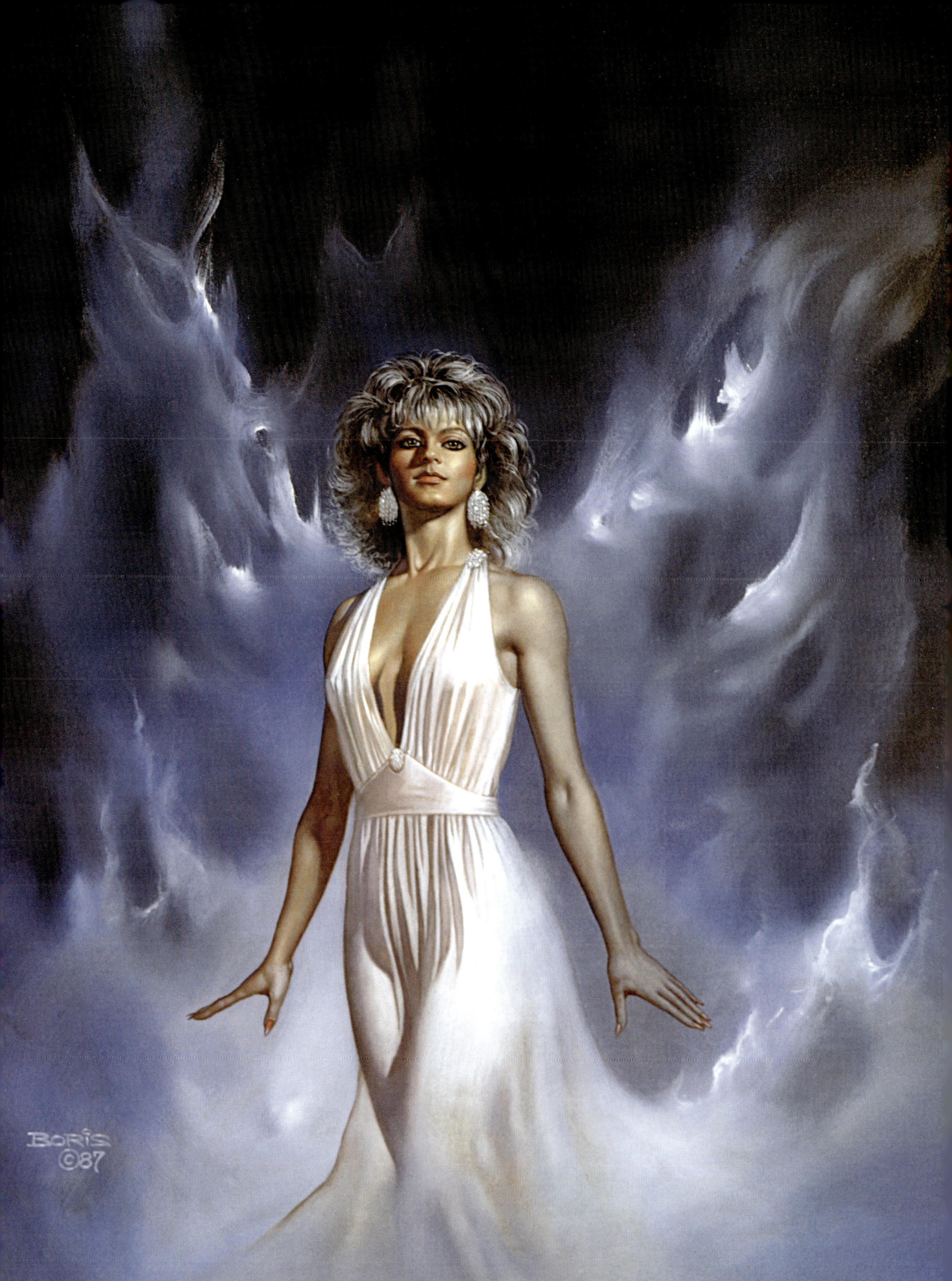
BORIS
©87

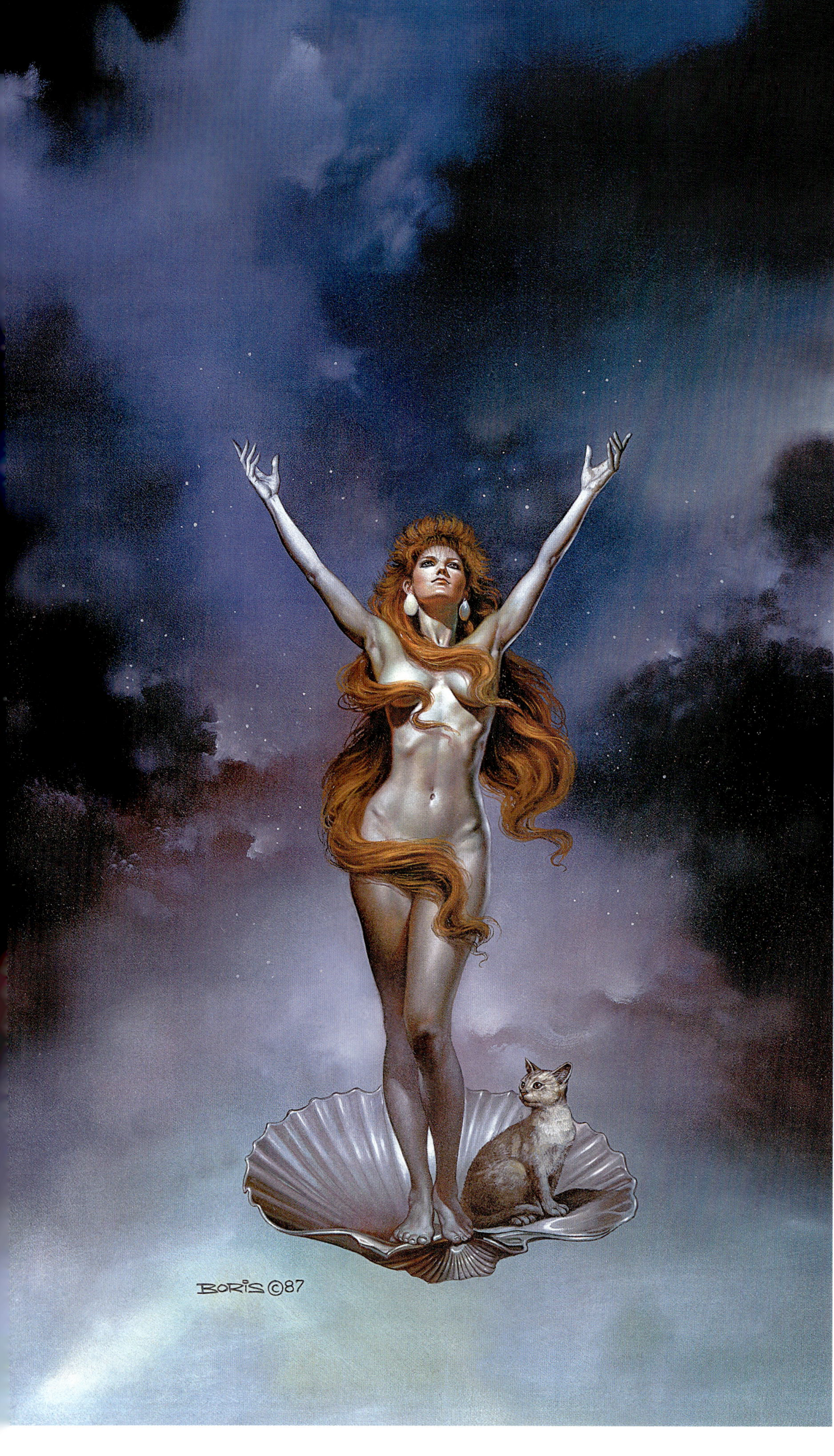

VENUS IN A HALF SHELL

1987, Boris *(left)*

This painting was commissioned as a take on Botticelli's famous *Birth of Venus* for a book jacket.

DUSK

2000, Boris *(right)*

From a series of pocketknife designs for the Franklin Mint. Originally they asked for just six ideas but the knives sold so well that the series was extended to eighteen. This was one of the last of them.

AQUARIUS

1987, Boris *(page 50)*

To make this zodiac sign a little different Boris chose a model of Korean descent, now living in the US.

CREATION

1989, Boris *(page 51)*

From the world myth series.

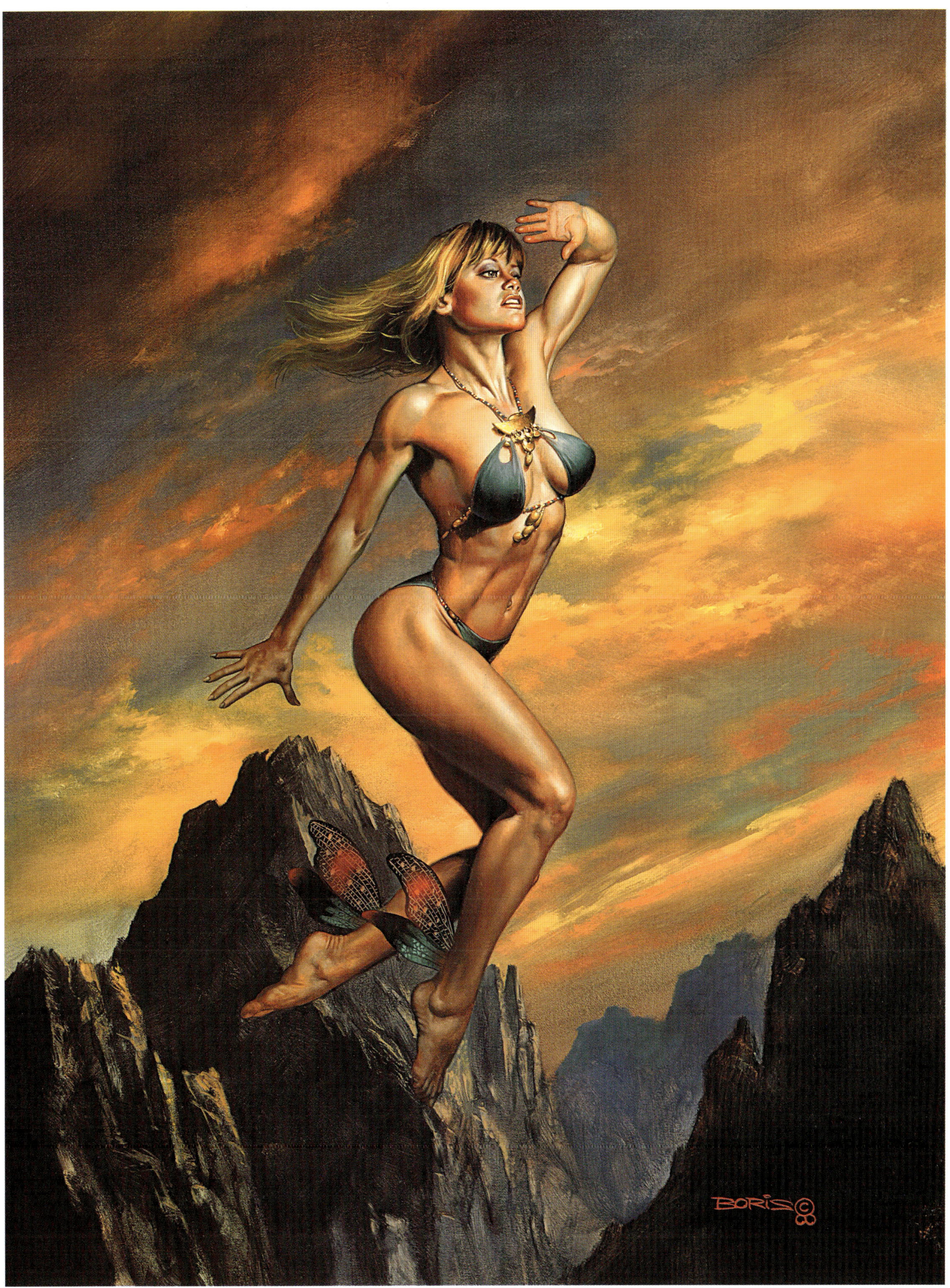
BORIS ©
88

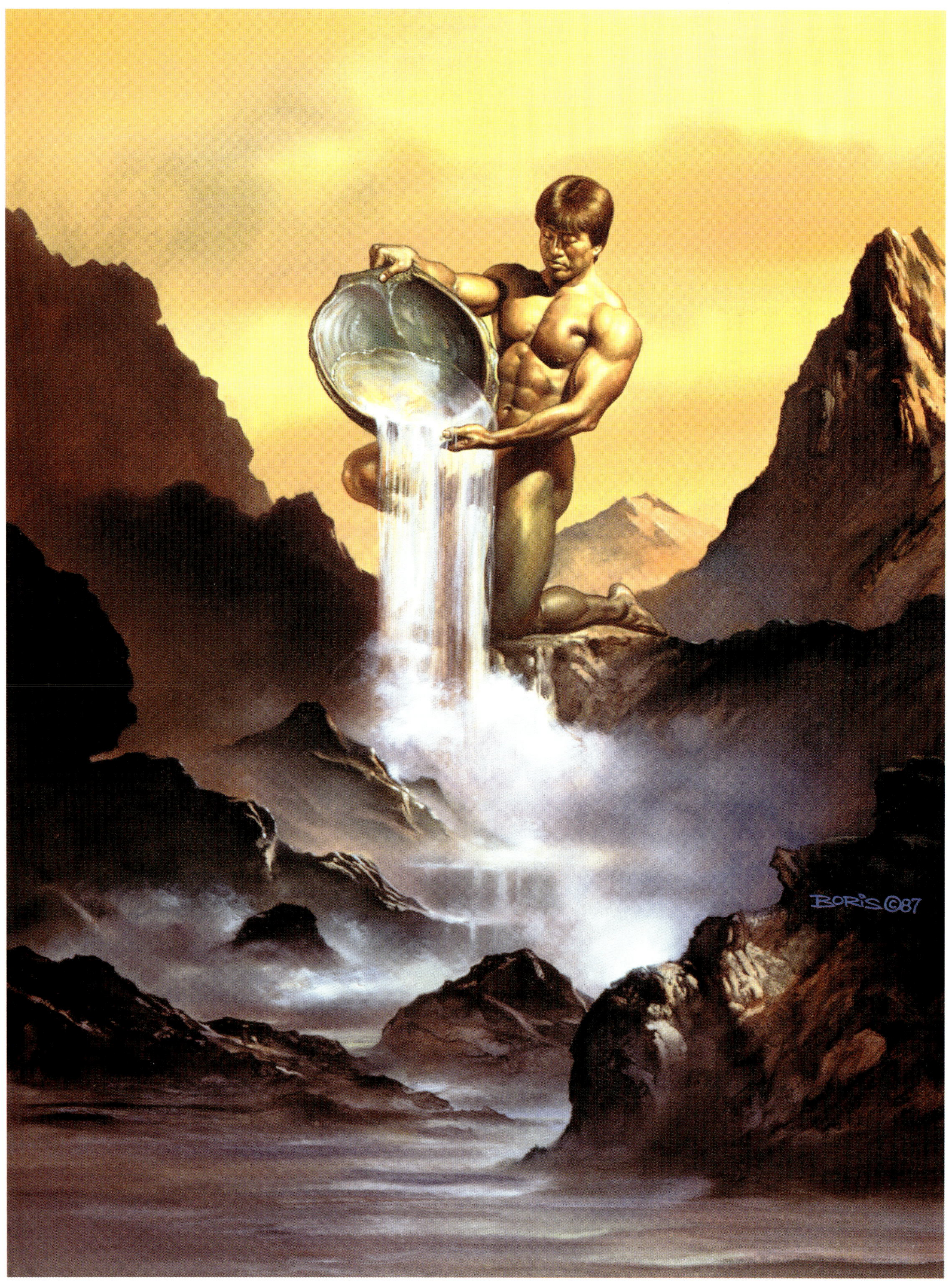
BORIS ©87

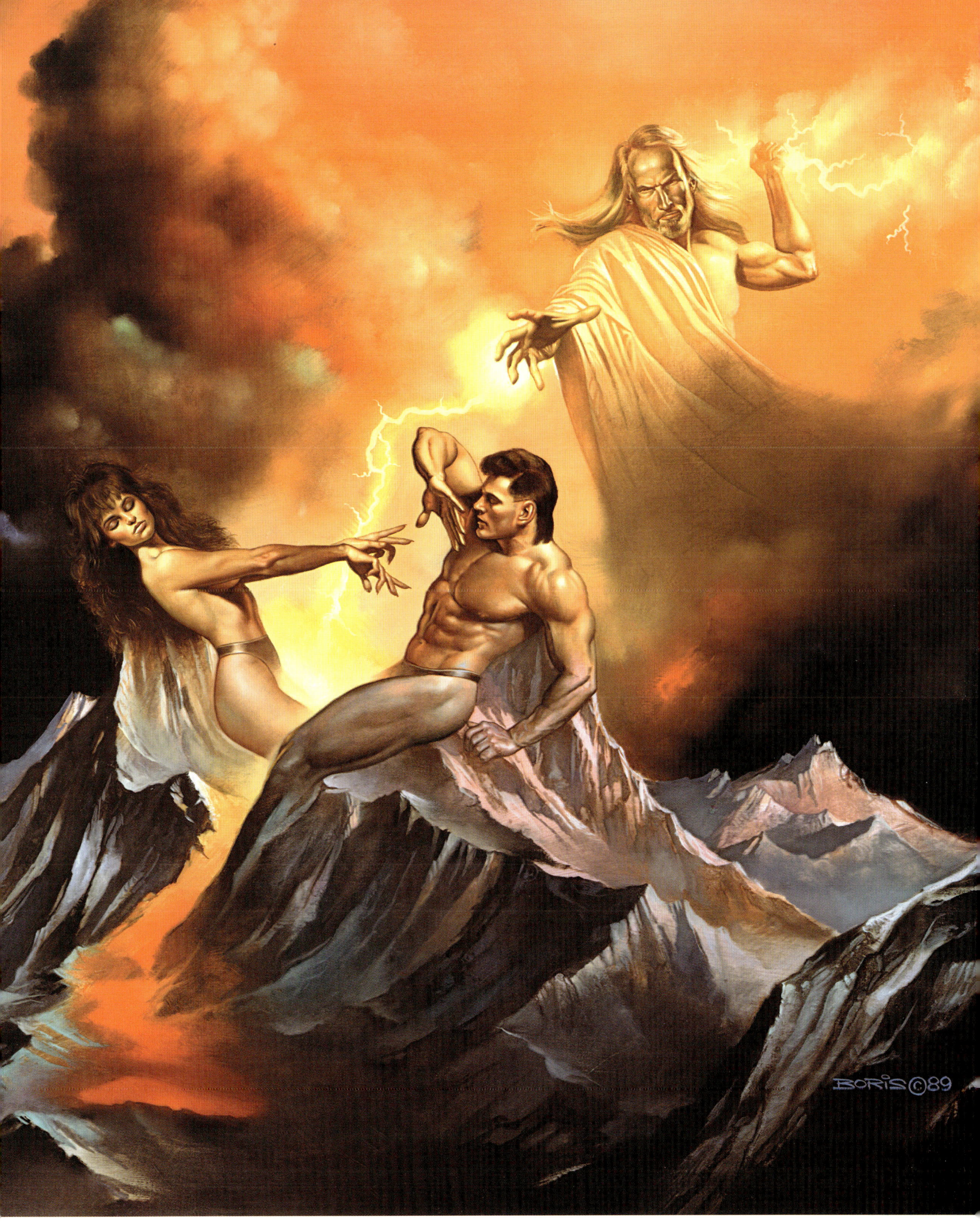
BORIS©89

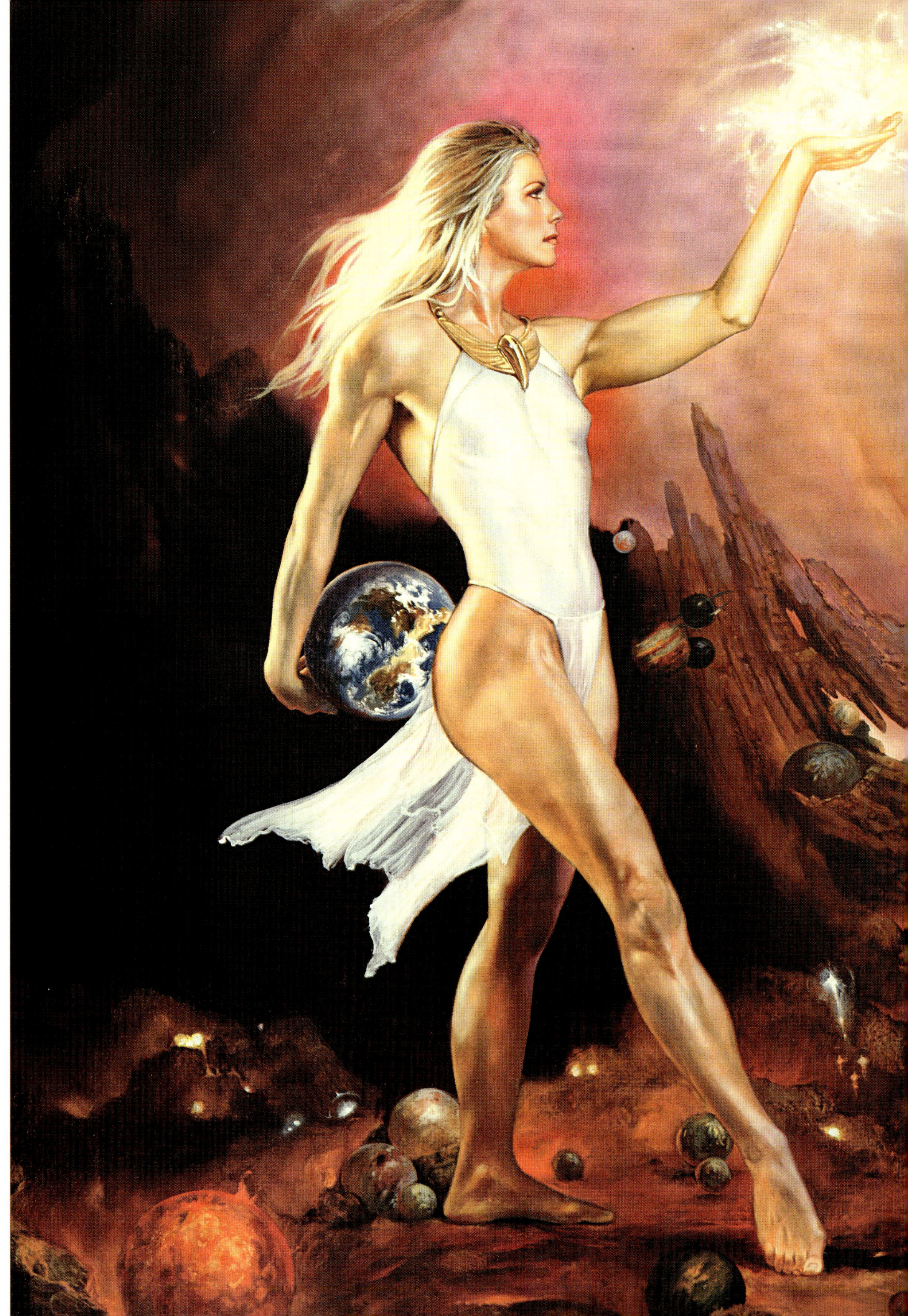

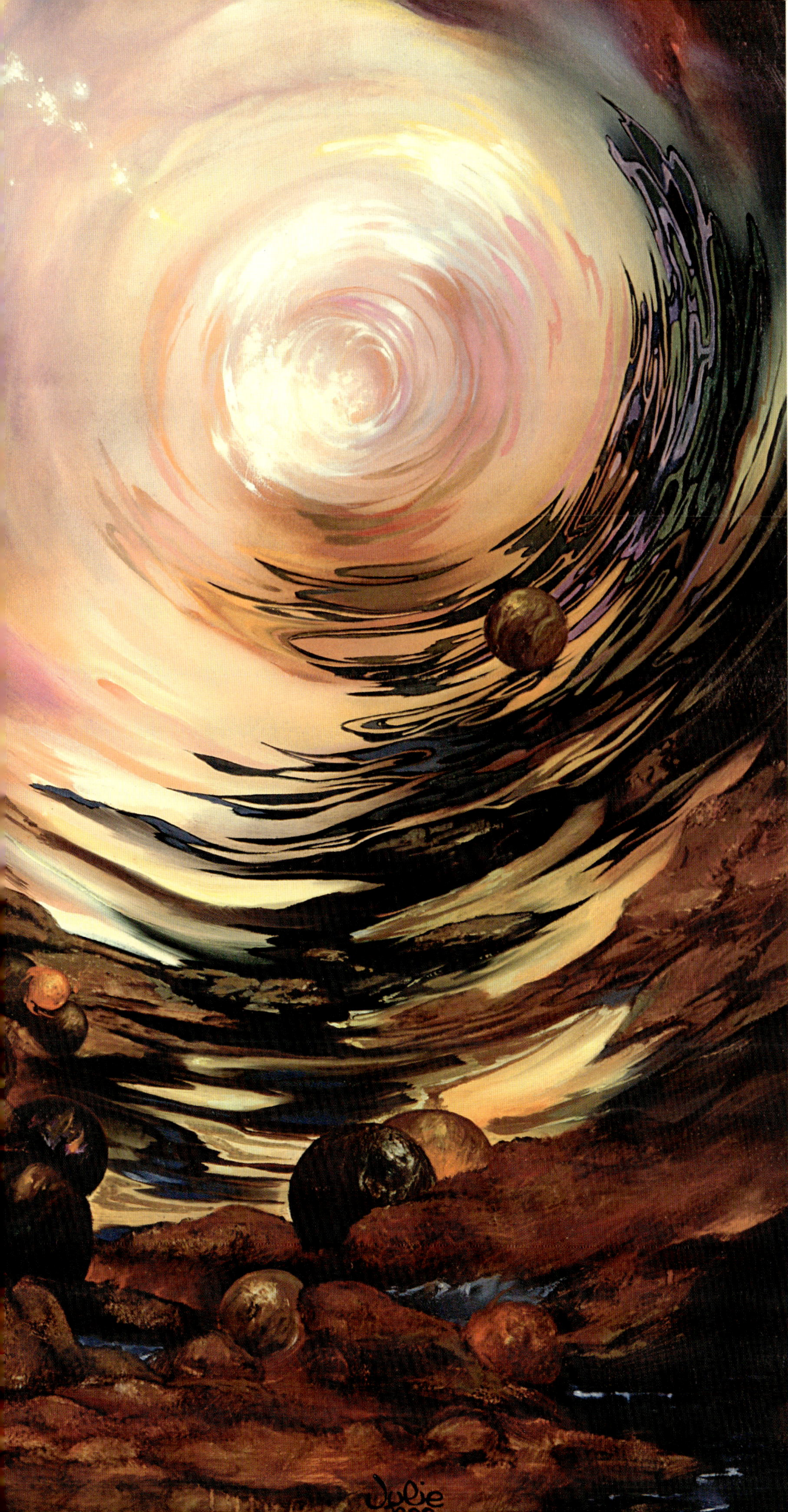

GALACTIC SPIN
2000, Julie

Julie was inspired for this by the model, Anja Langer, who flew over from Germany to pose for the artists: 'She was a very graceful person with some really beautiful ballet moves.' Julie stressed this by giving her a ballerina-type costume. The idea of the picture is that she is a cosmic female creating galaxies and spinning them off into space.

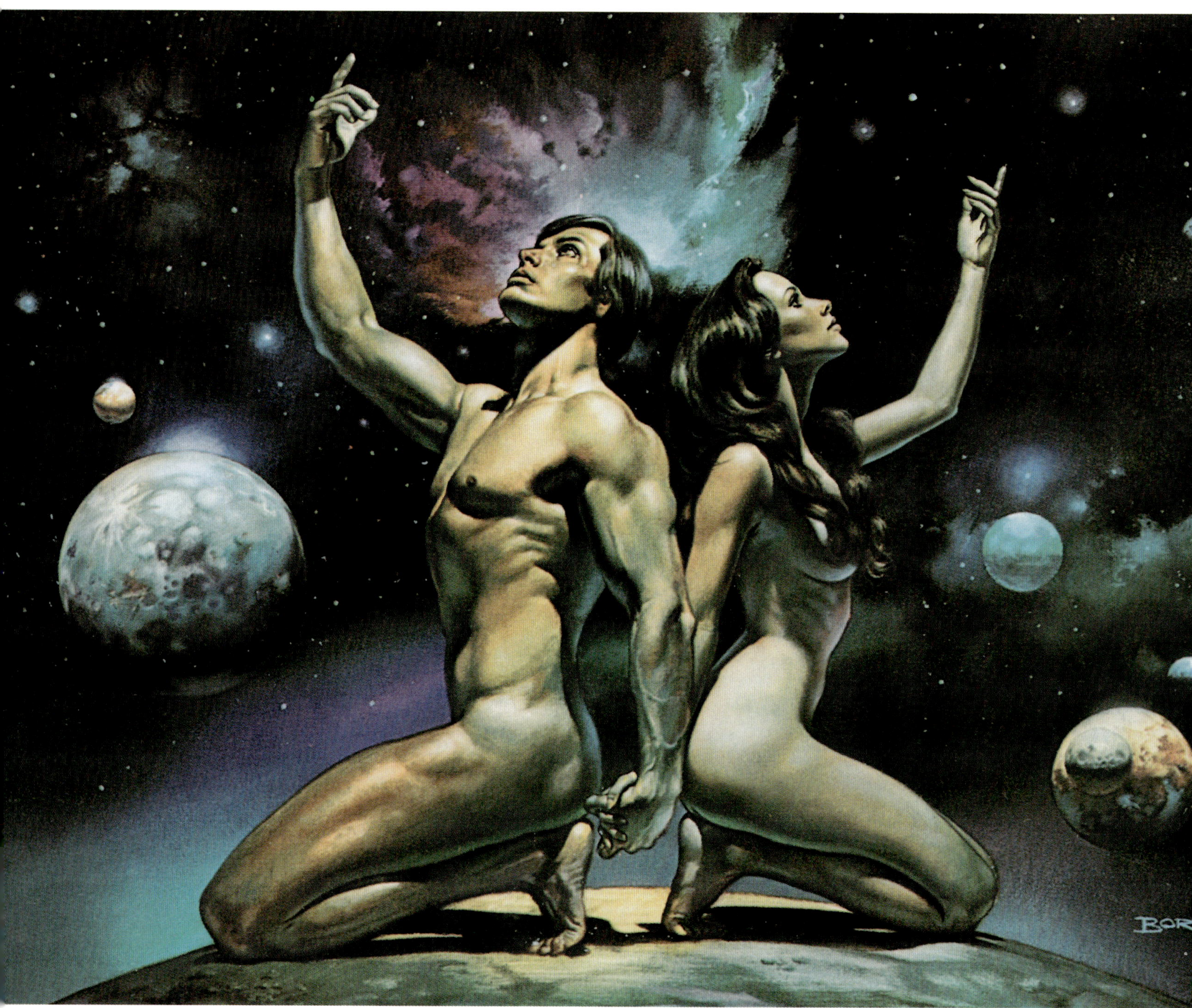

REACHING FOR THE STARS

1978, Boris *(above)*

A cover for the Science Fiction magazine *Future*. This was Boris's view of the future of mankind, launching out into the stars. Note the lack of a date, which he started adding to all his pictures soon afterwards. This has proved enormously helpful to people wanting to trace the development of his style because he otherwise finds it very hard to date his paintings accurately, having produced so many.

MAYAN LOVE

1979, Boris *(right)*

Boris loves doing very simple paintings without backgrounds occasionally, so all attention is focussed on the figures and their costumes. This was for a book cover.

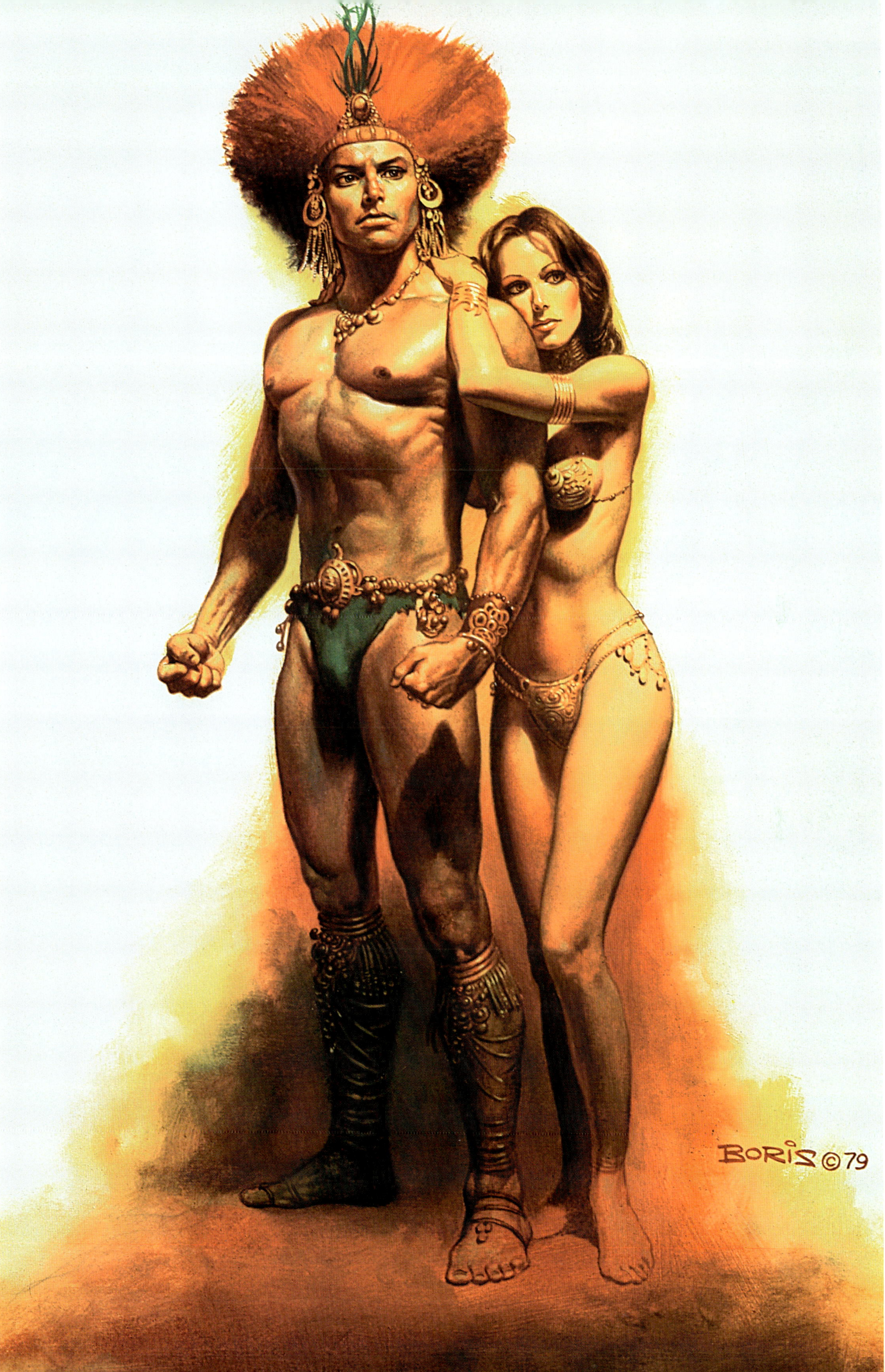
BORIS ©79

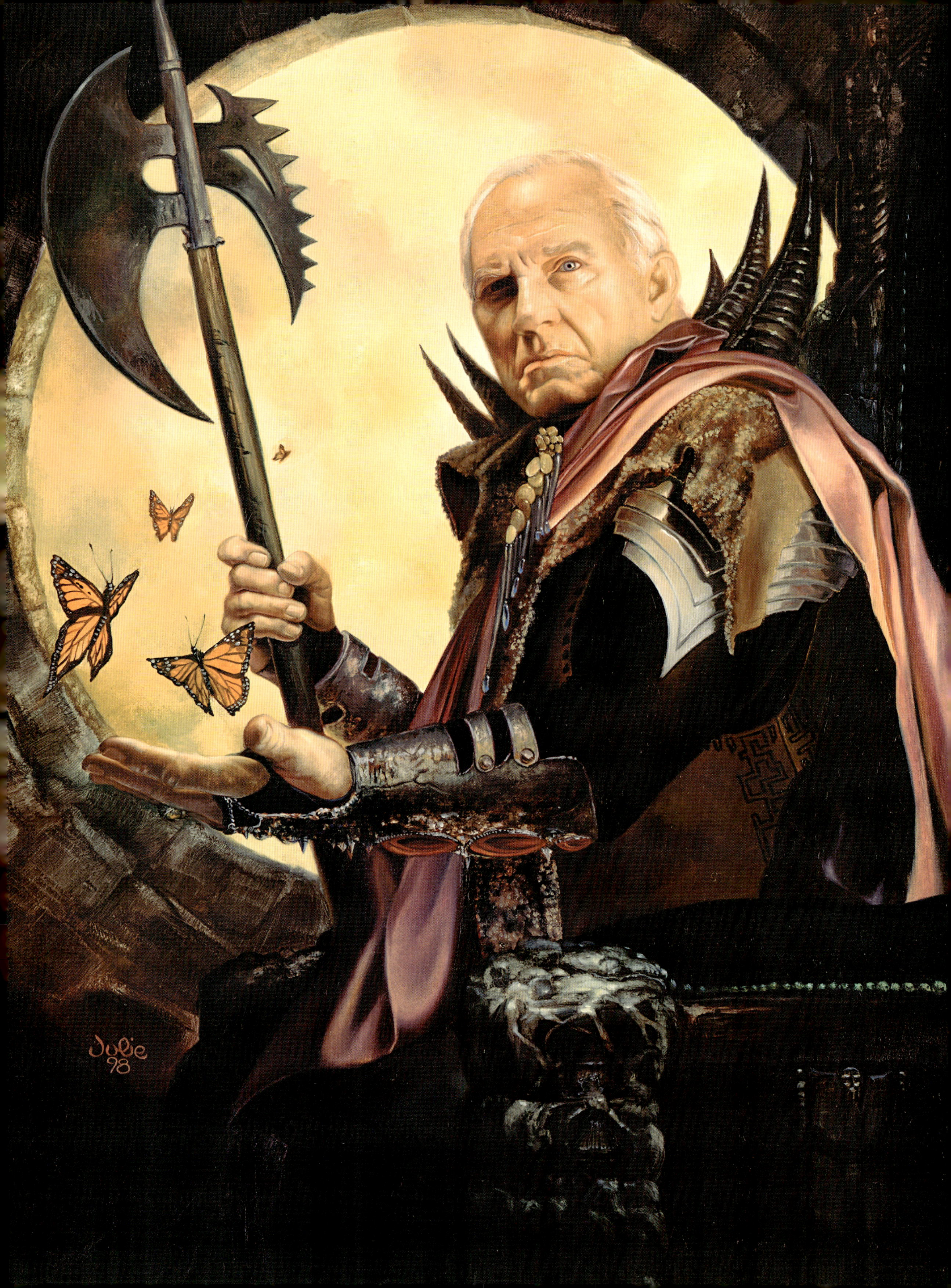
Julie
98

chapter 3

TIME TWISTING

Modern illustrators' use of photography to assist their paintings is ironic in a way since photography is popularly supposed to be what caused Fine Artists to abandon representative art a century or so ago. But one suspects there was more to it than that. Many Renaissance artists used the camera obscura for their portraits and the widespread use of mirrors by later artists, particularly in the Netherlands, to achieve perfect perspective is gradually being recognized.

One can see why a whole class of jobbing artists should want to take up the camera instead, because why spend days or weeks or even longer on getting a good likeness of people or places when a few minutes with a camera will do just as well? And one can see why their clients would also be relieved at having less of a drain on their purses, but for creative art the camera is just another tool. It can save time but it's no substitute for talent, drawing ability or imagination.

In Boris and Julie's case their use of cameras is complemented by countless hours drawing from life. The limitation of this is that most of their pictures call for figures in action, which is not that easy to draw from life. However, we begin this chapter with a few that could almost have been, though they weren't. The other advantage of photography is that it allows the capture of fleeting and spontaneous facial expressions that simply could not be held for any length of time any more than some of the more violent action poses.

The pictures in this chapter jump around a bit in time, hence the title. They demonstrate the wonderful freedom fantasy has to explore almost anything as long as it is not prosaic everyday reality. Imaginary and real pasts and futures are all grist to the mill. Medieval legend, Greek myth, space travel – anything is possible as long as it seems plausible enough to engage the imagination of the viewer. That is the key to successful fantasy because although anything is in theory possible, there are certain unwritten rules. They may not be apparent to people who have no taste for it, but a grasp of those rules, quite apart from their technical facility, is what puts Boris and Julie's paintings on such a pedestal.

THE CREATOR
1998, Julie

This is Julie's only painting of her father. Or rather, it is the only painting for which he acted as a model. Julie was impressed and quite surprised by the enthusiasm with which he entered into the part because many people find it awkward at first. What she was trying to capture in this picture is the complexity and contrariness of human nature. Here we have a decidedly mean character, armed and armoured to the teeth, yet he's releasing beautiful, gentle butterflies from his hand to fly out of the window into life.

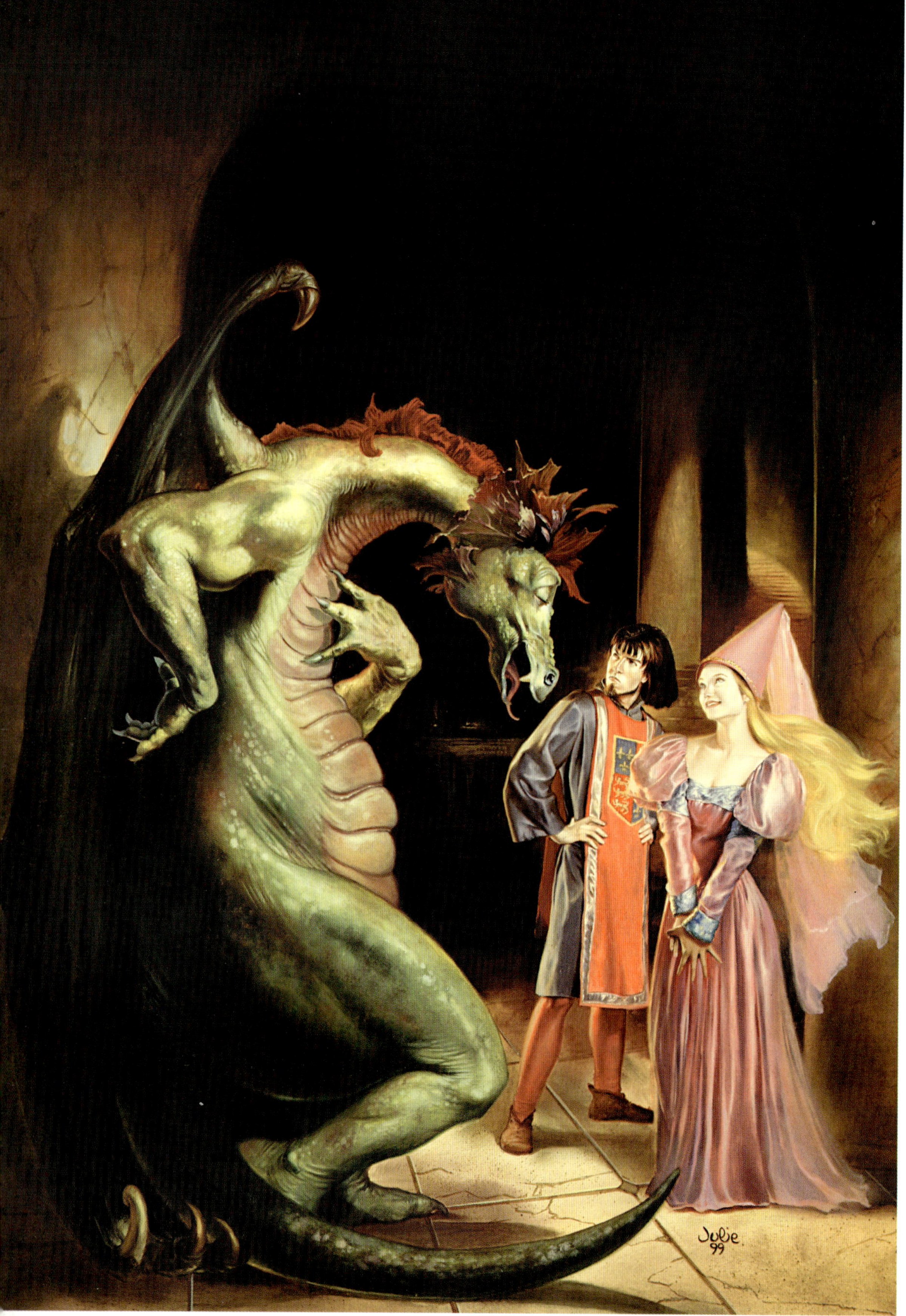

MR CHARMING

1999, Julie *(above)*

This was the cover for a Gordon Dickson book, an author that both Boris and Julie have illustrated. She loved the chance to inject a bit of humour into the picture – the young prince seething with jealousy as his lover allows herself to be seduced by the dragon's smooth-talking.

QUETZALCOATL

1992, Boris *(right)*

Most people find snakes repellent but Boris considers them among the most gorgeous of creatures. For his pains he was once bitten by a snake when he got a bit too carried away with examining it. Luckily it was not venomous. Anyway, here came a chance to translate some of that love into art with the Central American feathered serpent-god Quetzalcoatl.

PROMETHEUS

1997, Boris *(page 60)*

This was a private commission from a client who had this specific theme in mind. Such commissions are rare but Boris and Julie are always happy to take them if other commitments permit. Prometheus was the ancient hero who stole fire from the gods to brighten human lives, but paid the price of being chained to a rock to have his liver chewed endlessly by a vulture.

BACCHUS AND ARIADNE

1999, Julie *(page 61)*

After Ariadne, daughter of King Minos, helped Theseus escape the famous Minotaur's labyrinth, he treacherously abandoned her on the island of Naxos. But luckily this was the favourite haunt of the god Bacchus who rescued her and became her lover. The bold angle of this picture, designed to suggest movement and urgency, was suggested by creative movie camerawork.

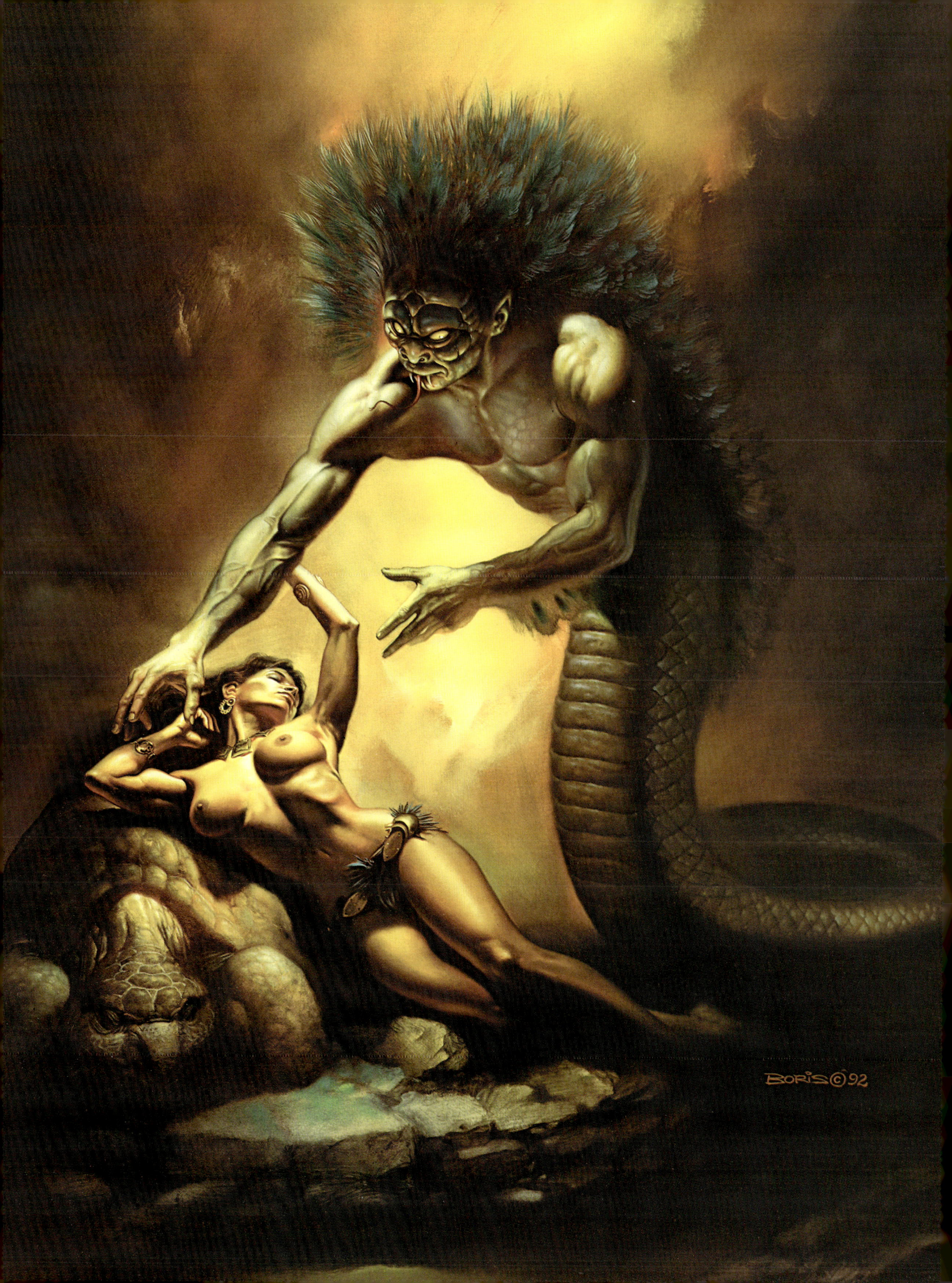
BORIS©92

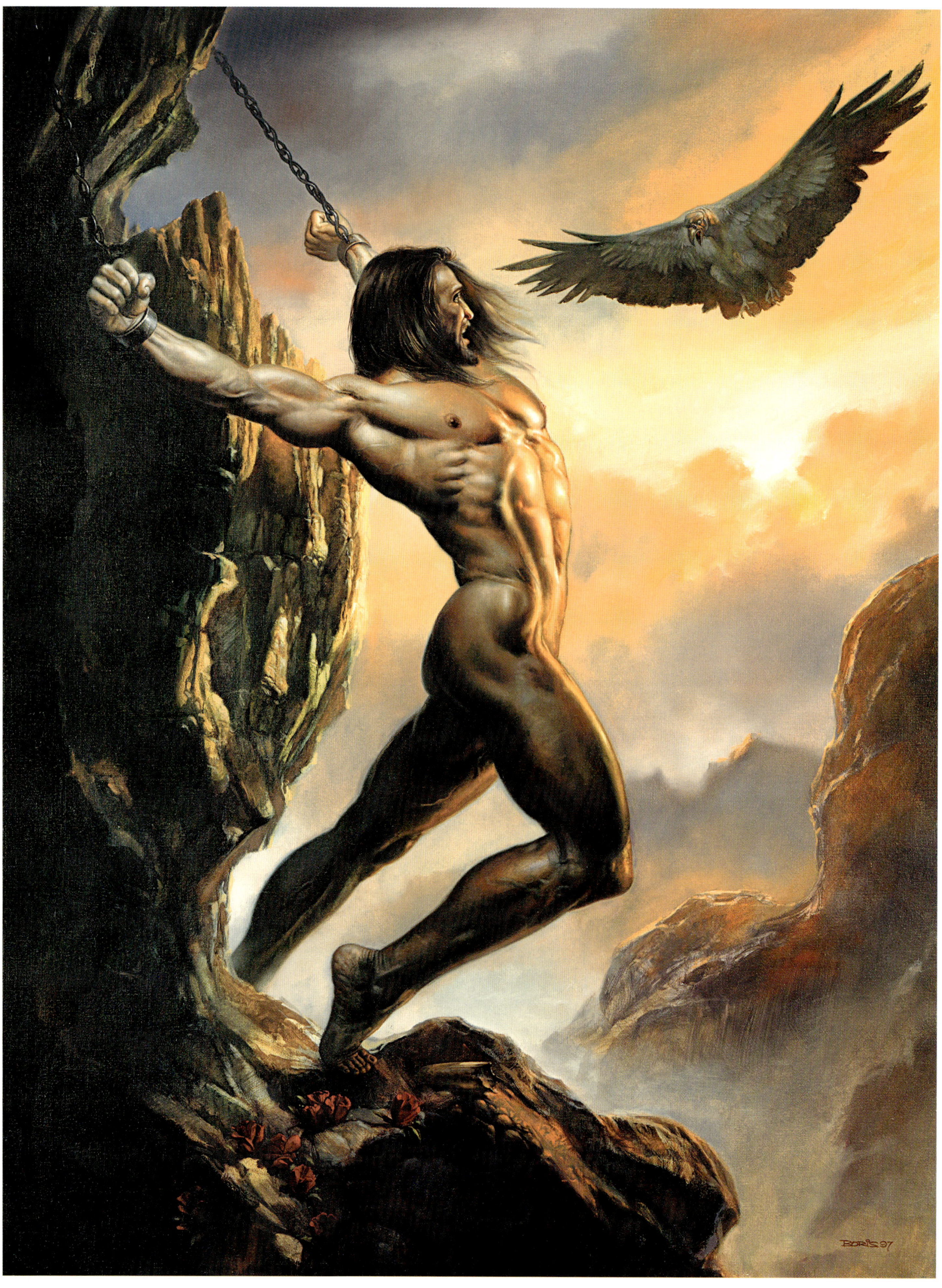
BORIS 97

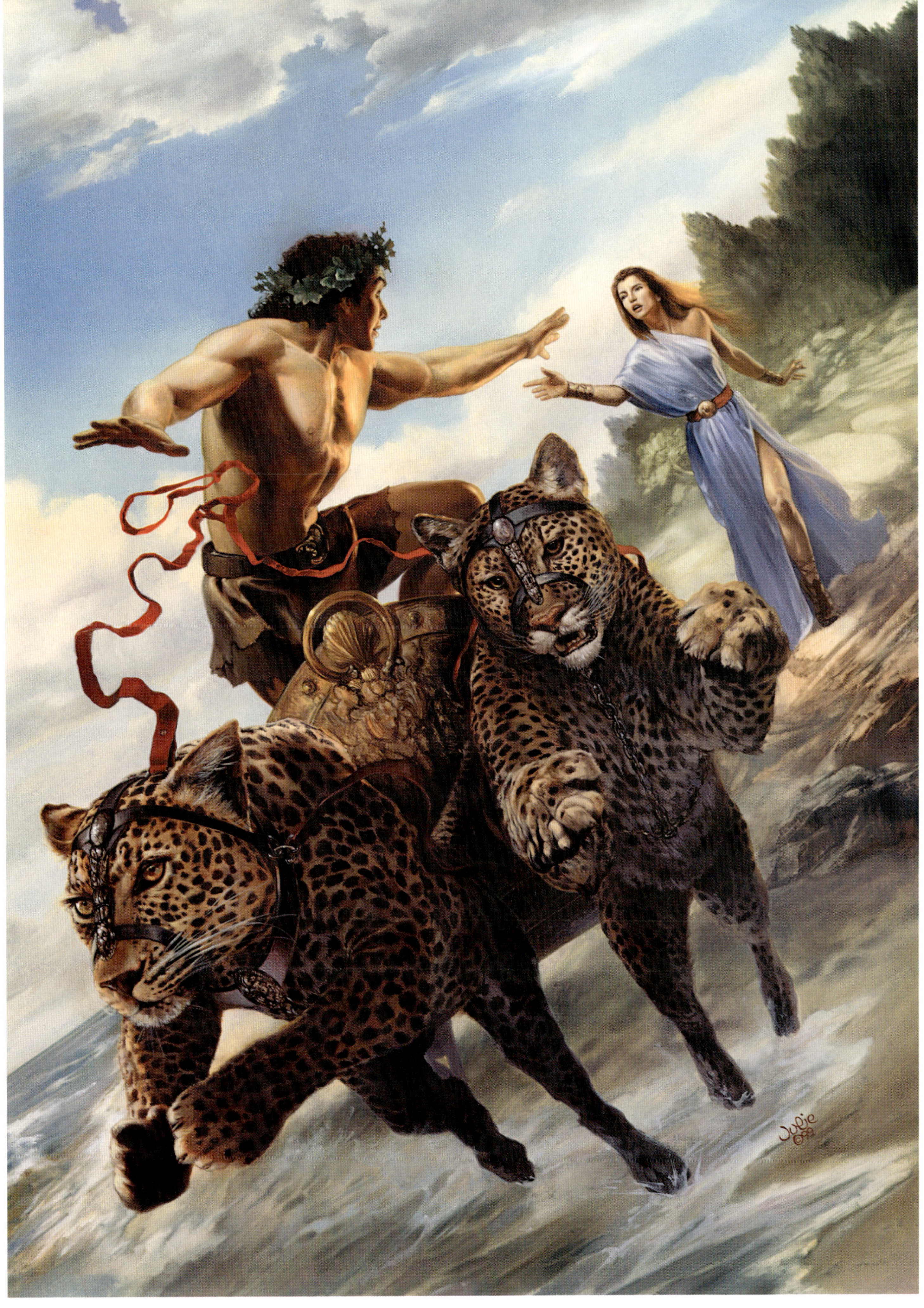

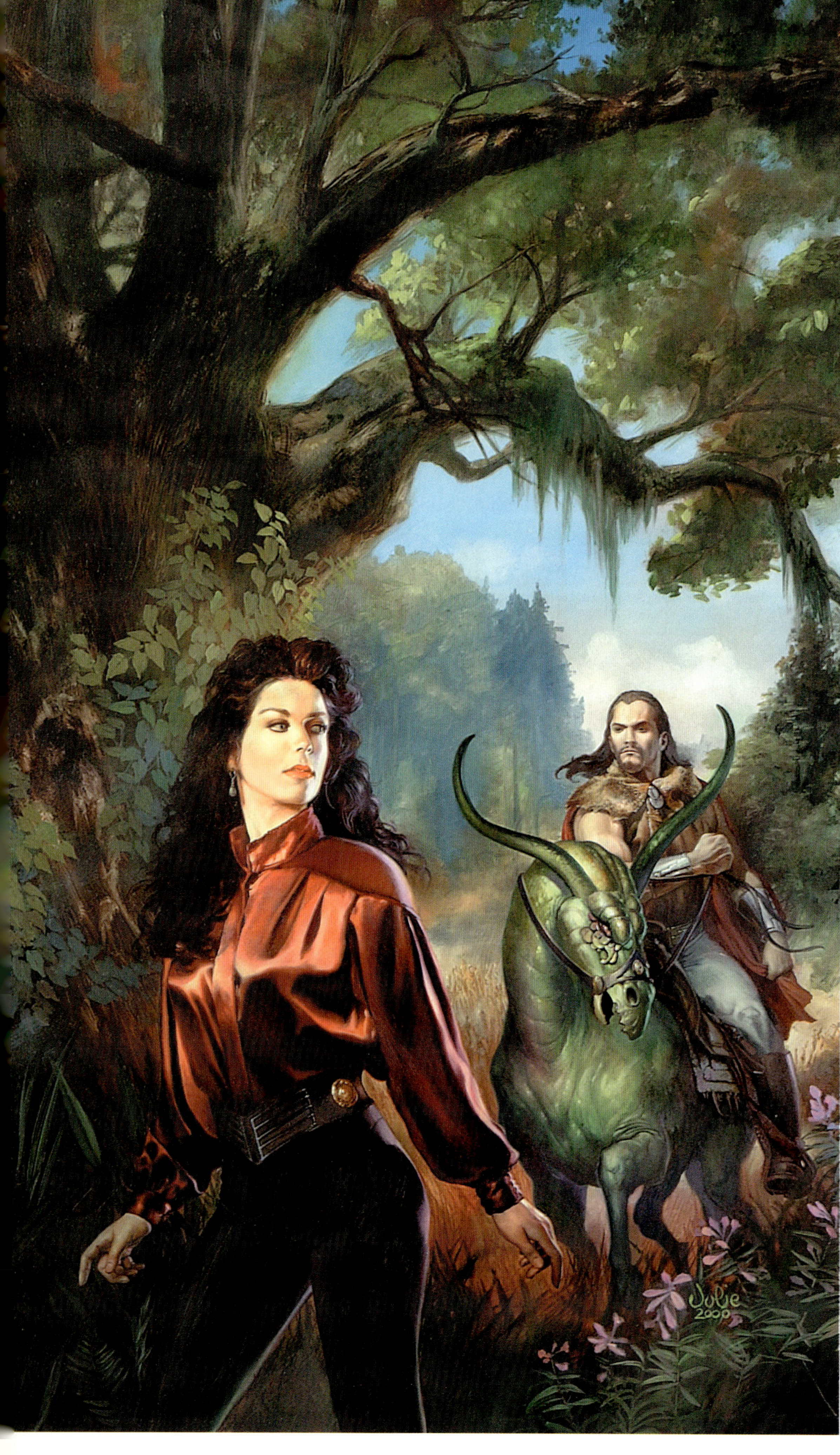

THE ENCOUNTER

2000, Julie *(left)*

Julie is rather more drawn to fantasies of the past than the future, while Boris is inclined the other way; but there is not a great deal in it. In practice they generally find something to enjoy in whatever kind of illustration comes along. This is one of several covers Julie has done for author Catherine Asaro, and she feels maybe she was chosen because of her portrayal of the very strong female characters in the books.

WOLF EYES

2000, Julie *(right)*

With a book cover like this the general concept is usually presented to an artist so creativity is kind of confined to the details. However, that can still be rewarding enough. In this case Julie had great fun painting the wolf, one of her favourite creatures. She also enjoyed having the two main characters stare straight out at the viewer with their contrasting attitudes – the wolf powerful and wise, the maid gentle and innocent yet determined. You have no doubt that between them they will triumph in their adventure.

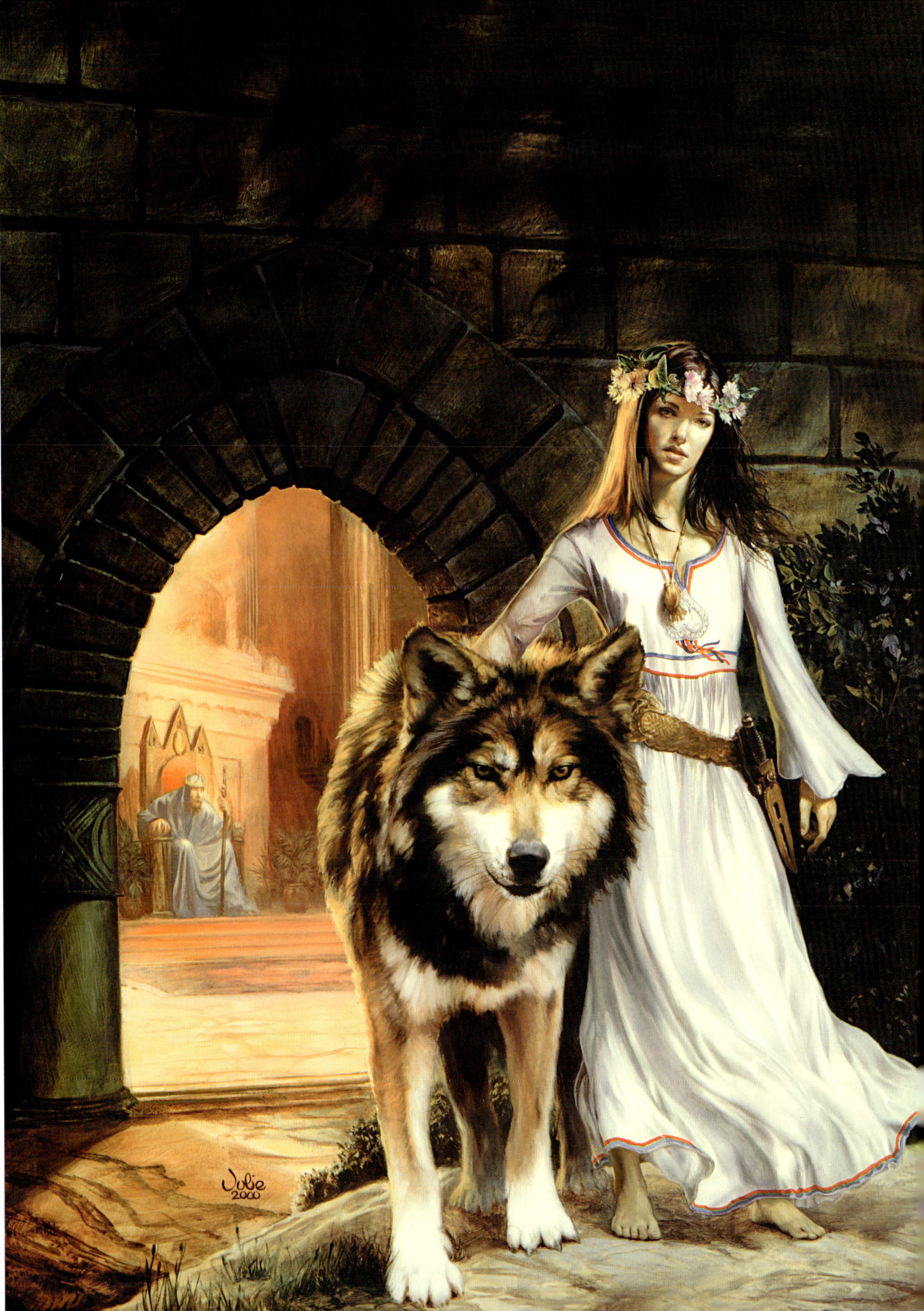
Julie
2000

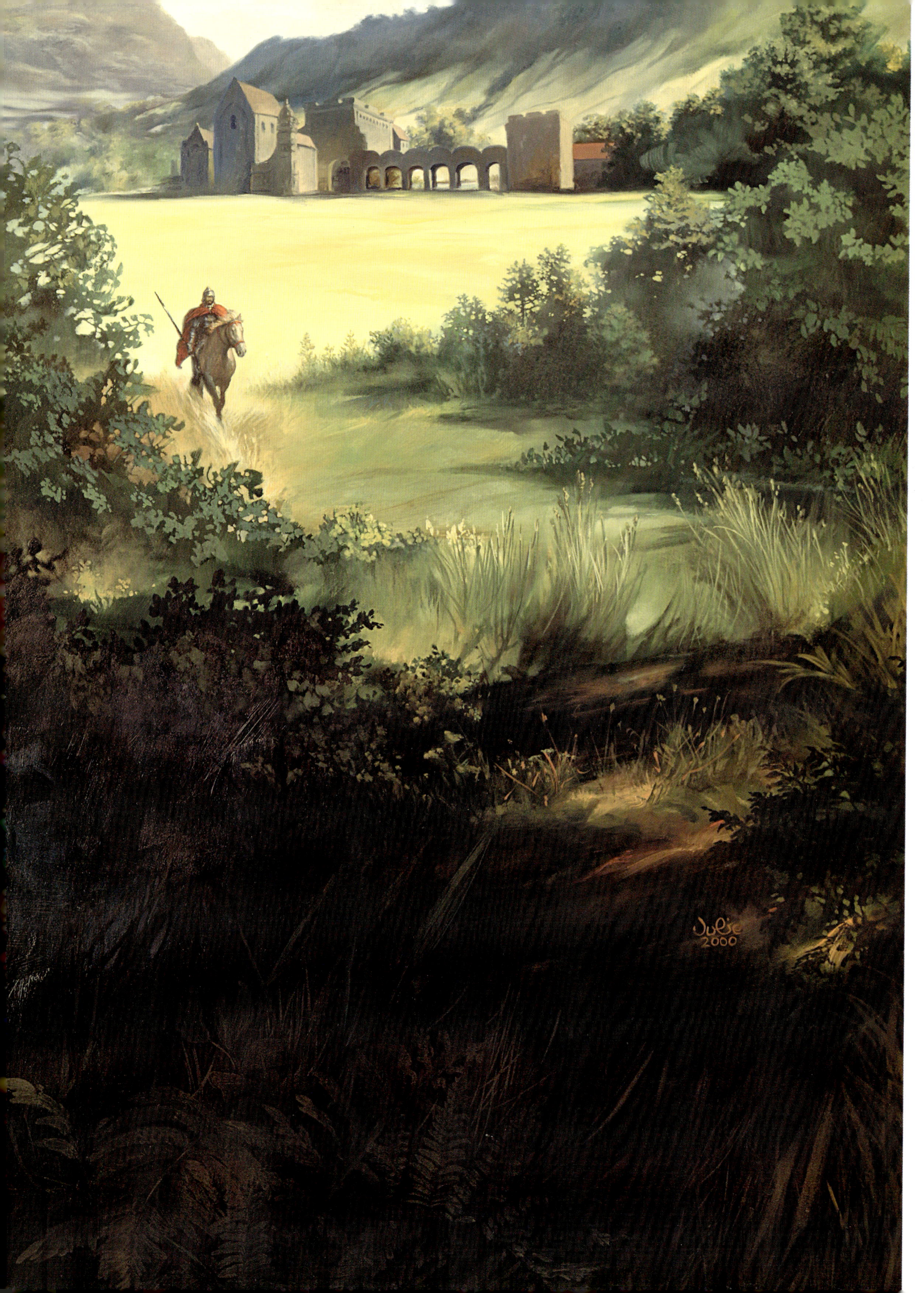
Julie
2000

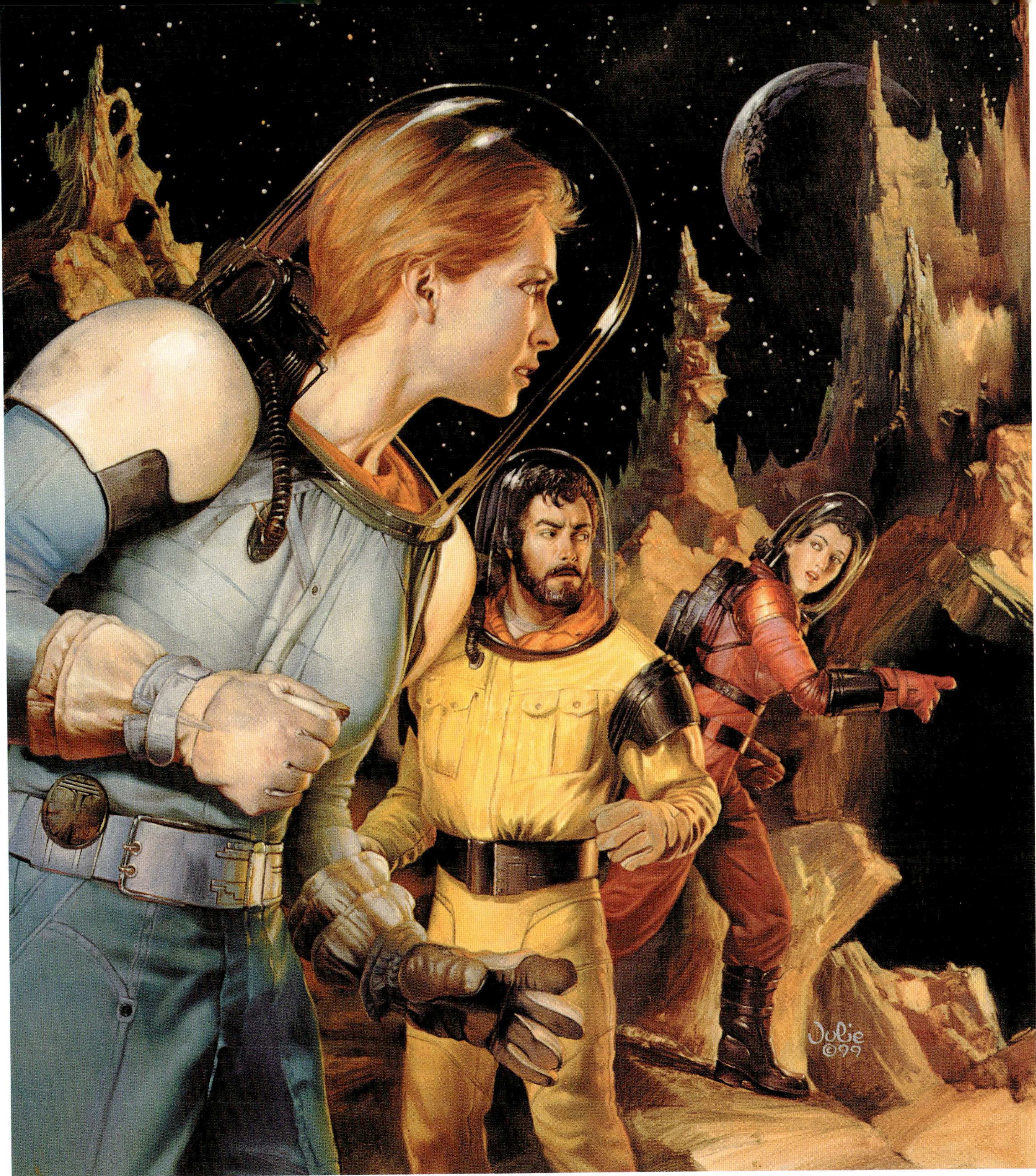

LLANTHONY

2000, Julie *(left)*

This book cover was well-timed because Julie had just met someone from Wales, where the story is set, and he sent her some photographs to get the feel of the place. Llanthony is a ruined abbey in an isolated valley of the Welsh Black Mountains and it looks pretty much exactly as Julie shows it here, remarkable really for someone who has yet to visit Wales. The slightly unusual composition was dictated by a need to have a dark area at the bottom to set off the title.

DISCOVERY ON ASTEROID X-72

1999, Julie *(above)*

Although this was a futuristic tale, it was not 'hard edged' Science Fiction so Julie aimed in this illustration for the old-fashioned feel of the 60s SF shows that she grew up with, like Lost in Space. Her models' space suits and equipment were improvized from materials that came to hand plus some reference to technical books about space travel and this, Julie says, was a lot of fun in itself – making everyday things into something totally different.

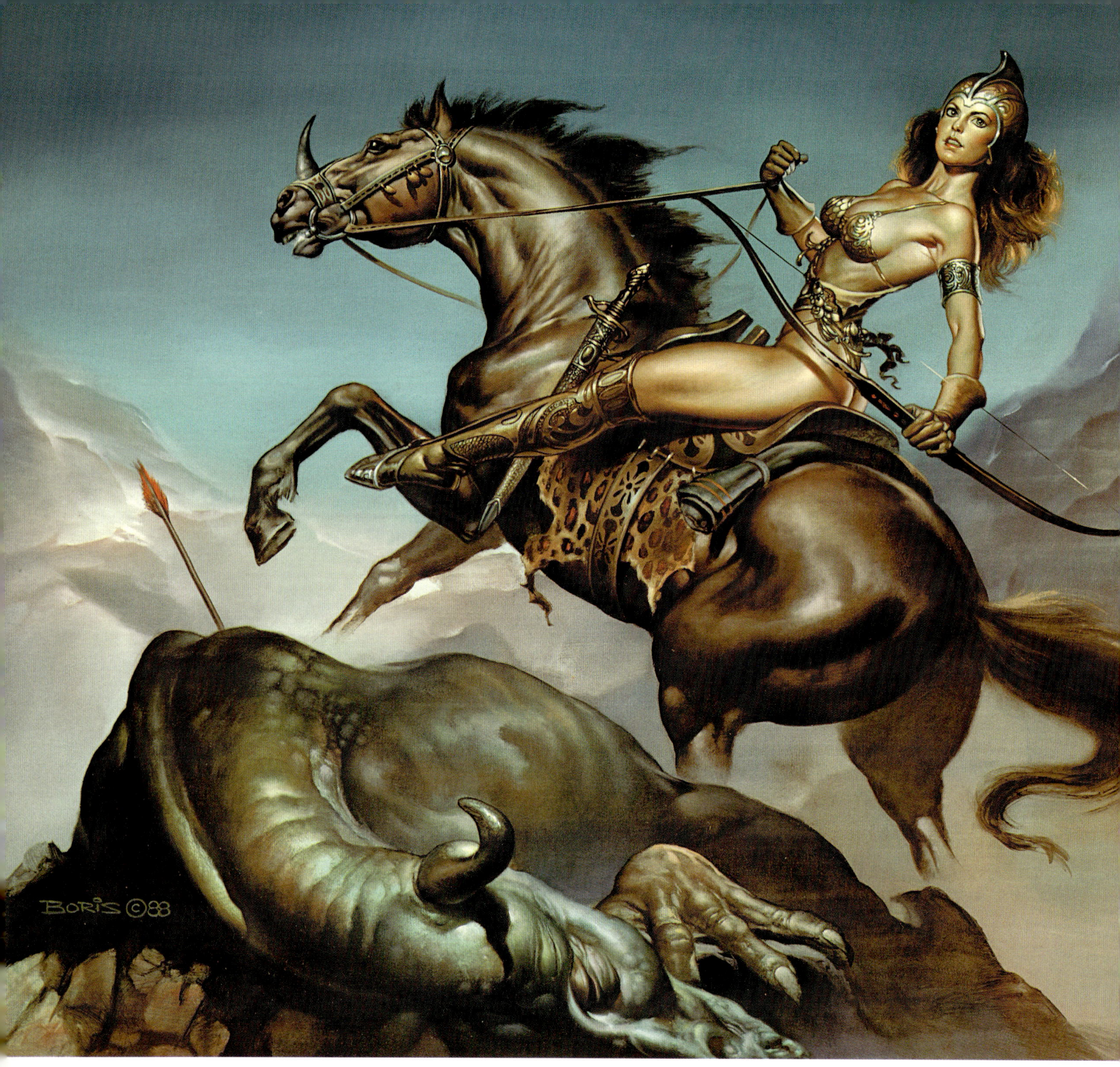

DIANA THE HUNTRESS

1988, Boris *(above)*

Horses are another of Boris's great loves and he takes every chance to paint them: 'I love the way they move and their musculature, especially in summer when they shed much of their fur.' He used to keep his own horses in fact but found it too time-consuming for comfort and ended it when his last one went lame.

THE MANTICORE

1992, Boris *(right)*

More often than not Boris's monsters have recognizably human elements in their constitutions. Partly this is because it can add to their menace but mainly it's because his endless love and fascination with the human body comes through.

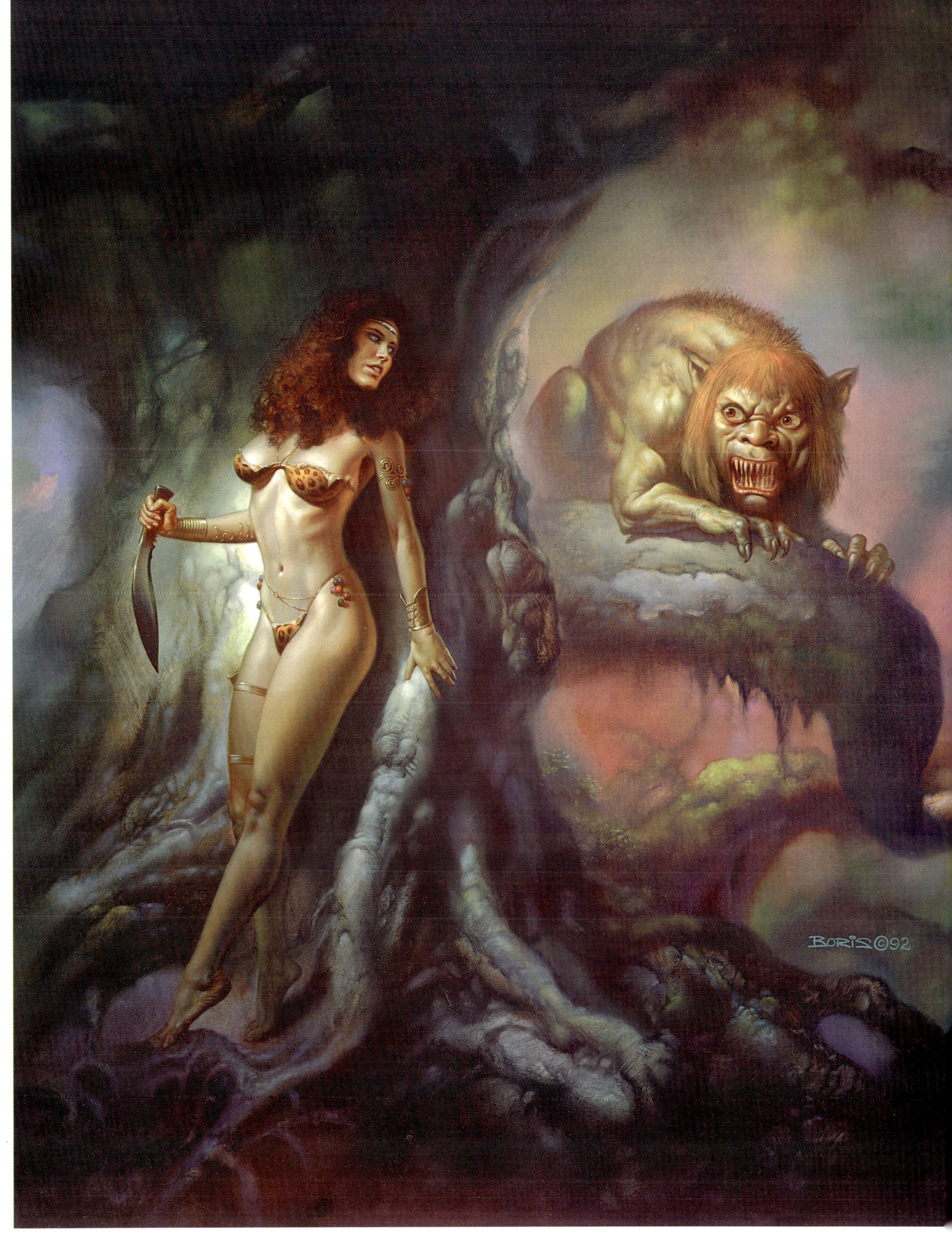
BORIS©92

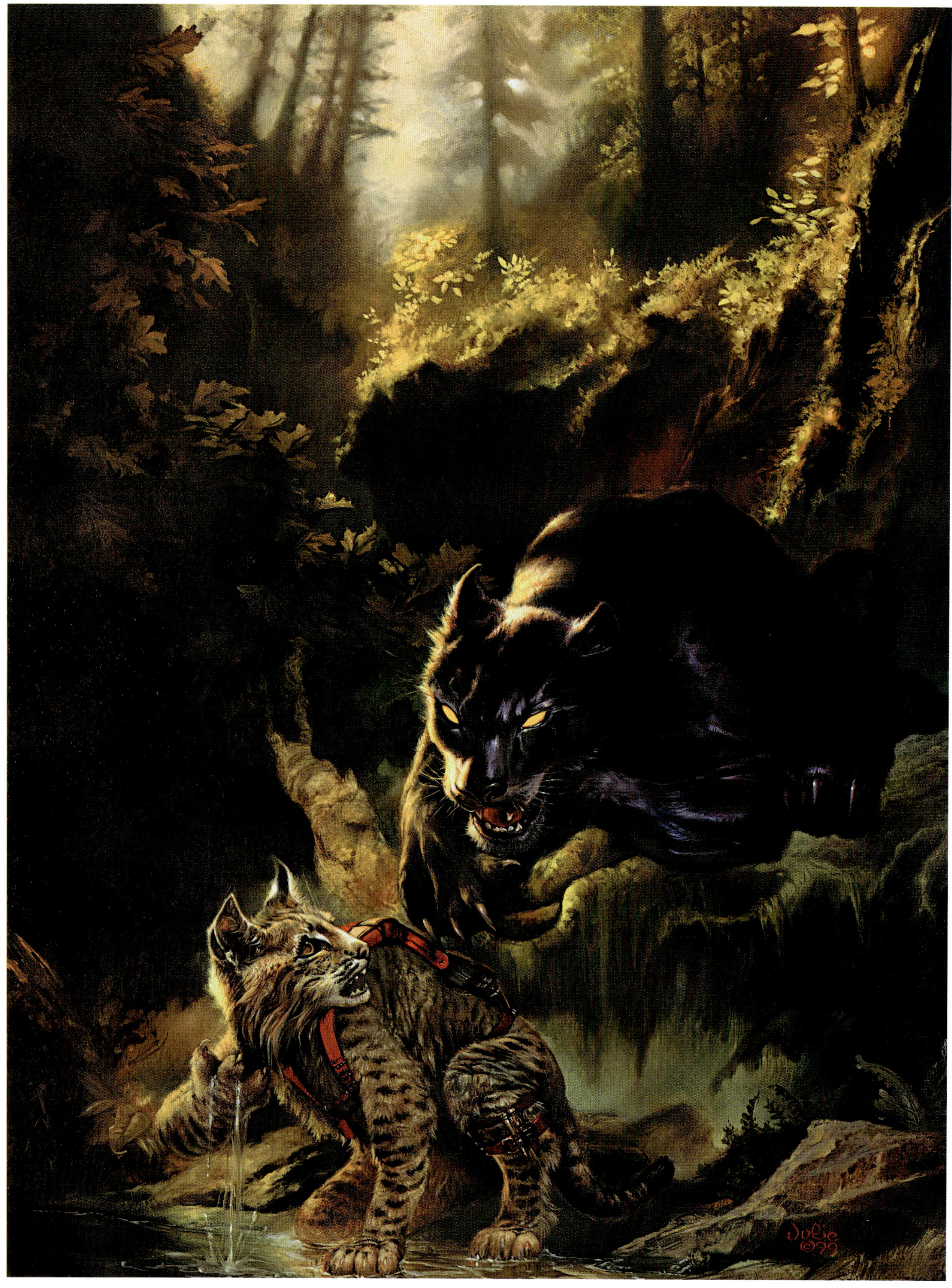

MAGIC FOREST

1999, Julie *(left)*

This picture combined two of Julie's favourite themes – animals and 'woodsy areas'. The challenge was to create a scene that looks completely lifelike at first, but is actually impossible. Looking closer we see that the smaller cat has a backpack and the animals seem to be engaged in verbal conversation.

FISHING

1993, Boris *(right)*

Boris has often been fascinated by the metallic and jewel-like appearance of many fish, so here he decided to push this further to a fantastic extreme where the monstrous fish is actually made of living metal and gems.

JASON AND MEDEA

2000, Julie *(page 70)*

We see Jason the Argonaut making off with the Golden Fleece, unaware yet that an angry giant has caught up with them. Boris posed for both Jason and the ogre. Stylistically Julie was aiming for a slightly Maxfield Parrish feel to the painting. She's a great admirer of his distinctive use of colour and dreamy backgrounds, so here was seeing how much she had learned from him.

PEDRUM

1993, Boris *(page 71)*

This is largely a study in textures, particularly between the female's soft skin tones and the animated stone of her attacker, who is springing into life from their rocky perch. We see one of its hands fractured off but still gripping the woman's arm, suggesting a troublesome removal later!

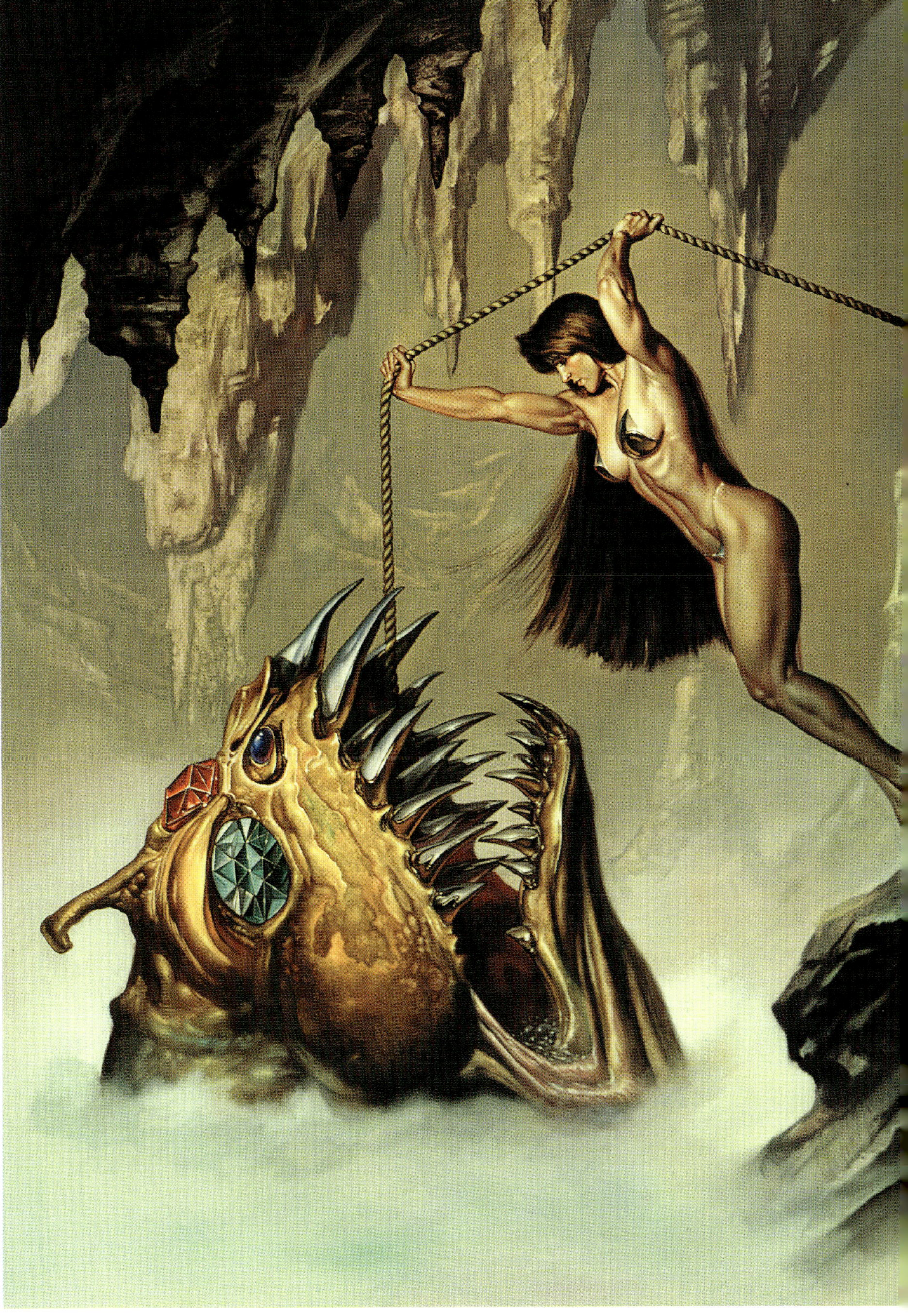

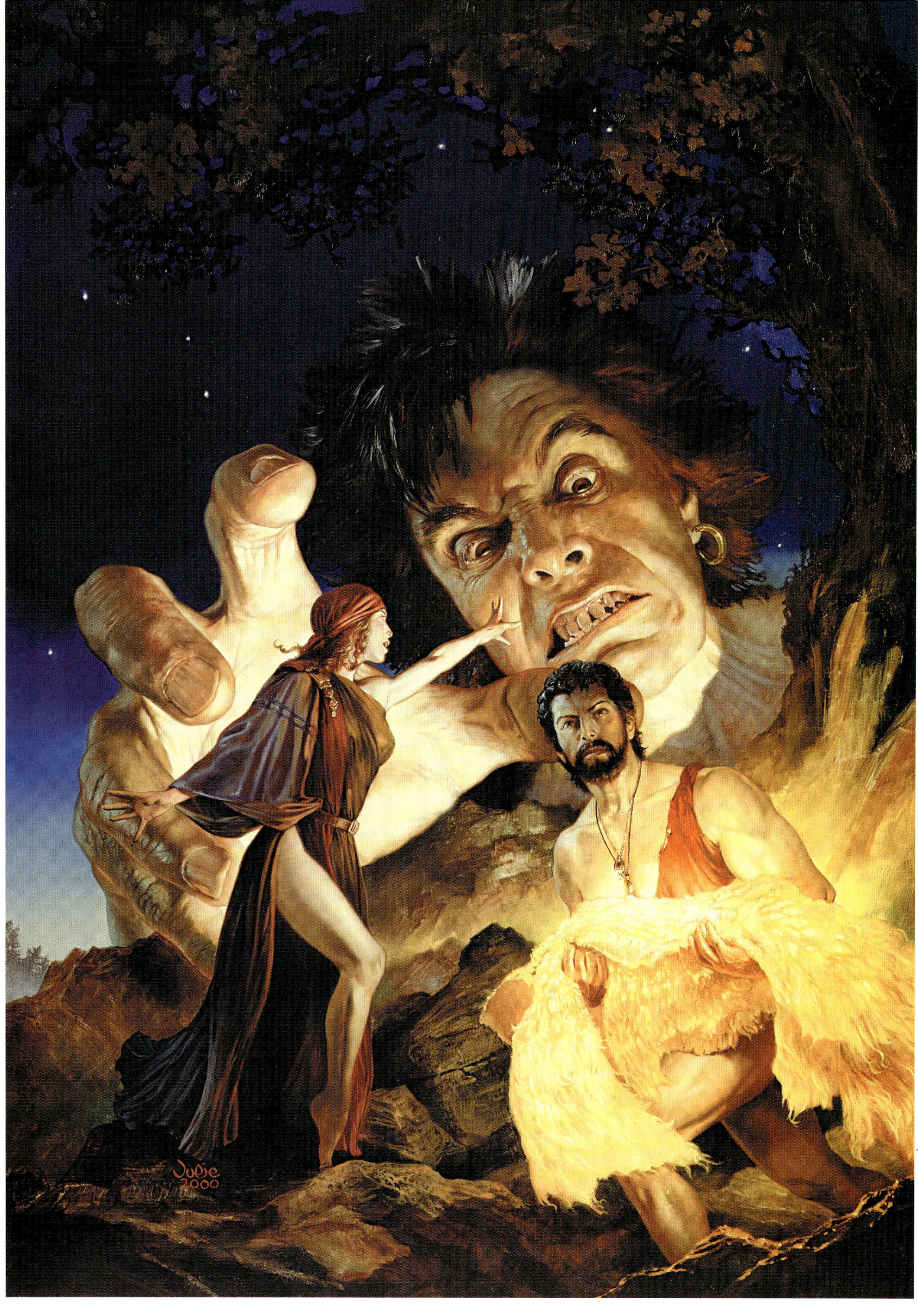

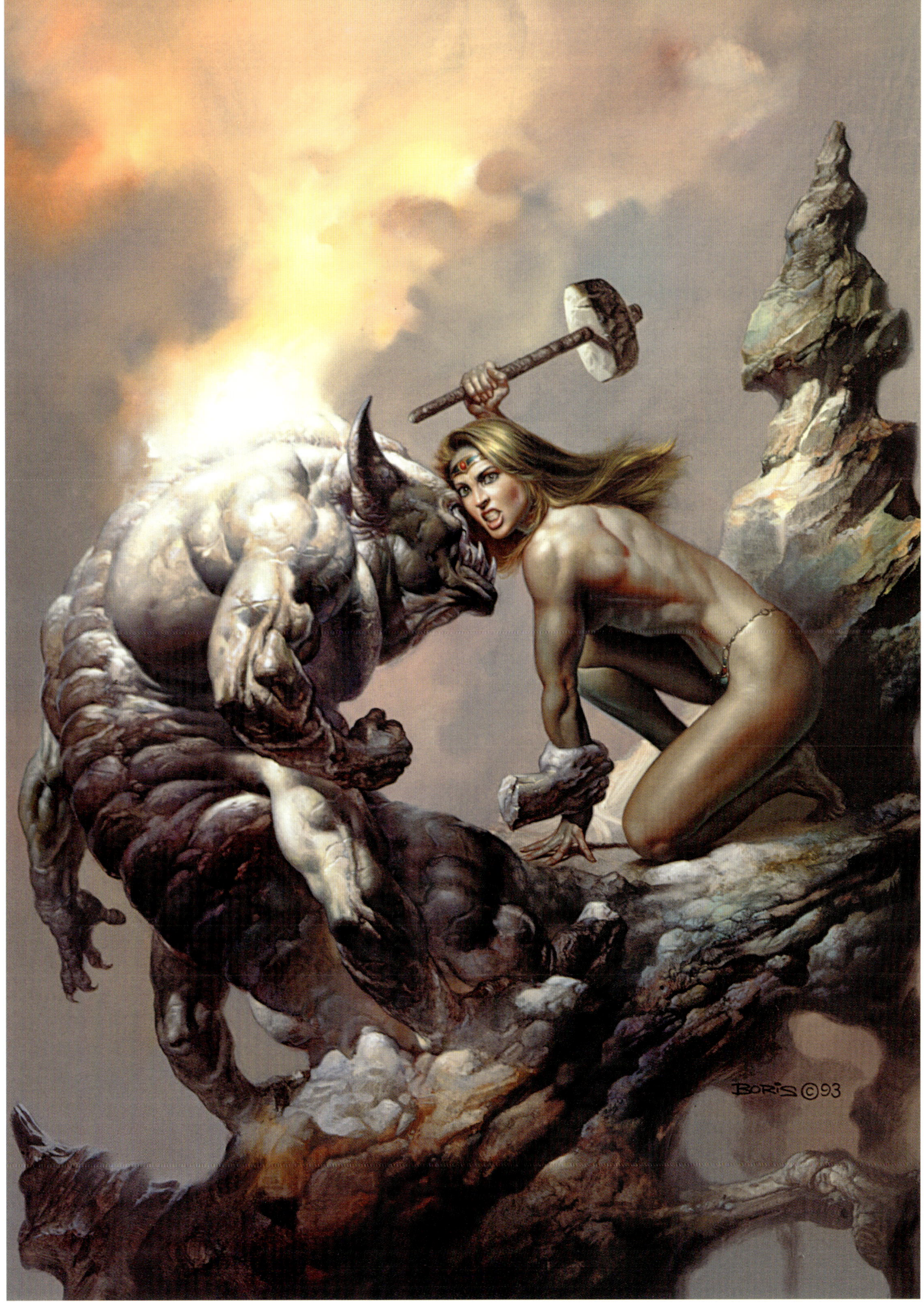
BORIS ©93

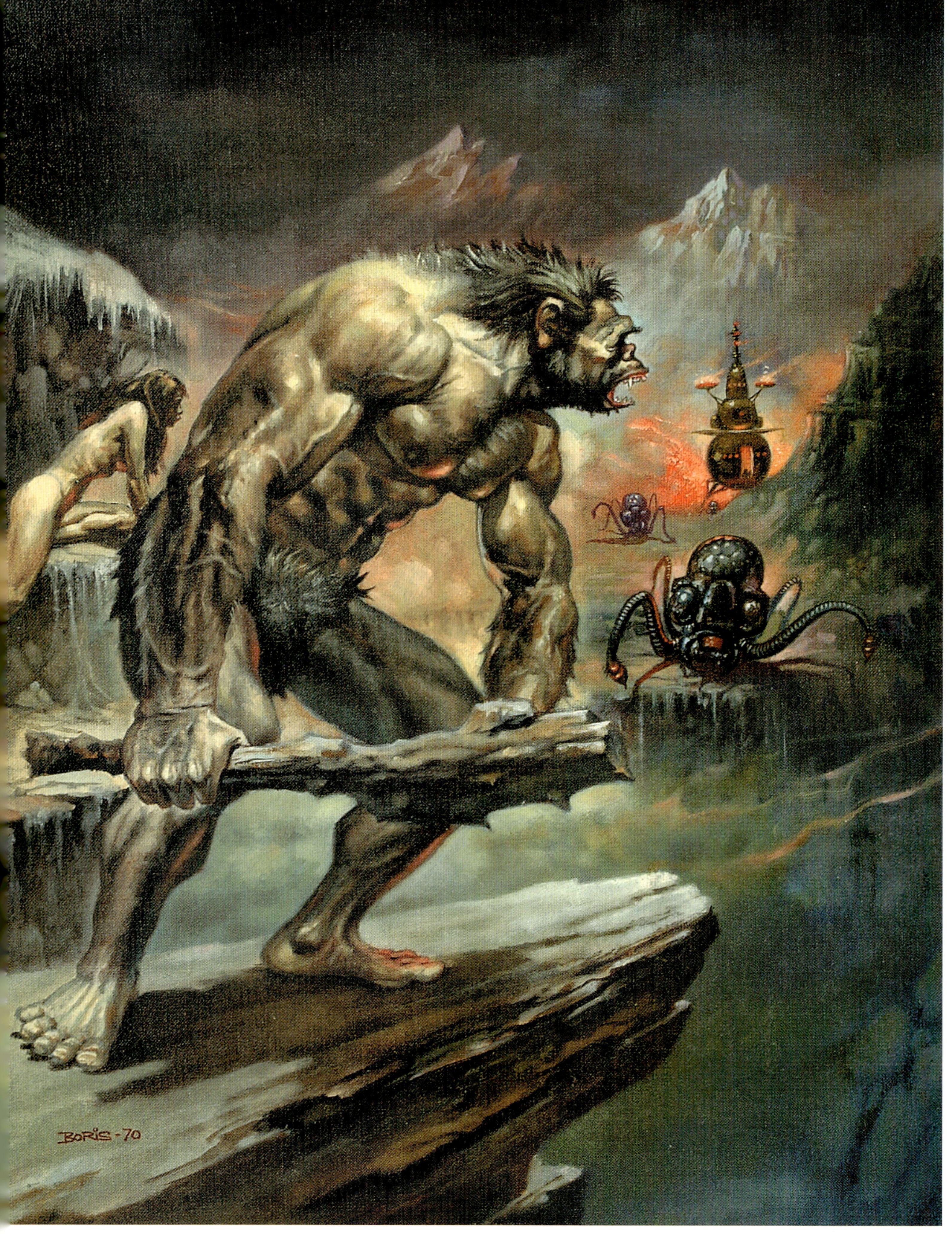
BORIS-70

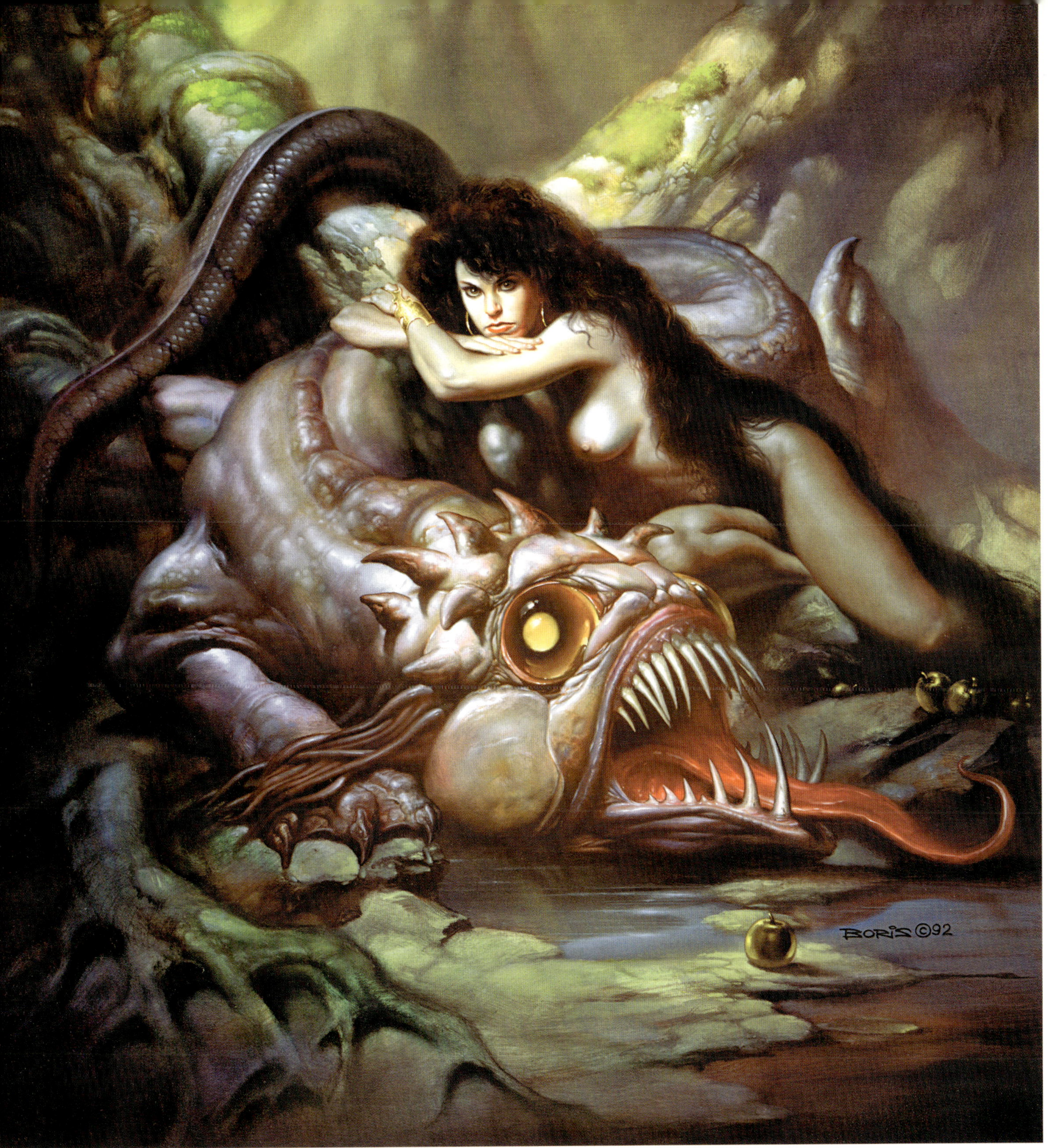

CRO-MAGNONS

1970, Boris *(left)*

A very early picture and in fact Boris's very first fantasy illustration for a publisher. It looks rather rough to him now, but it's fun to see the differences (and similarities for that matter) compared with recent paintings.

GOLDEN APPLES

1992, Boris *(above)*

This makes a good contrast with Cro-Magnons for the degree of 'polish' Boris now gives his paintings. He really enjoyed the contrast between the female and the grotesque, even slightly silly, monster. Its teeth look threatening but its attitude is almost that of a baby. With the female there is also a contrast between her pale skin and flowing black hair that frames her face and upper body in such a way that the eye of the viewer is drawn straight there.

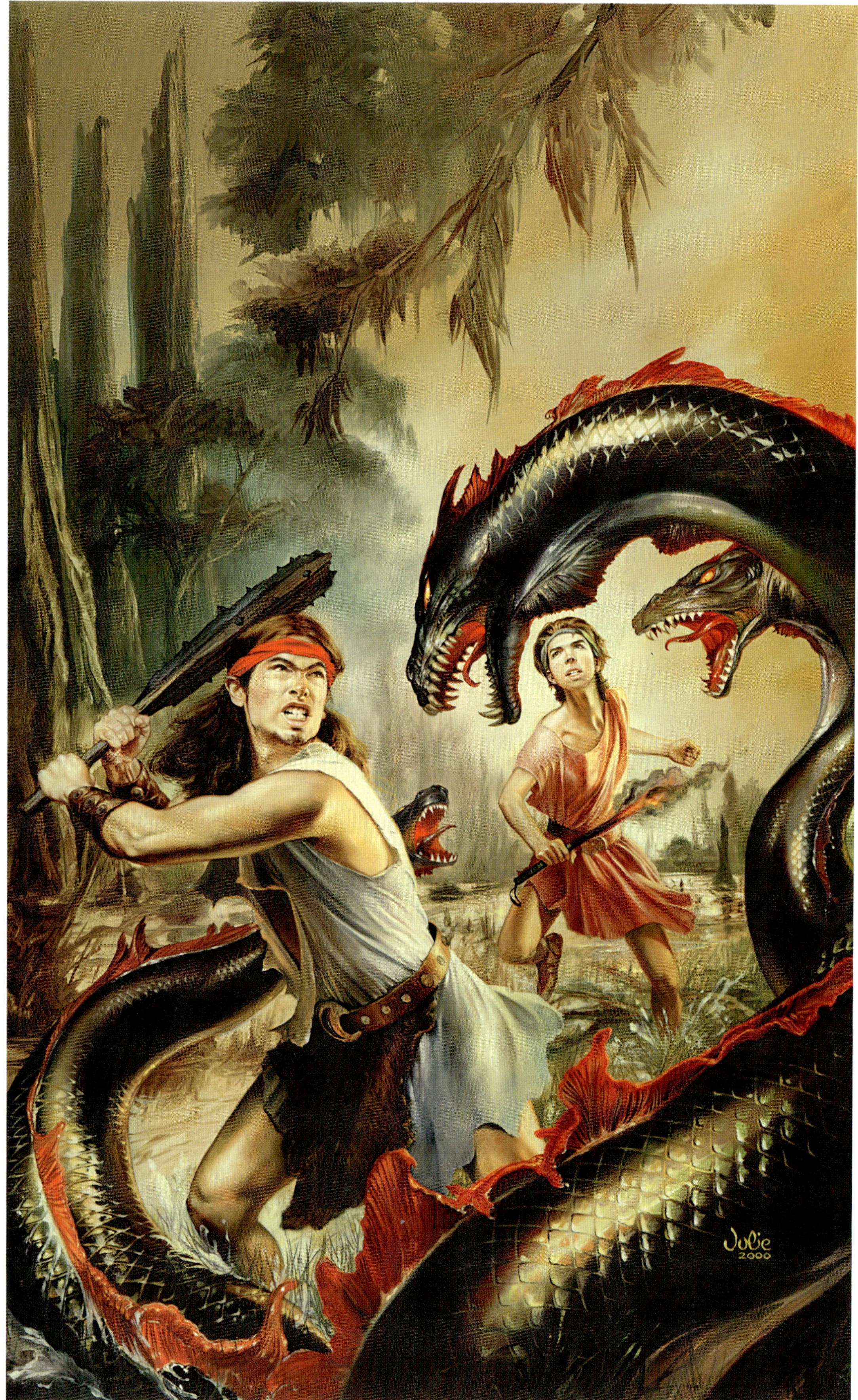

HERCULES AND THE HYDRA

1999, Julie *(left)*

Julie grew up in the swampy bayous of southeastern Texas, so when she was asked to paint this scene for a book cover, the background 'almost painted itself'. She enjoys the illusion of depth in this painting, and is rather pleased with her Hydra.

PREDATORS

1990, Boris *(right)*

Someone once praised Boris for the sensuality of his trees, and he was pleased because that is his aim. While admitting that 'we don't see too many trees like this in real life' he loves bestowing on the twisting forms an almost animal litheness. They are also useful devices lending a sense of depth and distance to a picture.

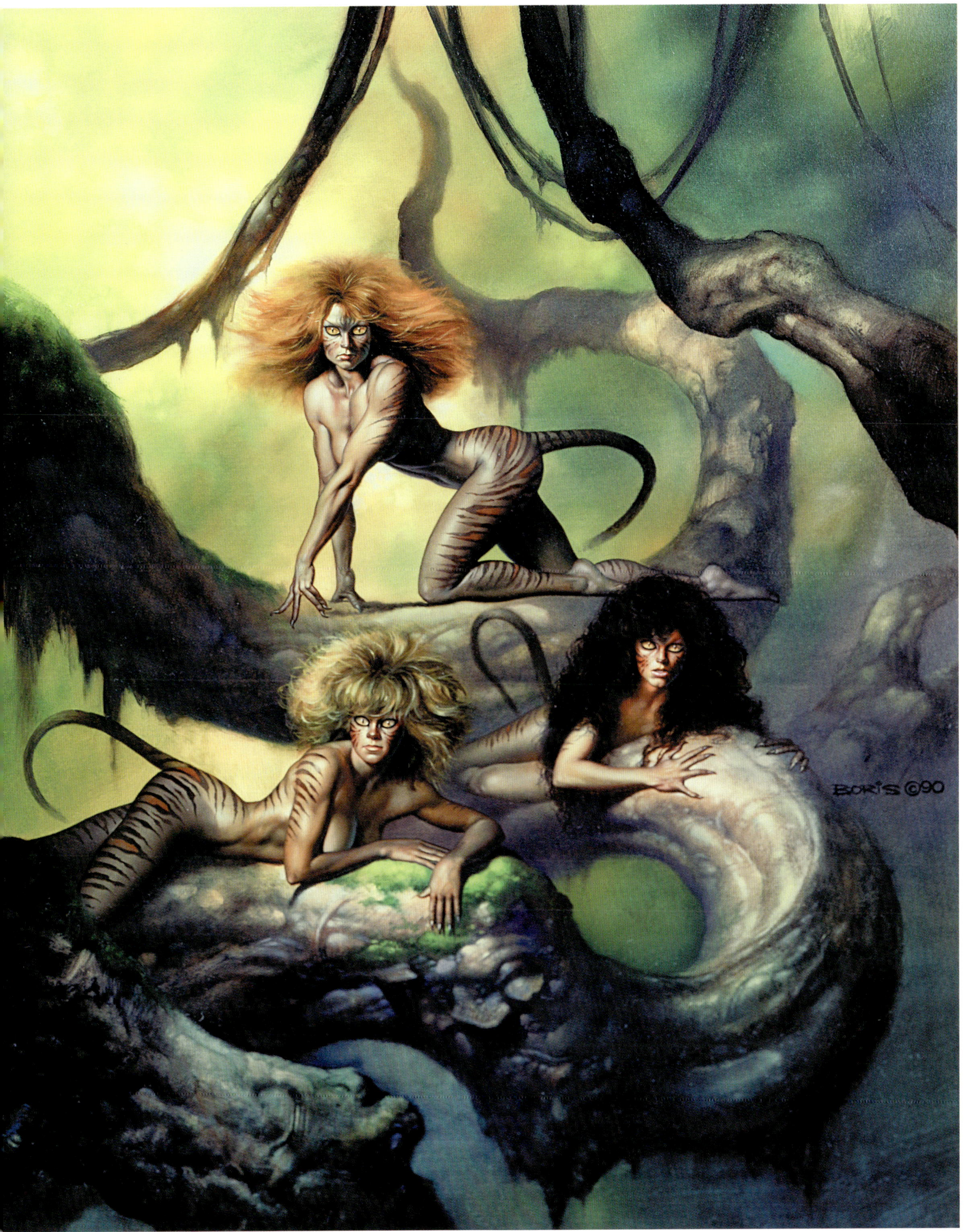
BORIS ©90

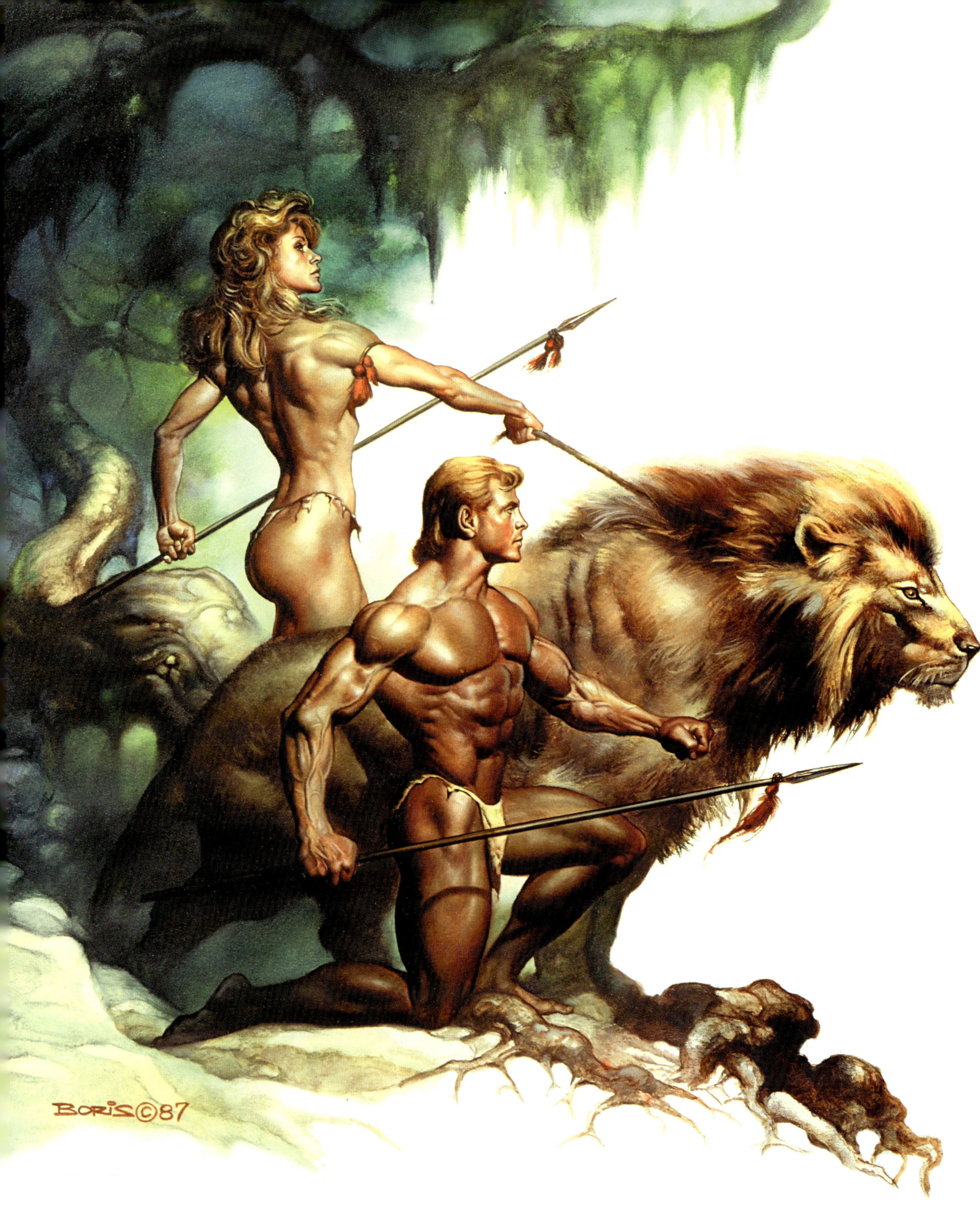
BORIS©87

LEO

1987, Boris *(left)*

The interesting thing about this astrology picture, says Boris, was bringing together the three main elements – woman, man and lion. They're different genders and species but are united by all being magnificent specimens of their kind. They are also united by a similar majesty of pose that suggests they are engaged on some joint quest that overrides their differences. So it is the tension between their similarities and differences that makes the picture.

THE ARRIVAL

1999, Julie *(right)*

This was a calendar picture which meant Julie could paint more or less what she wished. Her starting point was simply wanting to work with these particular colours – the theme and mood developed from there. She is now very pleased with the stormy atmosphere surrounding the couple, broken by the ray of pale sunshine; also by the precarious rock and water. The female began as a blonde but this hot pink colour gave her a more unpredictable edge. As to the symbolizm Julie says: 'A lot of times we don't think about the symbolizm of what we're painting, it's simply a visual thing. We like to just paint whatever makes us happy when we look at the picture.'

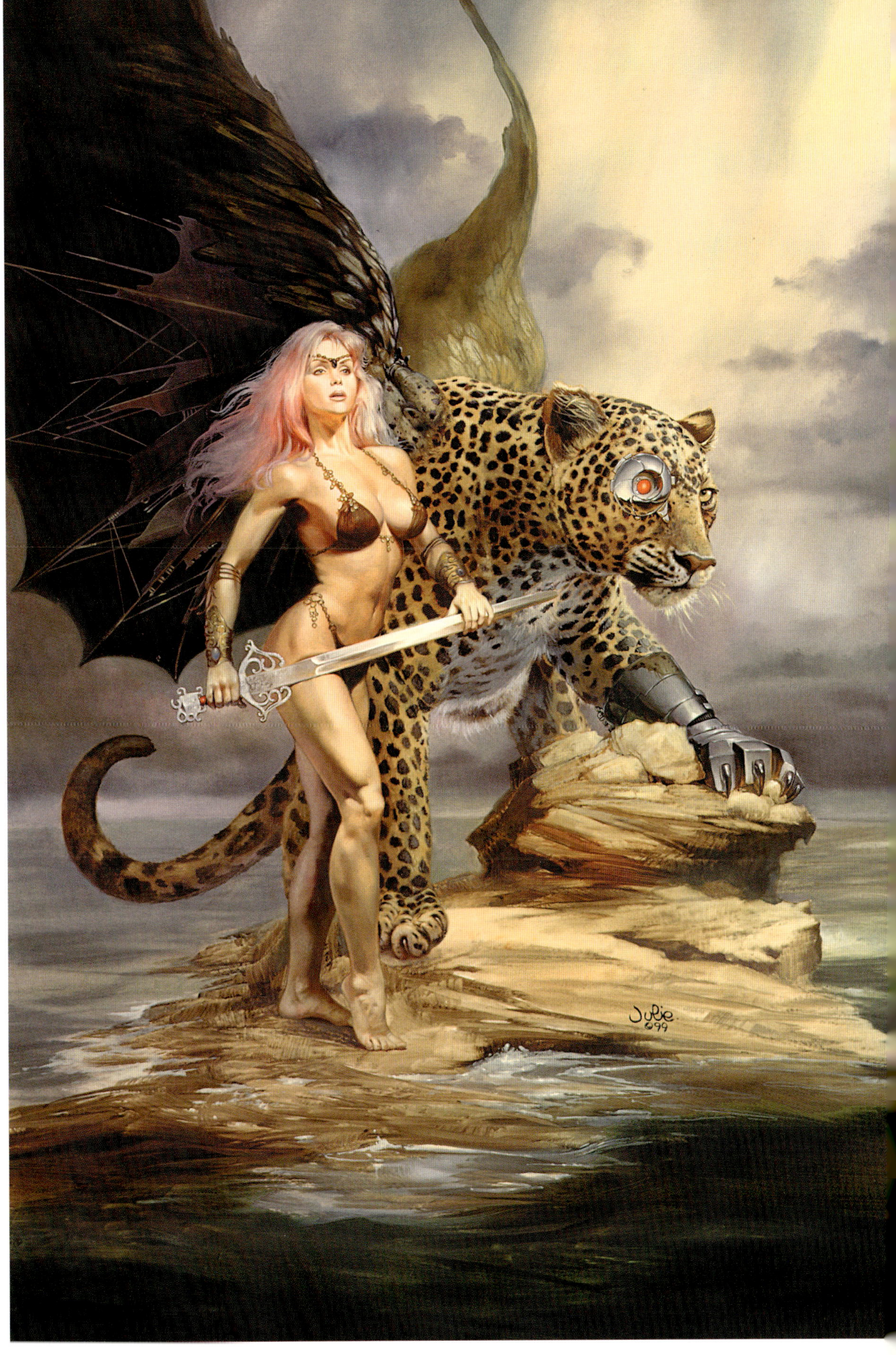

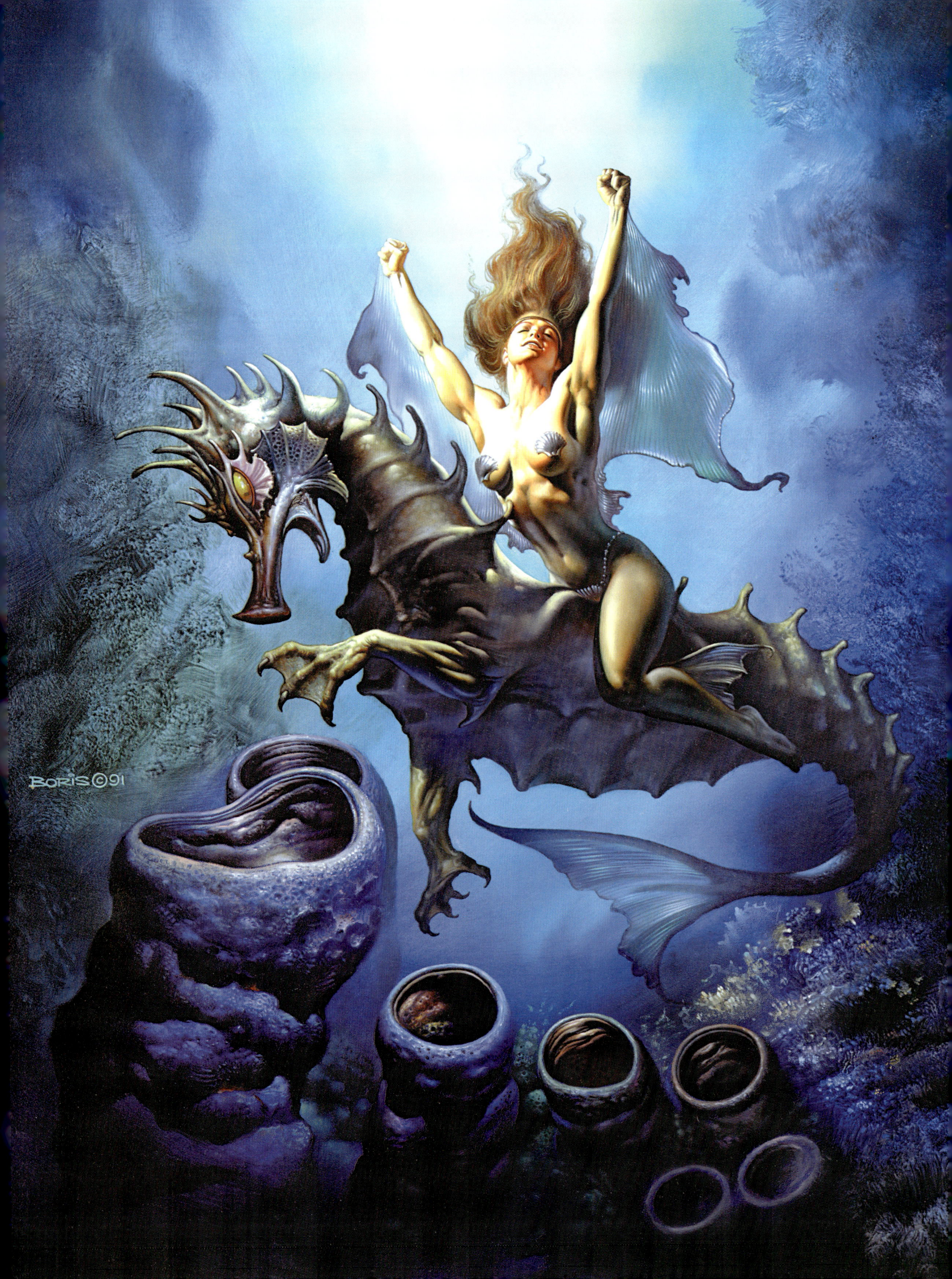
BORIS©91

chapter 4

In illustration one is always to some extent setting out to achieve an aim that is chosen in advance. You don't just sit down and paint whatever comes into your head. Usually there is a story or idea asking to be expressed. What is impressive about Boris and Julie is that they have a distinctive style that shows through in their pictures, even though clients who kind of knew what they wanted to begin with dictated over half of them to a greater or lesser extent. But what those clients also wanted was the personal touch, the magic, which the artists do put into whatever they paint. They usually succeed in coming up with a surprise, no matter how tight the brief.

This flexibility and willingness to accommodate themselves to the job in hand is what makes them such professionals. Having a personal vision that puts its stamp on whatever they do is what also makes them artists who stand head and shoulders above the crowd. Where they do manage to achieve nearly complete artistic freedom is in their calendars where they are asked basically just to be themselves and express that vision. But there is no great gulf between the two kinds of work, as we see them here side by side. Without a caption it is often hard to tell the difference. Something personal goes into whatever they paint and that lifts it above the mundane.

In illustration, as in life, there is always a fine balance between being original and self-indulgent. If the artist's personality swamps the subject, well, the chances are that they won't be asked again. But if they don't manage to make something original of it the same applies. There are no end of other artists eager to try their hand. It is a tightrope act and it often takes courage to be yourself at the same time as satisfying the demands of other people. What shines through in Julie and Boris's paintings is that despite being consummate professionals they are also totally untainted by cynicism and in love with what they do.

HIPPOCAMPUS
1991, Boris

Although he cannot swim, Boris is an enthusiastic scuba diver and loves the sensation of flying through strange surroundings. It is where the inspiration comes from for pictures like this, much of whose reference comes from Boris's own photos.

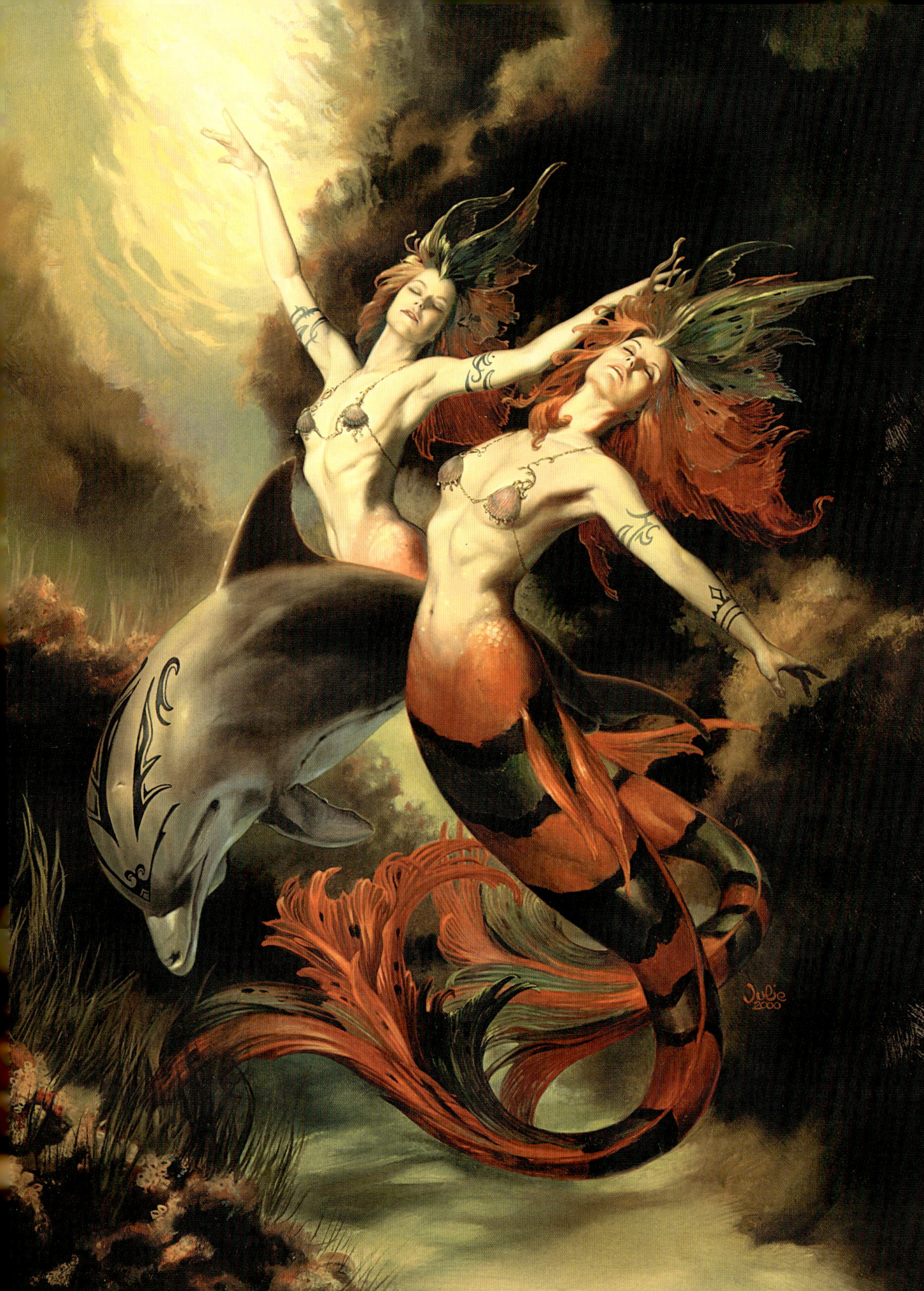

NEPTUNE

1990, Boris *(right)*

People are familiar enough with mermaids and mermen but often forget that the granddaddy of them all (in Greek and Roman myth anyway) was Neptune, father of the Tritons who enforced his underwater rule. When Neptune was courting his wife Amphititre he was aided by a friendly dolphin. In reward he set it among the stars as a constellation we can still see today.

TWIN VISIONS

2000, Julie *(above)*

'It seems like all girls love mermaids,' says Julie. 'I also really have a fascination with dolphins, so that is kind of what happened here. I wanted these three to have the same tattoos to show they're a team.' Another inspiration was an Edmund Dulac illustration of mermaids she saw about thirty years ago. Instead of the usual blues and greens associated with mermaids he had used reds and golds, so that is what Julie wanted to try here, and she is very happy with the result. Originally there was only going to be one mermaid, but she had so many good shots of this model to choose from that having two suddenly seemed a good idea. It saved making a decision on which was best.

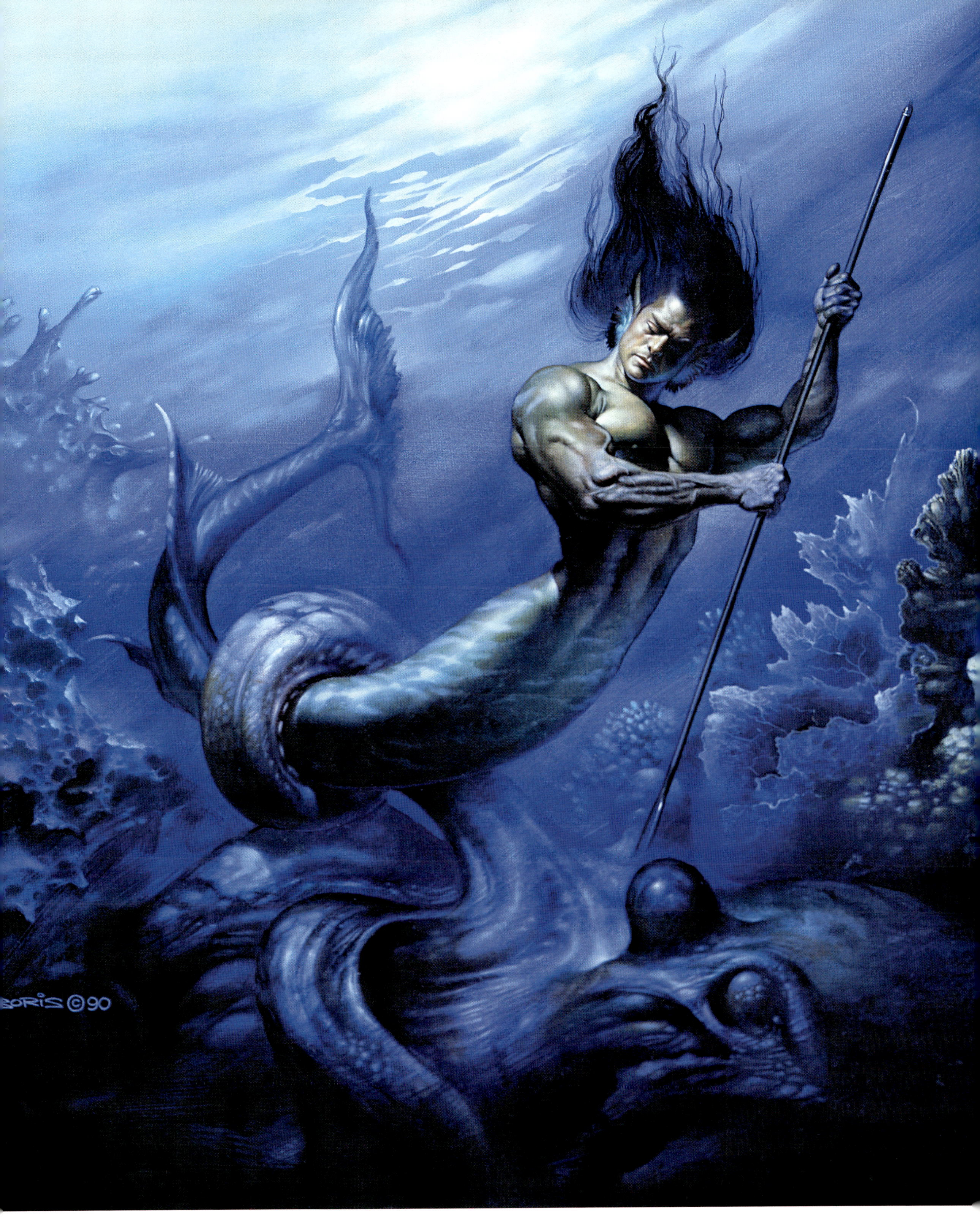
BORIS ©90

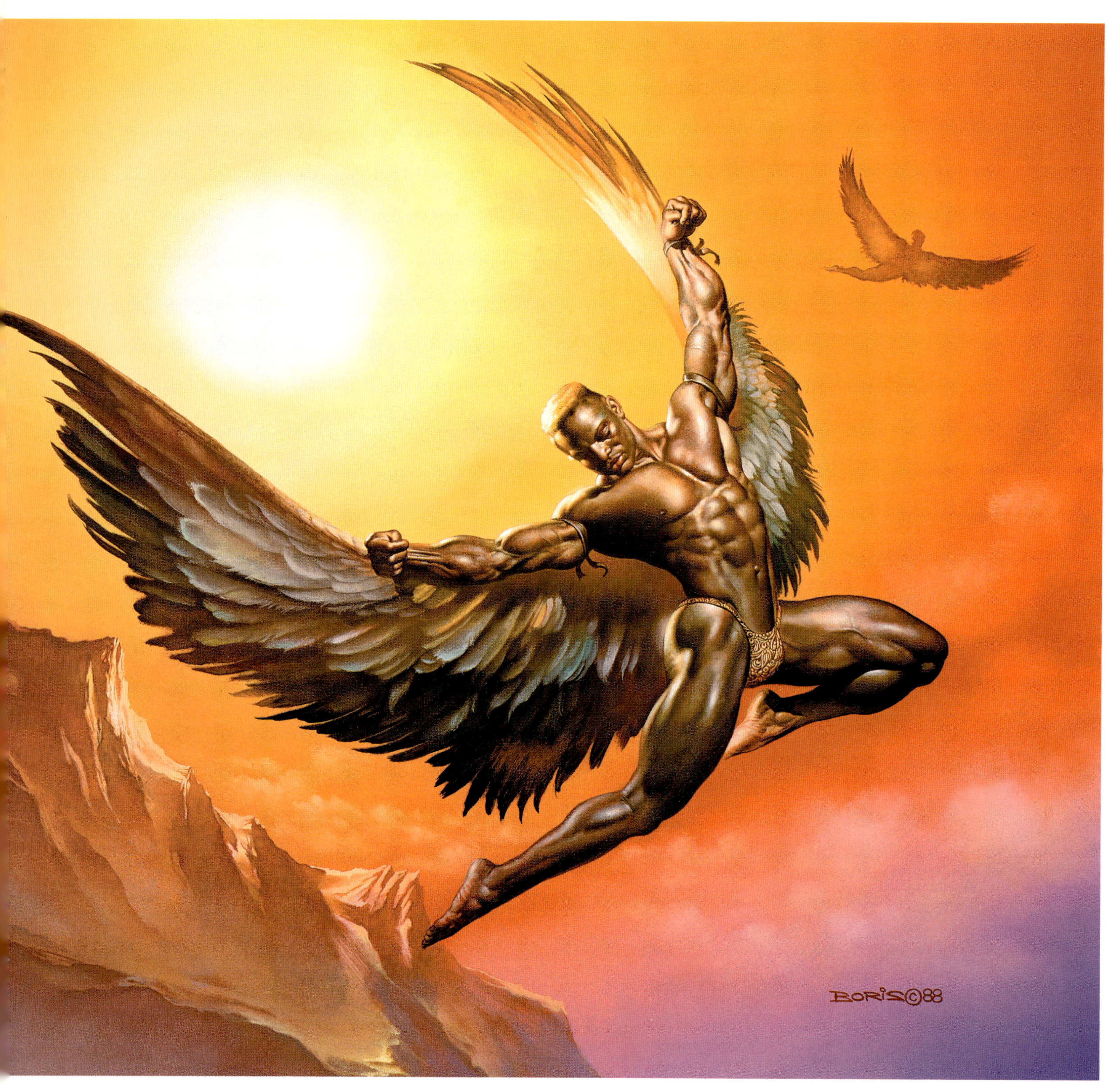
BORIS©88

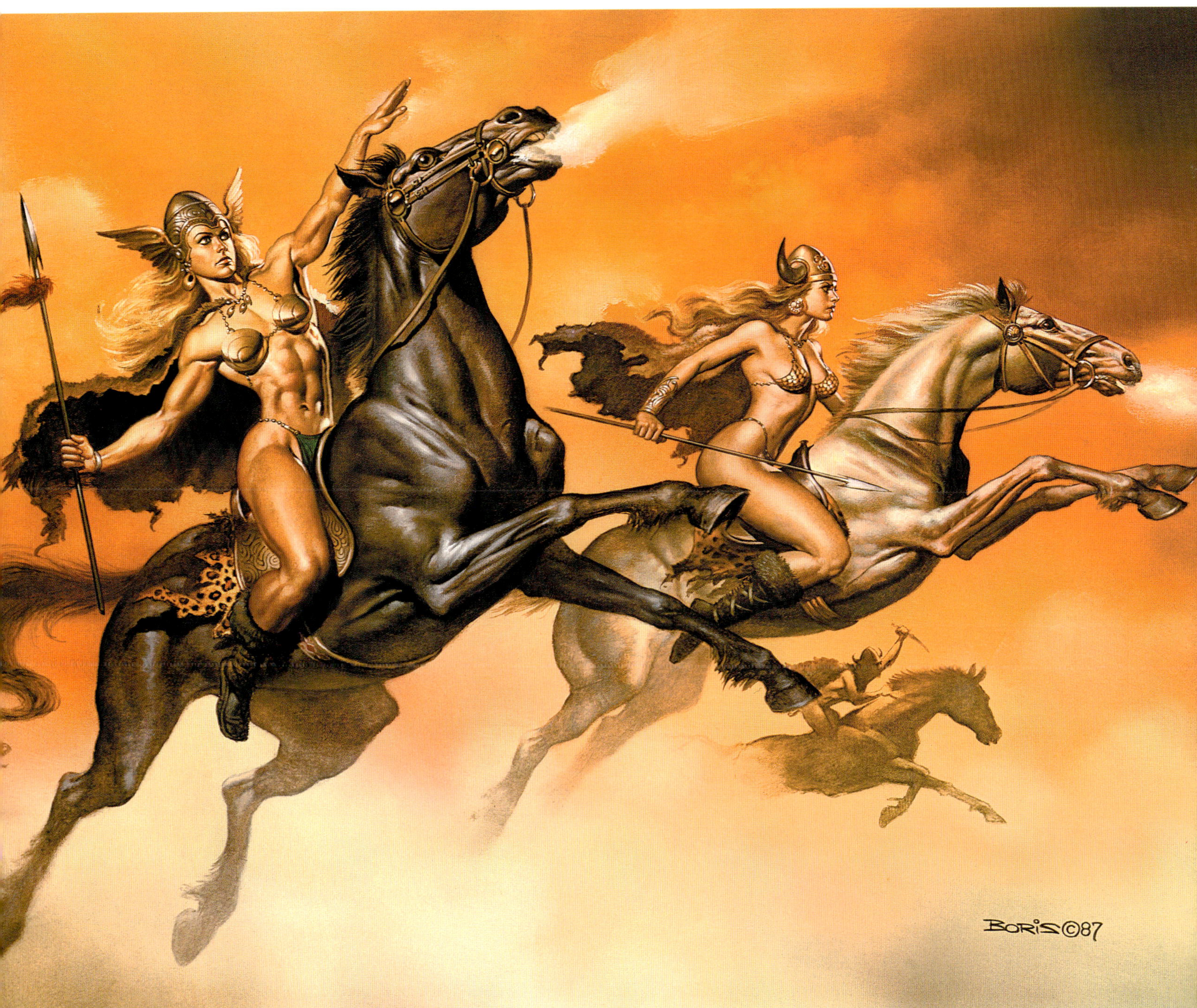

ICARUS

1988, Boris *(left)*

A rather unconventional portrayal of the hubristic Greek hero. Boris enjoys being controversial like this, and after all ancient Greek statues still are largely responsible for our idea of the perfect human physique.

VALKYRIES

1987, Boris *(above)*

Just an excuse really to paint beautiful, powerful women and horses.

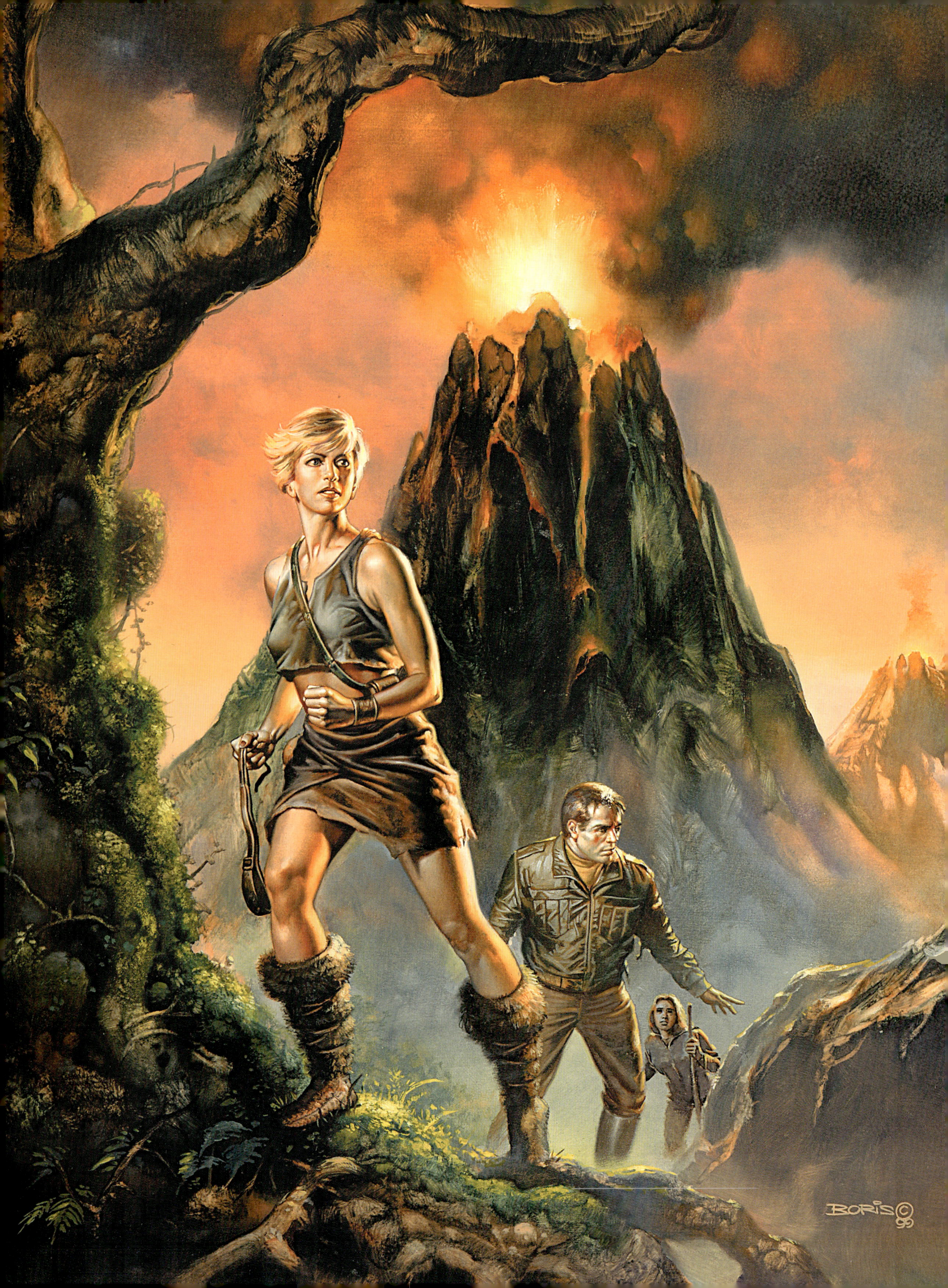
BORIS©
99

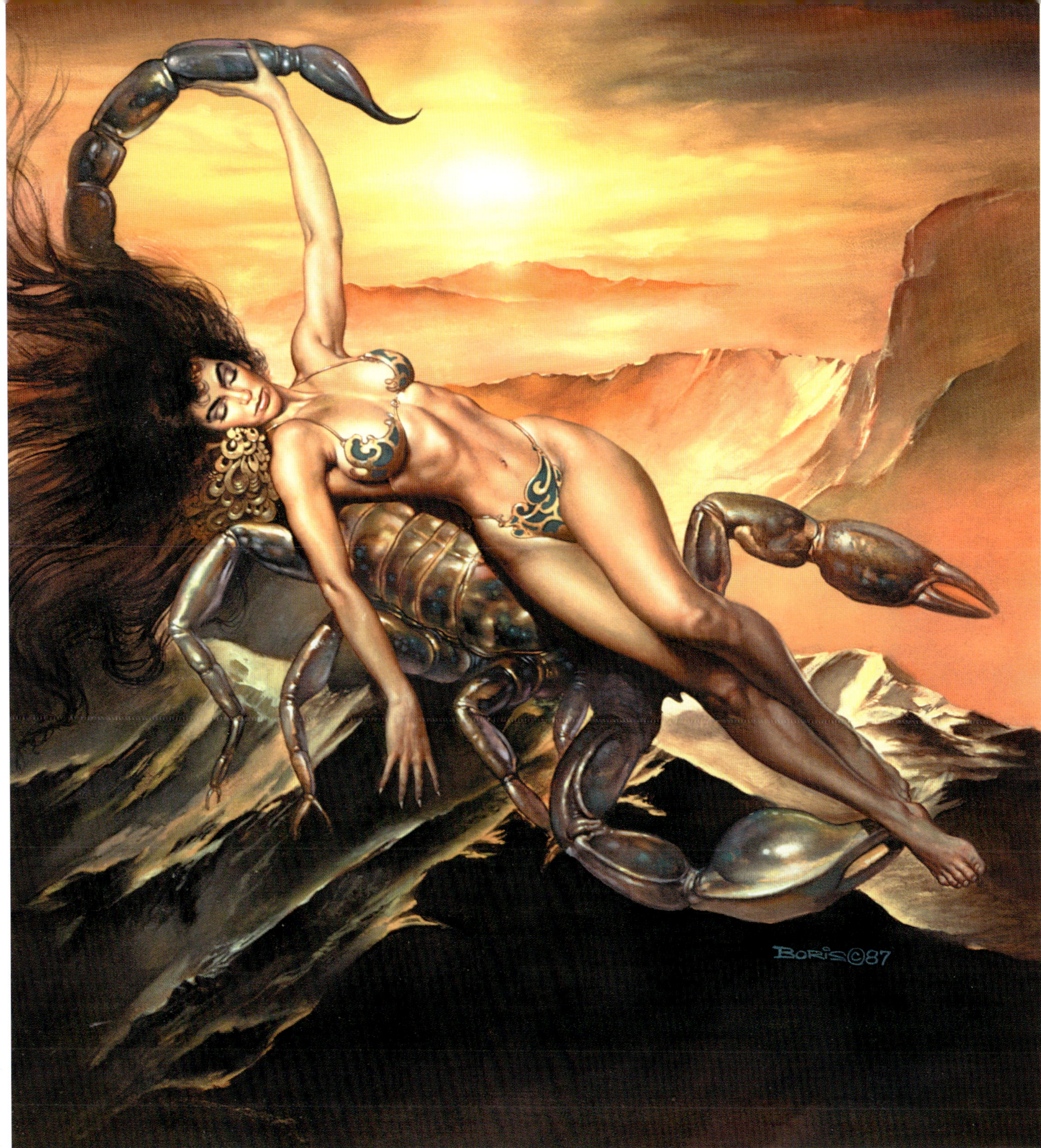

VOLCANO

1999, Boris *(left)*

A variation on a favourite theme. Boris and Julie once visited Hawaii and had the chance to study volcanoes at first hand. Boris: 'It was wonderful to see so many volcanoes. And there were miles of black lava – very eerie and surrealistic and different to what I'd imagined'.

SCORPIO

1987, Boris *(above)*

Boris actually loves scorpions, spiders, insects and the like and has a large library of his own close-up photos: 'They're beautiful creatures when enlarged in a way most people don't ever see'.

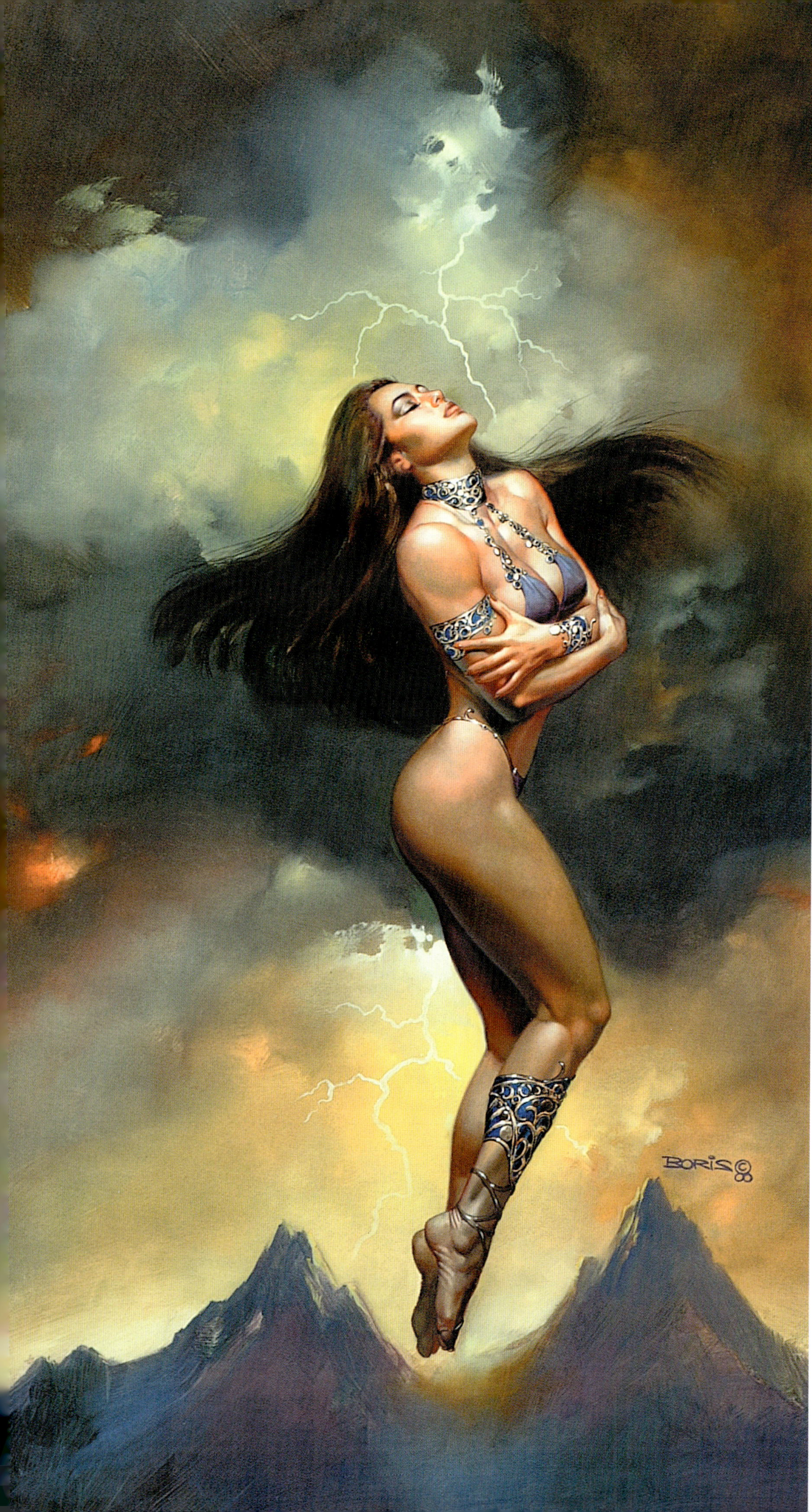

GODDESS OF THUNDER
2000, Boris *(left)*

A pocketknife design for the Franklin Mint. Boris: It was fun to be allowed the opportunity to work on single figures like this with very simple backgrounds – just enough to indicate the mood of the piece, in this case thunder'.

ABDUCTED
1987, Boris *(right)*

Boris allowed himself some artistic license here because of course there is no way that this creature's wings could support its own massive body, let alone the woman's as well. But that is the beauty of fantasy – one is allowed to bend rules for the sake of effect because in these other worlds the rules of possibility are assumed to be different.

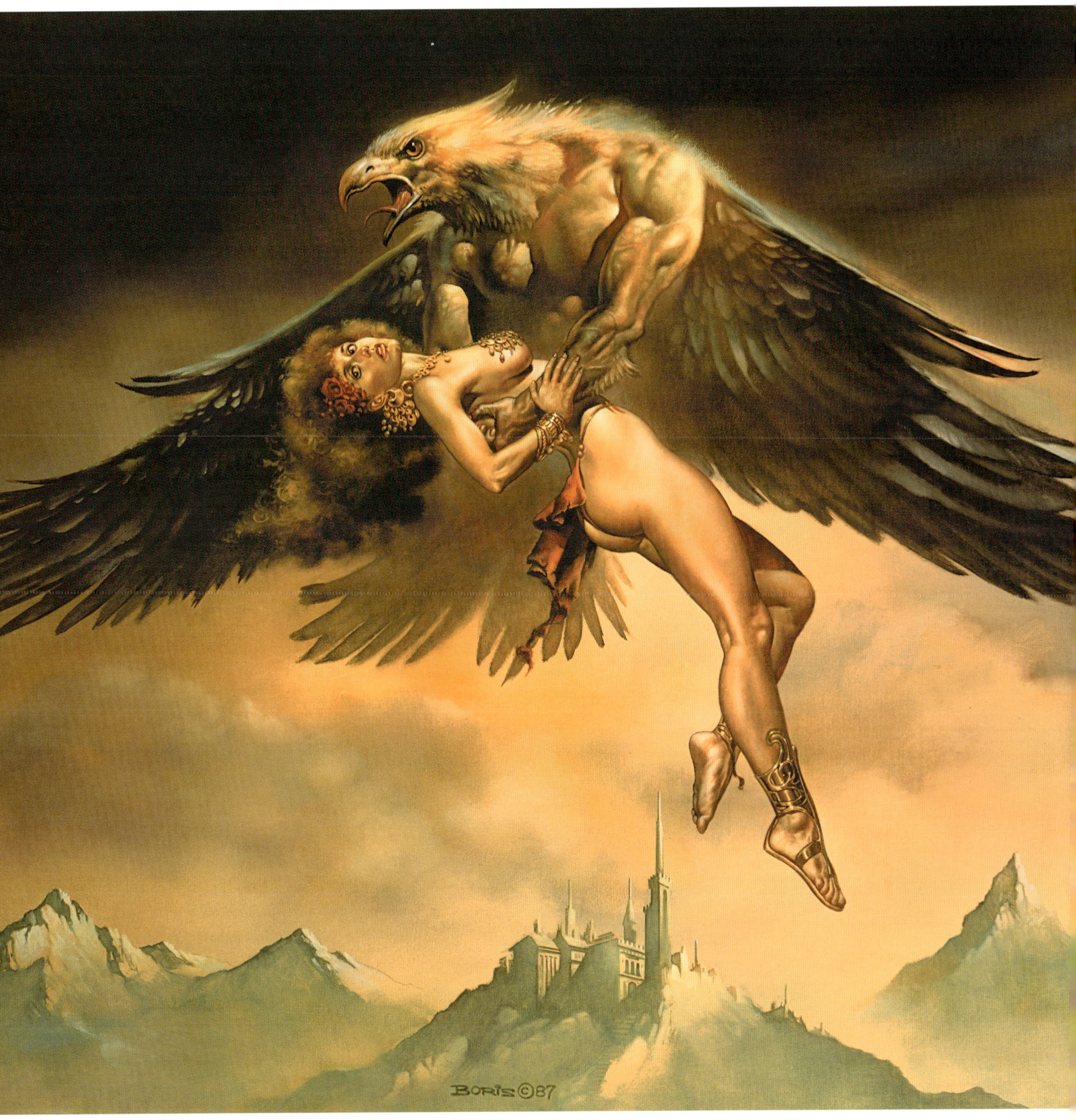
BORIS ©87

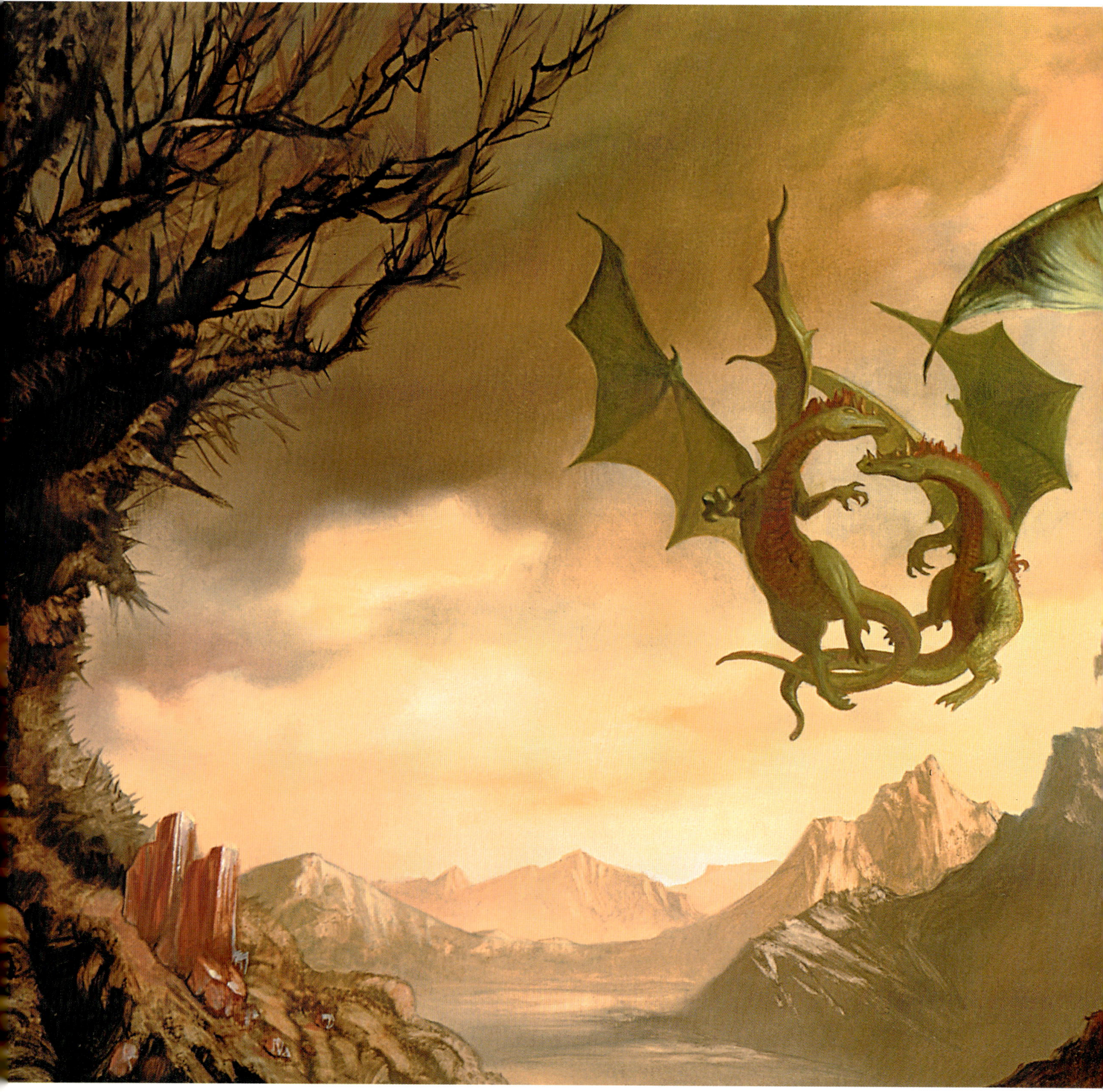

DRAGON OF THE RUBIES
1999, Julie

The idea here is that the dragon in the foreground is standing guard over the gems springing up out of the ground, while the other two dance playfully in the sky. The picture was designed for the possibility of being printed on a ceramic mug so the left and right sides connect to make a seamless join.

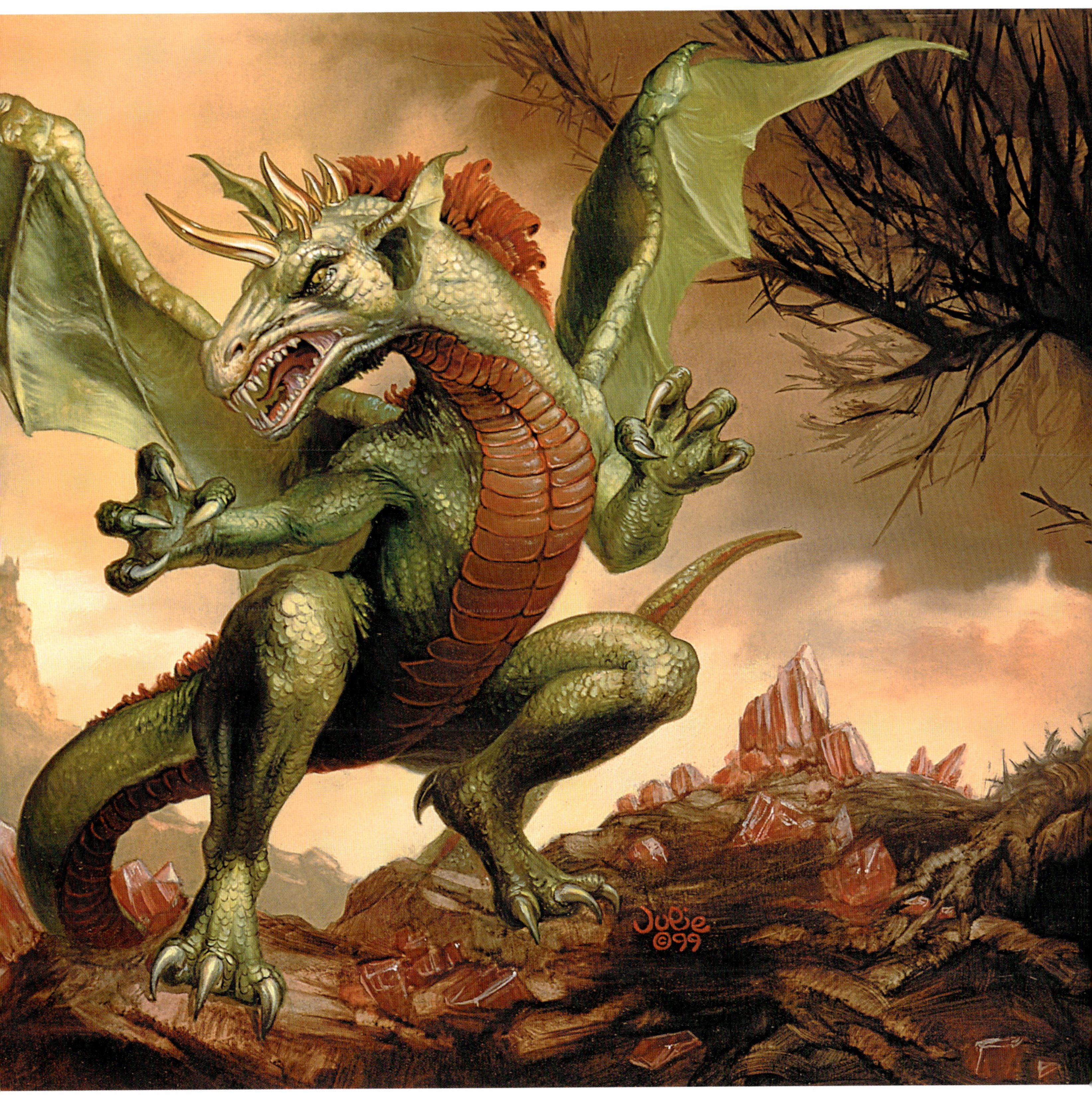
Julie
©99

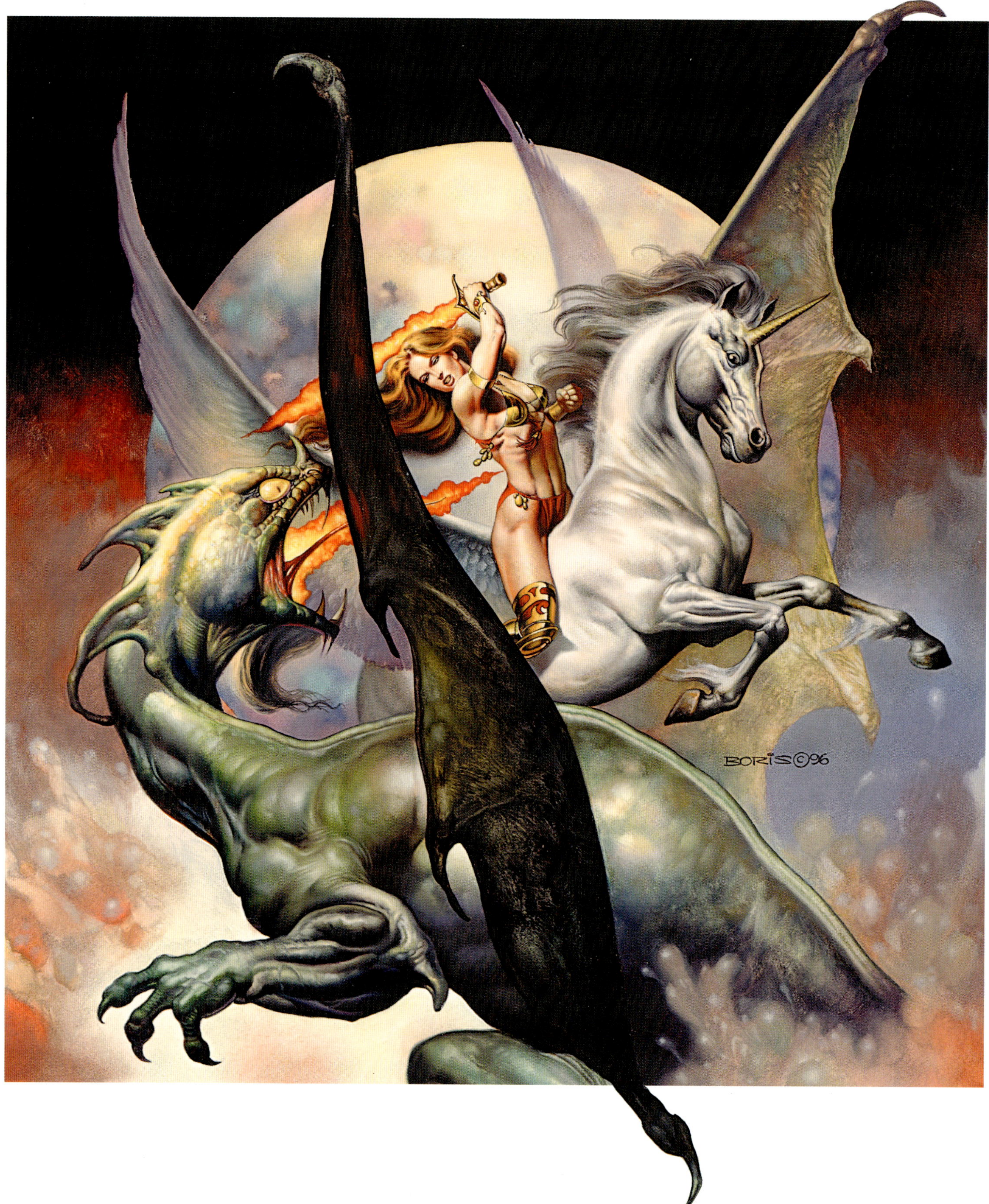

WHITE PEGASUS

1996, Boris

This calendar illustration offered a chance to exercise Boris's ongoing fascination with wings, whether they be feathered, scaled or insect wings.

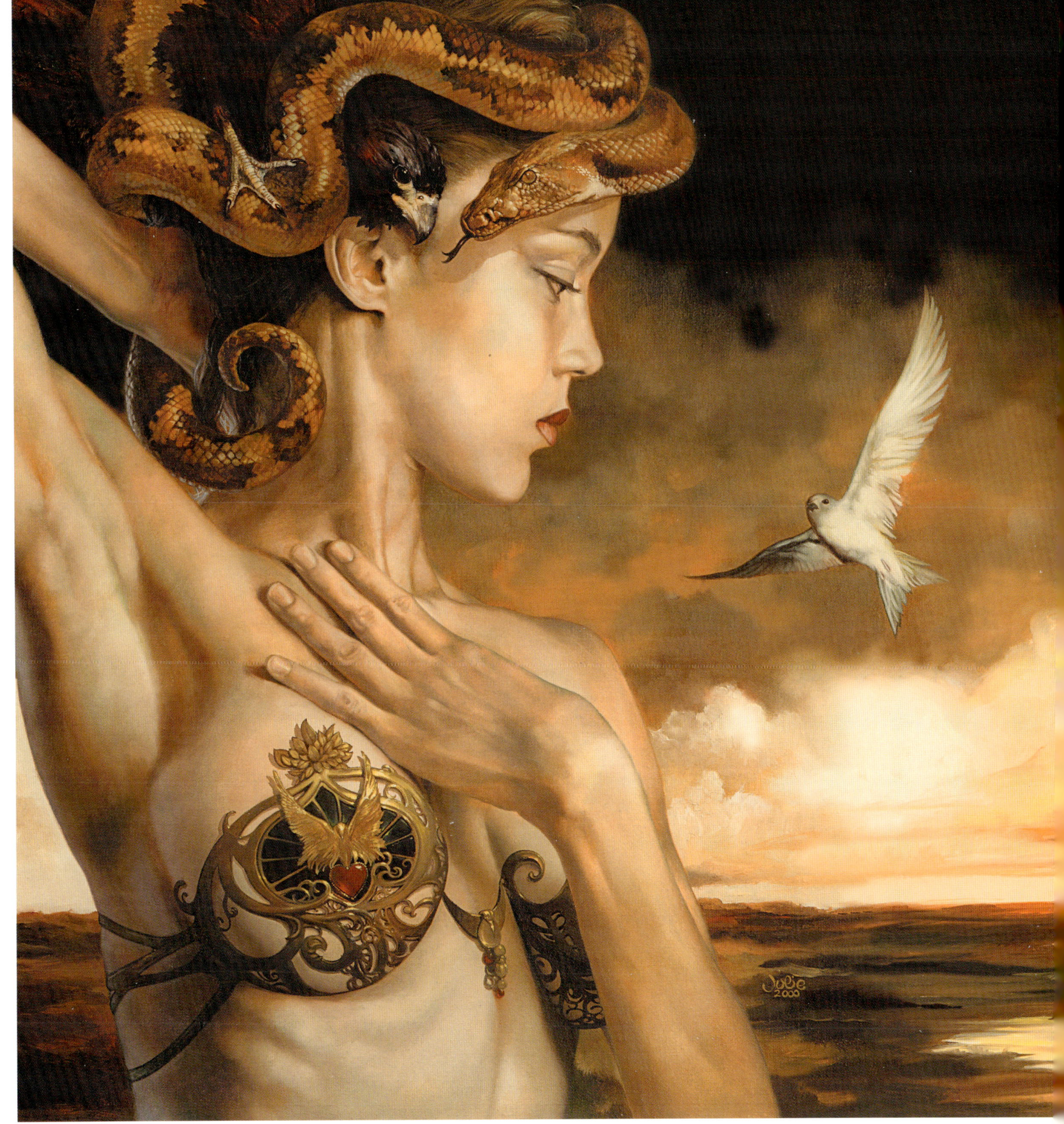

PRISONER OF HERSELF

2000, Julie

More surrealistic than a typical fantasy picture, Julie aimed to express here a sense of how people can often create their own hell. The snake stands for self-delusion while the two birds represent different aspects of the subject. The white one is calling for her to free herself from self-inflicted torments. The bleak landscape is where those torments and delusions have led her. Nevertheless, the picture does have a strange and haunting beauty.

FATHER TIME

Julie, 1999

This book cover called for lots of atmosphere – a large painting with a lot of background. By happy chance it snowed just as Julie was about to start, so all she had to do for the background is step out and take a look at her backyard. The look she aimed for in the main character is that she is plainly not happy with her circumstances or company, but resigned to them. She is battle-weary, worn down and feeling the weight of her years, but still determined to press on.

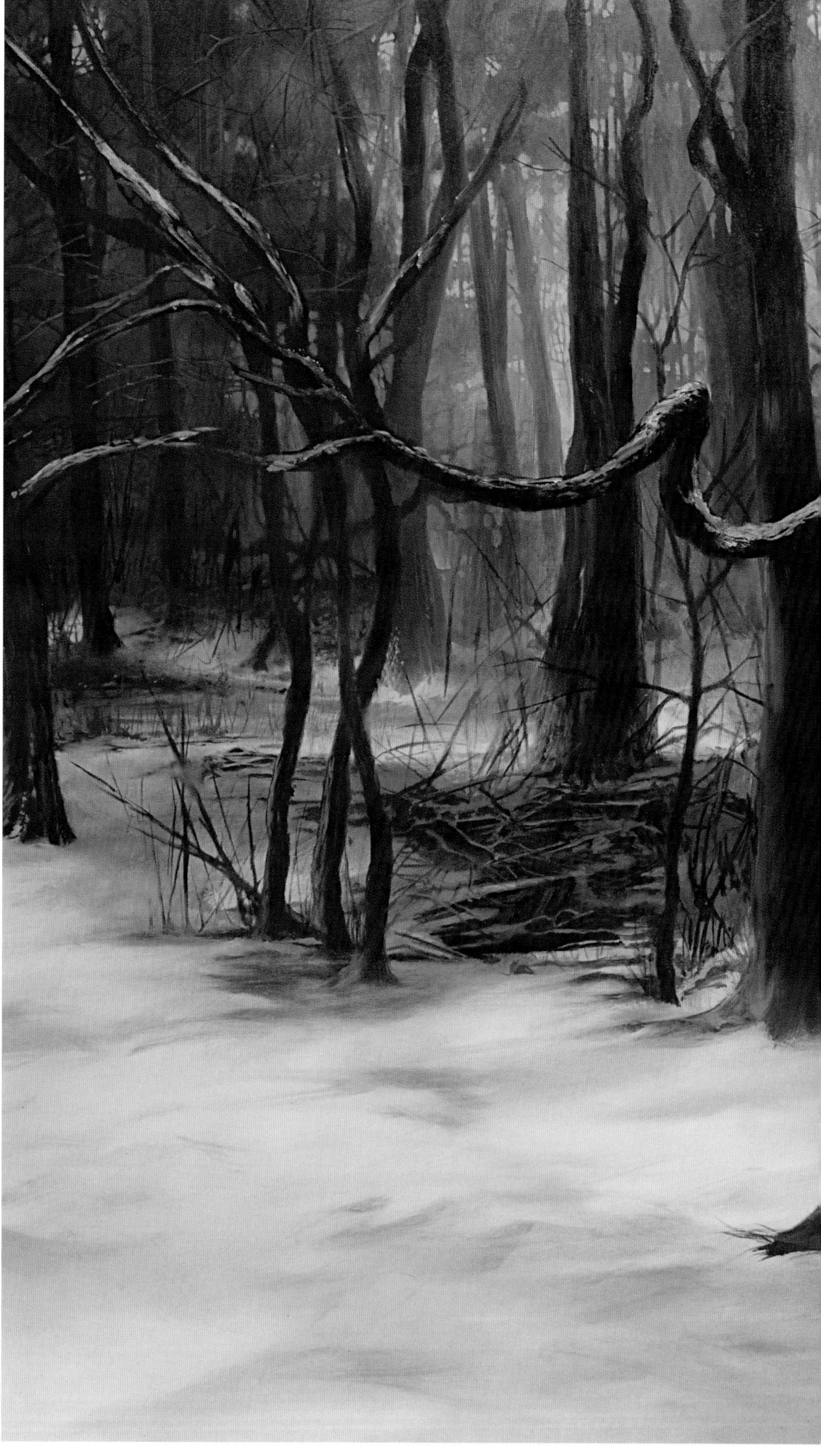

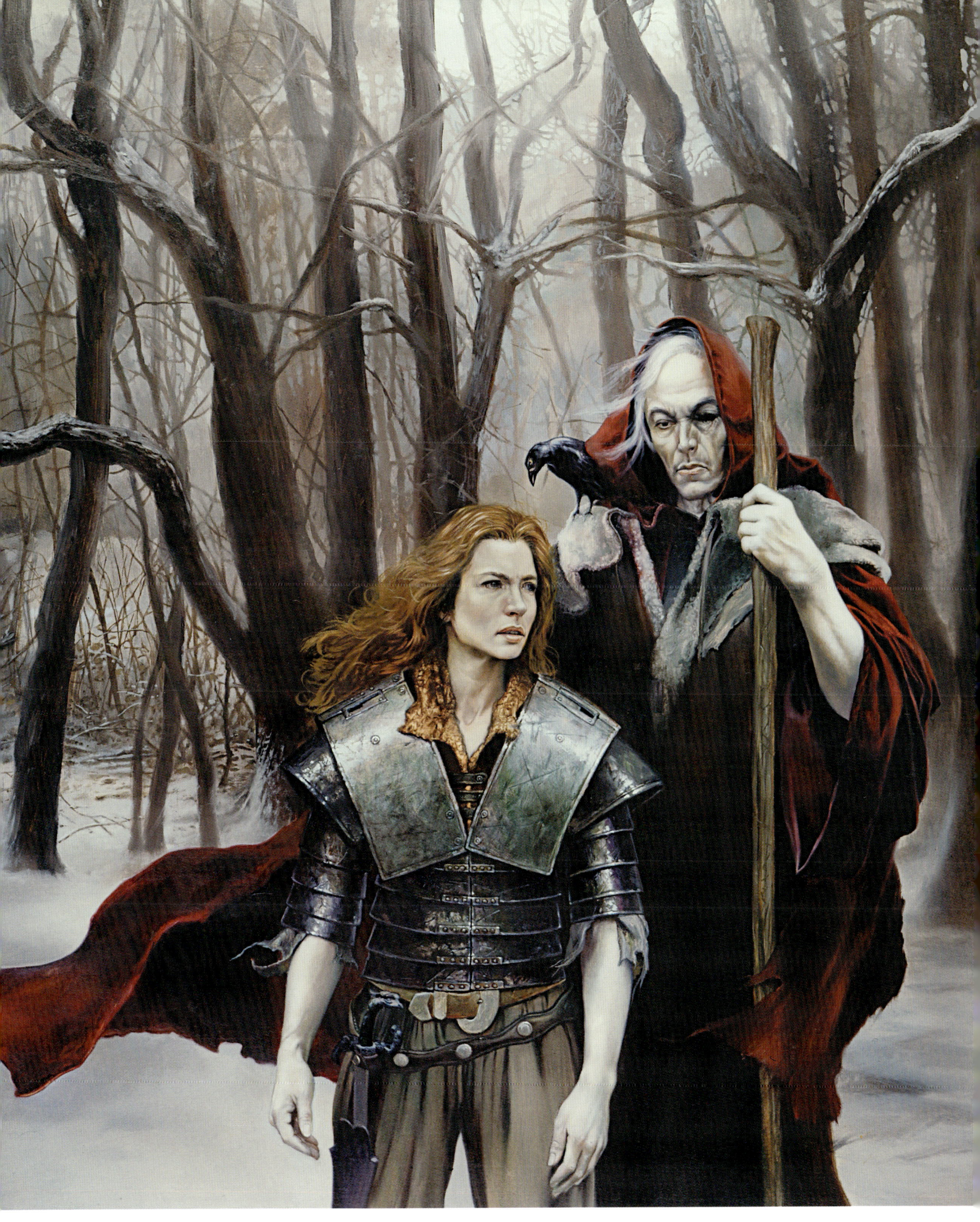

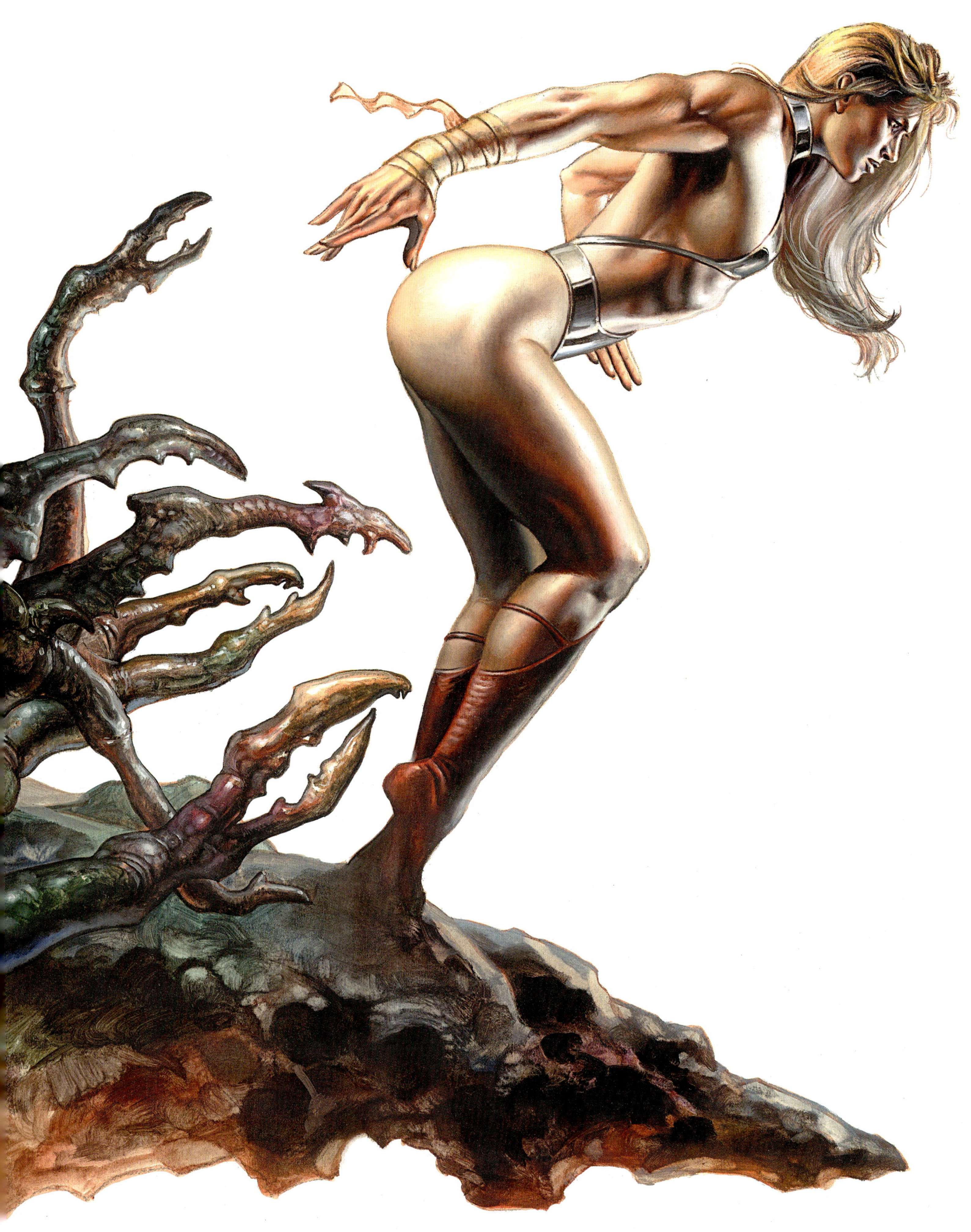

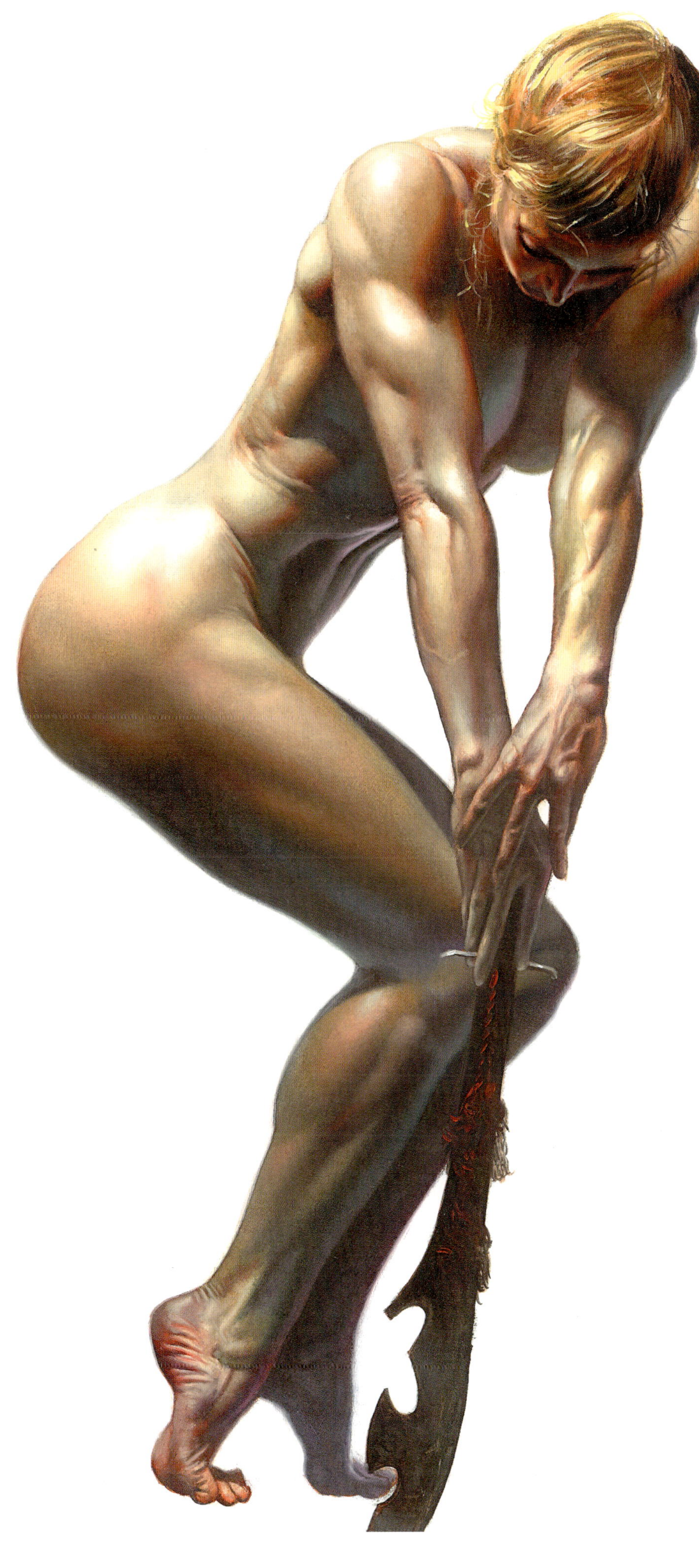

PARTING OF THE SEAS

1999, Boris *(details)*

These two details were part of an interesting experiment involving computers. The idea was to paint the background and figures separately and then overlap them digitally. It was enjoyable but in the end he and Julie thought: 'What's the point? It's easier just to paint them in place'.

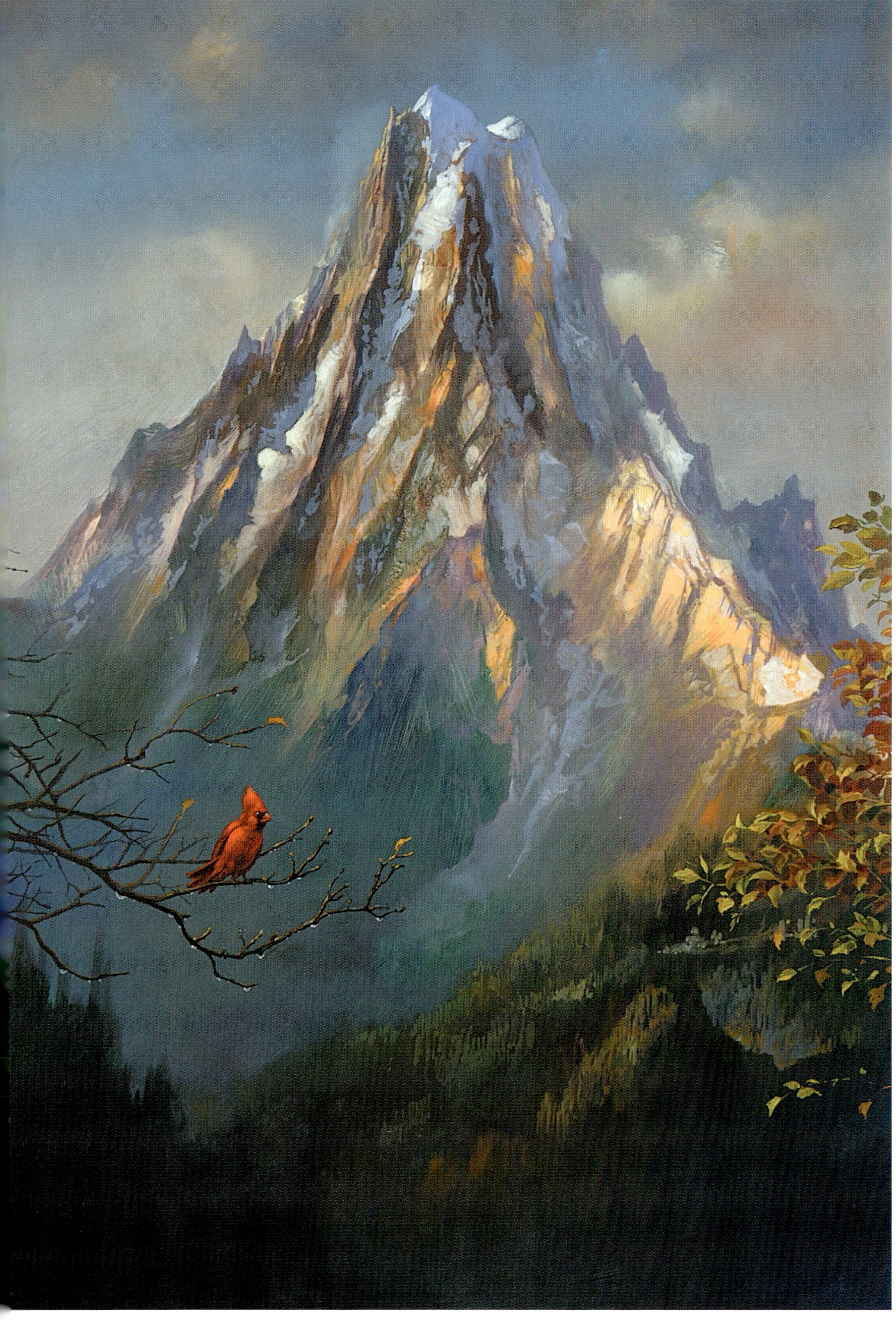

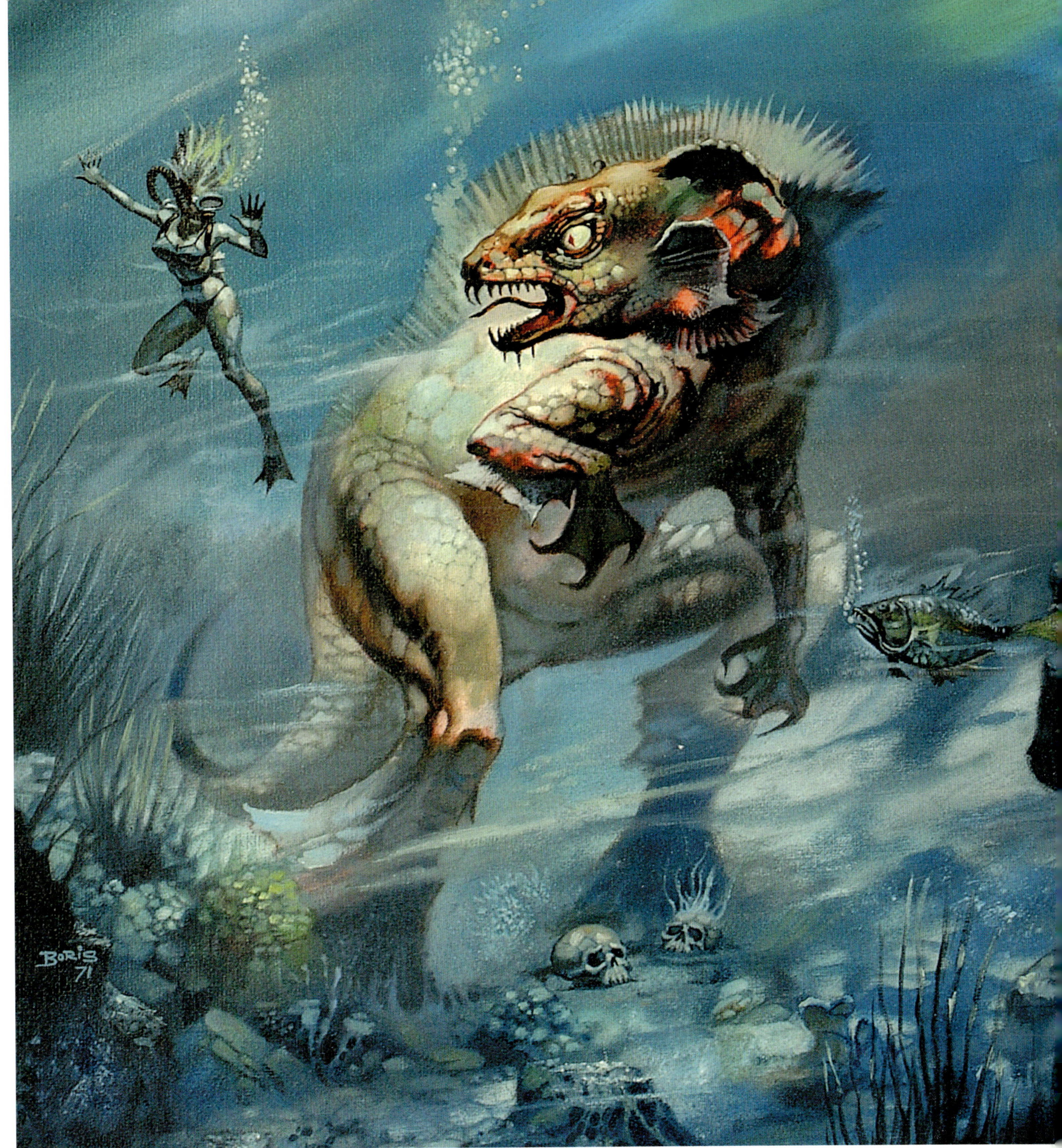

MOUNTAIN SONG
2001, Boris *(left)*
This experimental piece was the first in a possible series of environmental pictures showing the forces of nature. Boris would have liked to show just a mountain but the bird adds a touch of life and colour.

CREATURE FROM THE ABYSS
1971, Boris *(above)*
An early cover for Nightmare comic. Boris still likes the humour of the piece with monster and diver equally startled by the other's presence. Many people overlook this in his pictures, the humour is quite subtle, especially when on the surface some wildly dramatic scene is being illustrated.

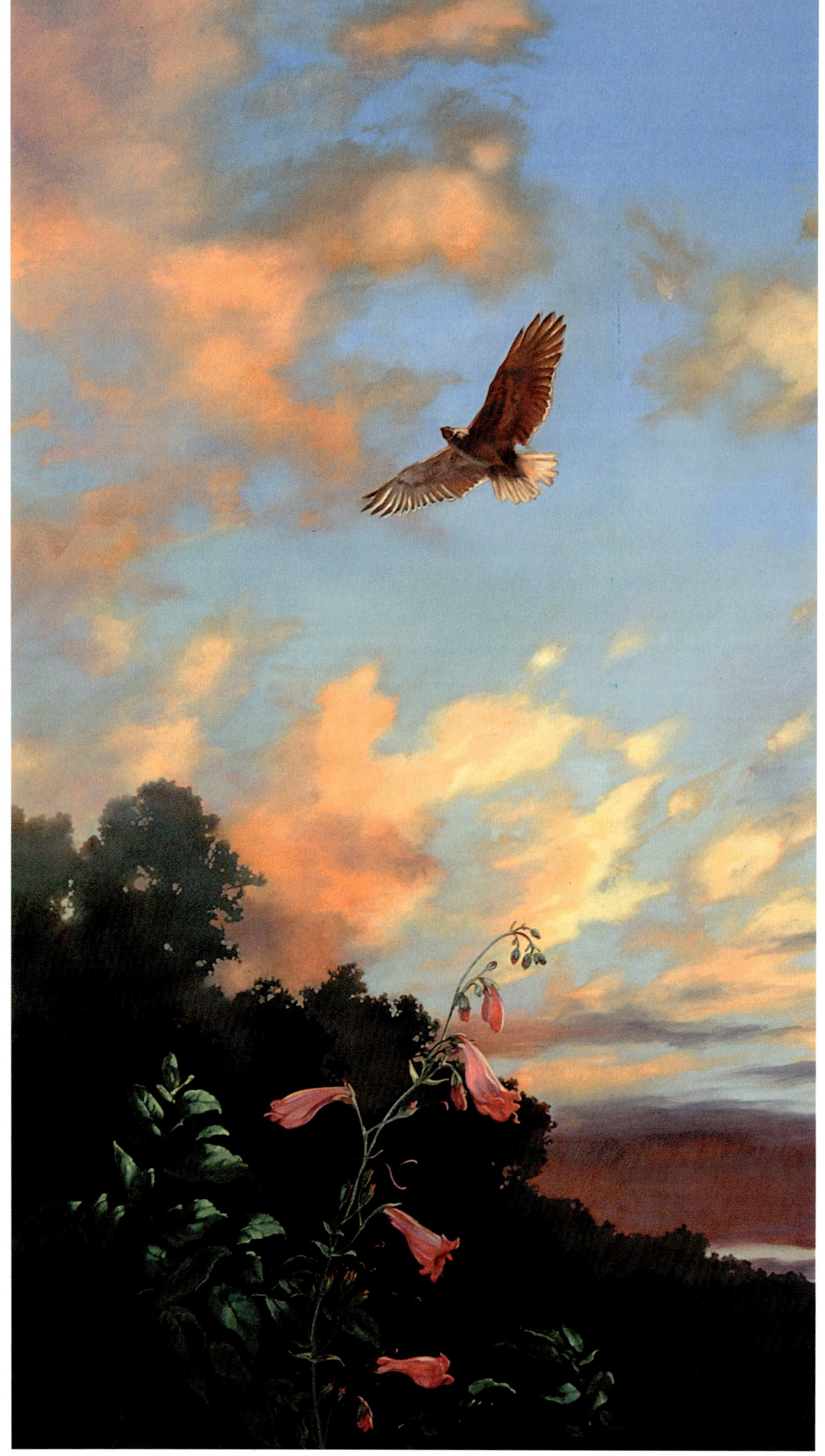

SKY

2001, Julie *(left)*

Julie's matching piece for Mountain Song (page 96). In the end they didn't follow through the idea of a series, but may return to it in the future.

FOREST FIRE

1999, Julie *(right)*

This was for a book cover so once the publishers had chosen a scene, the action was largely determined by the story. It was a good chance to combine action with detailed background.

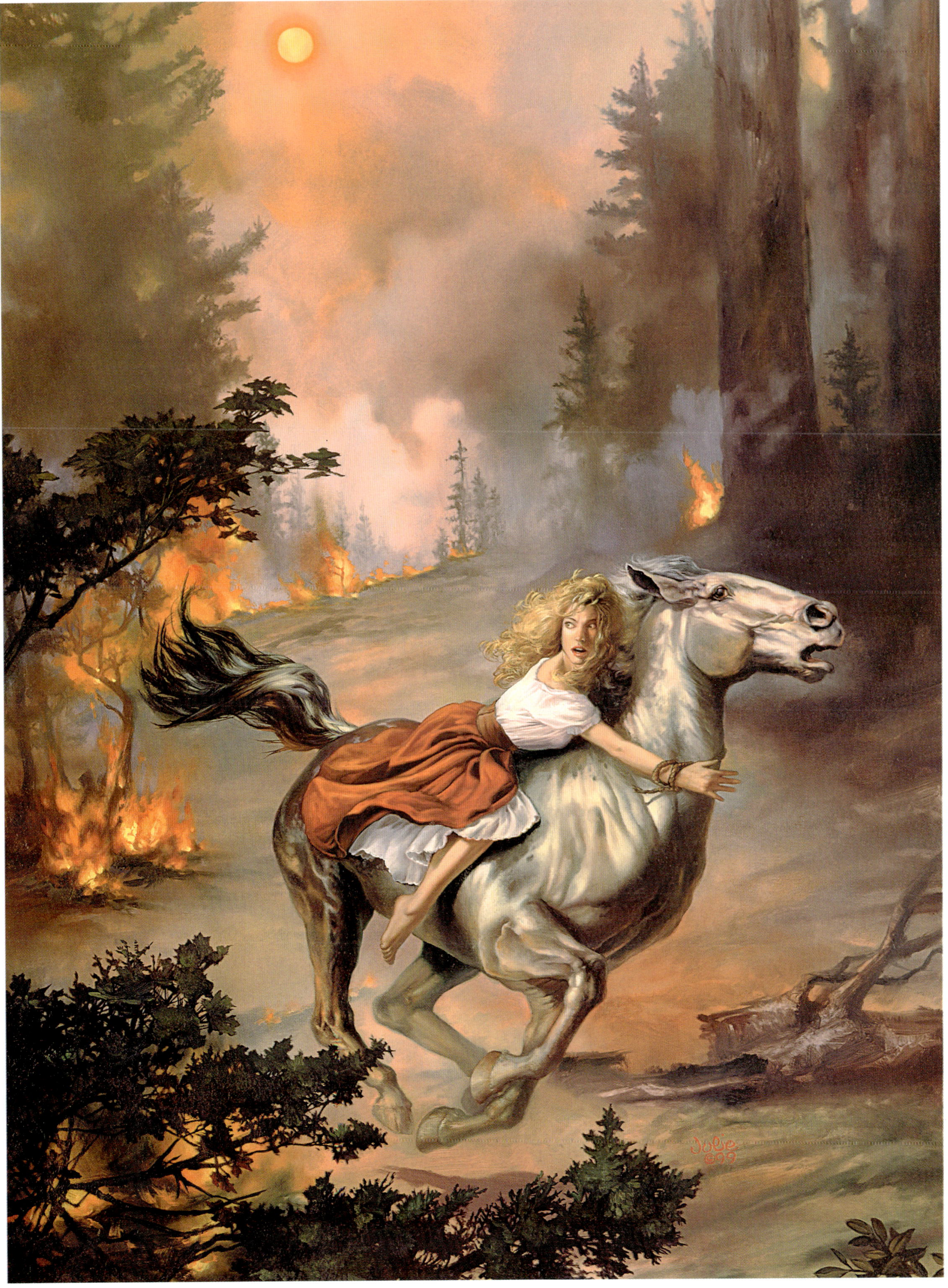

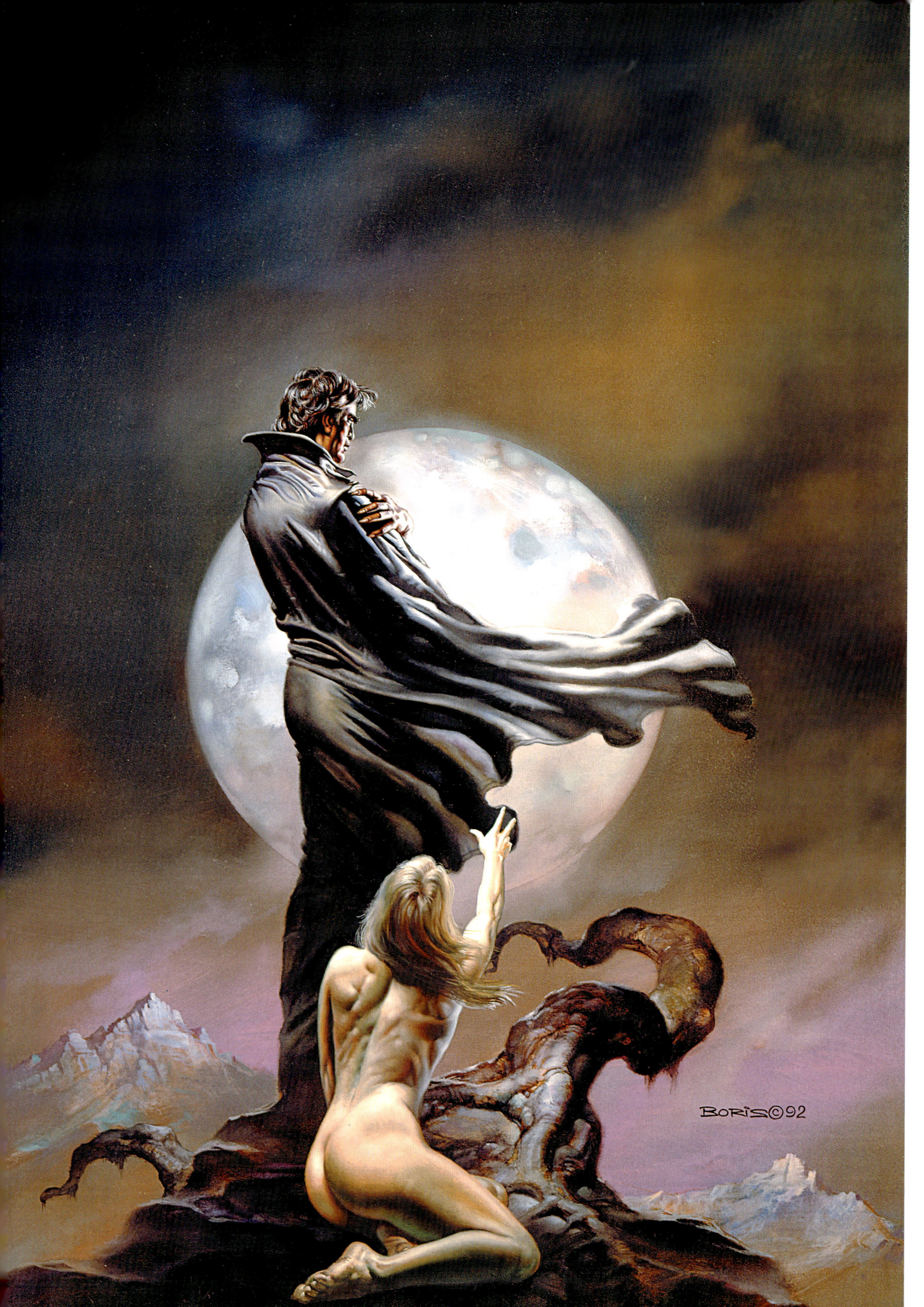
BORIS©92

DRACULA

1992, Boris *(left)*

This is a rare example of Boris reworking a painting. It was a cover for Bram Stoker's novel and appeared without the female figure. This was to depict the vampire's loneliness, which it did, but Boris was just not happy till the female was added later: 'Although as far as the painting goes it means he is no longer alone, the attitude of the woman shows he is still unreachable'. The general response Boris has had from the improved version seems to bear this out.

MUTANT

2001, Julie *(right)*

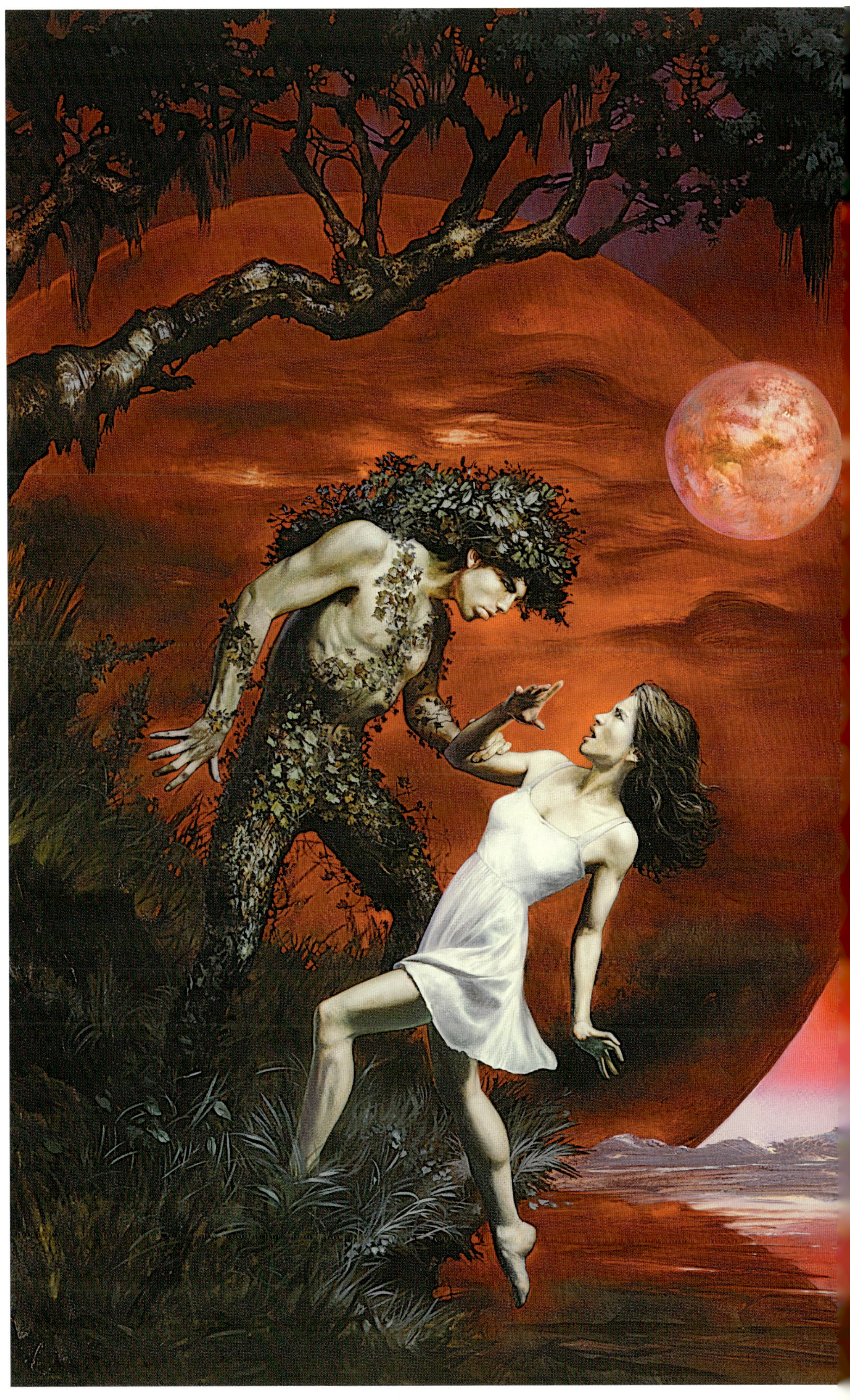

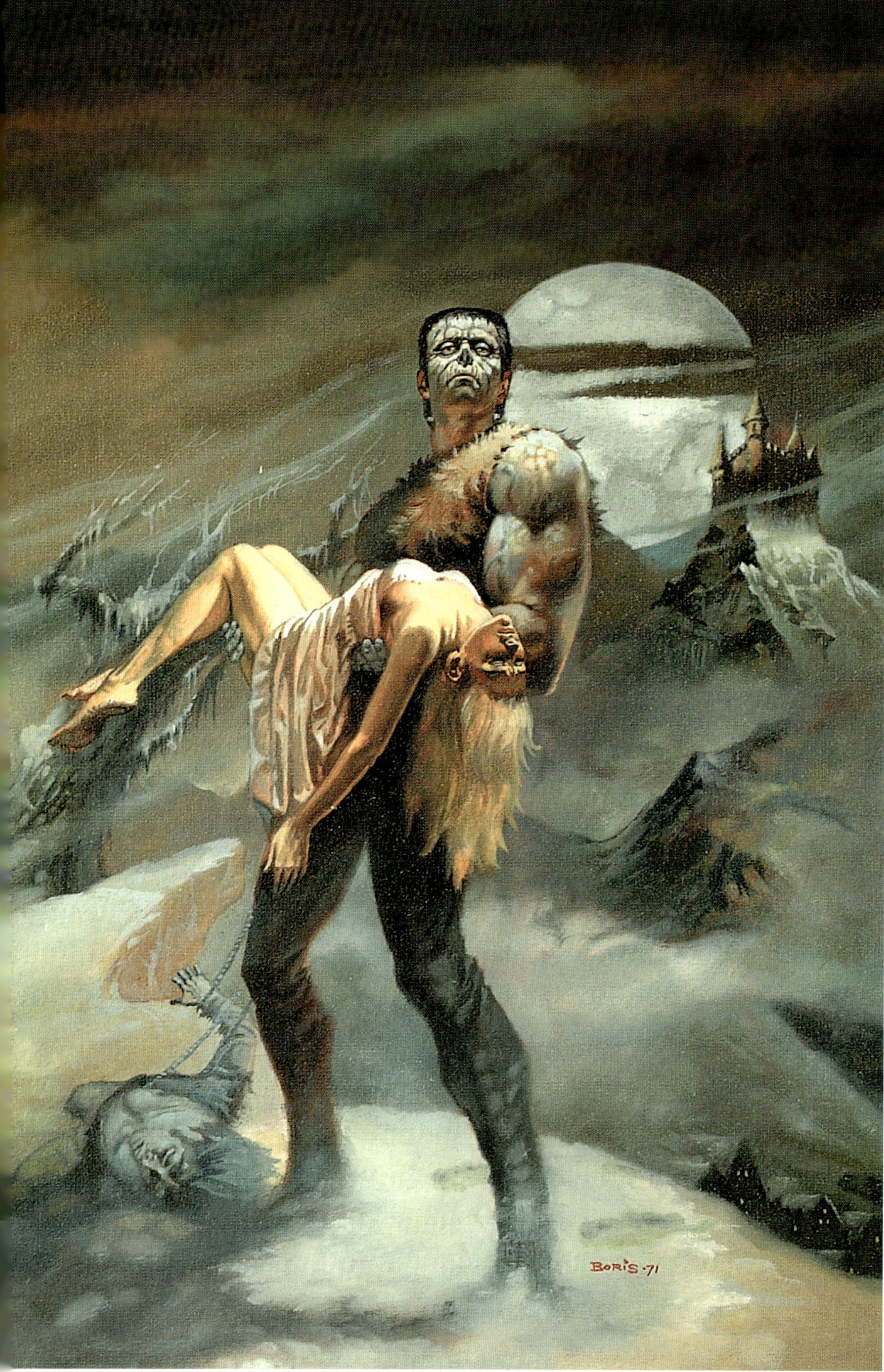

FRANKENSTEINS MONSTER

1971, Boris *(left)*

An early comic book cover showing the development of Boris's characteristic style. His son Dorian, who was about six at the time, was the first model for the girl in order to get the proportions of the two main figures right. Then, in case you were wondering, Boris asked a female to take the same pose for the final composition.

FETCH

1970, Boris *(right)*

Another cover for *Nightmare*. Boris can find much to criticize in these early pictures but as historical documents they make an interesting contrast with current work.

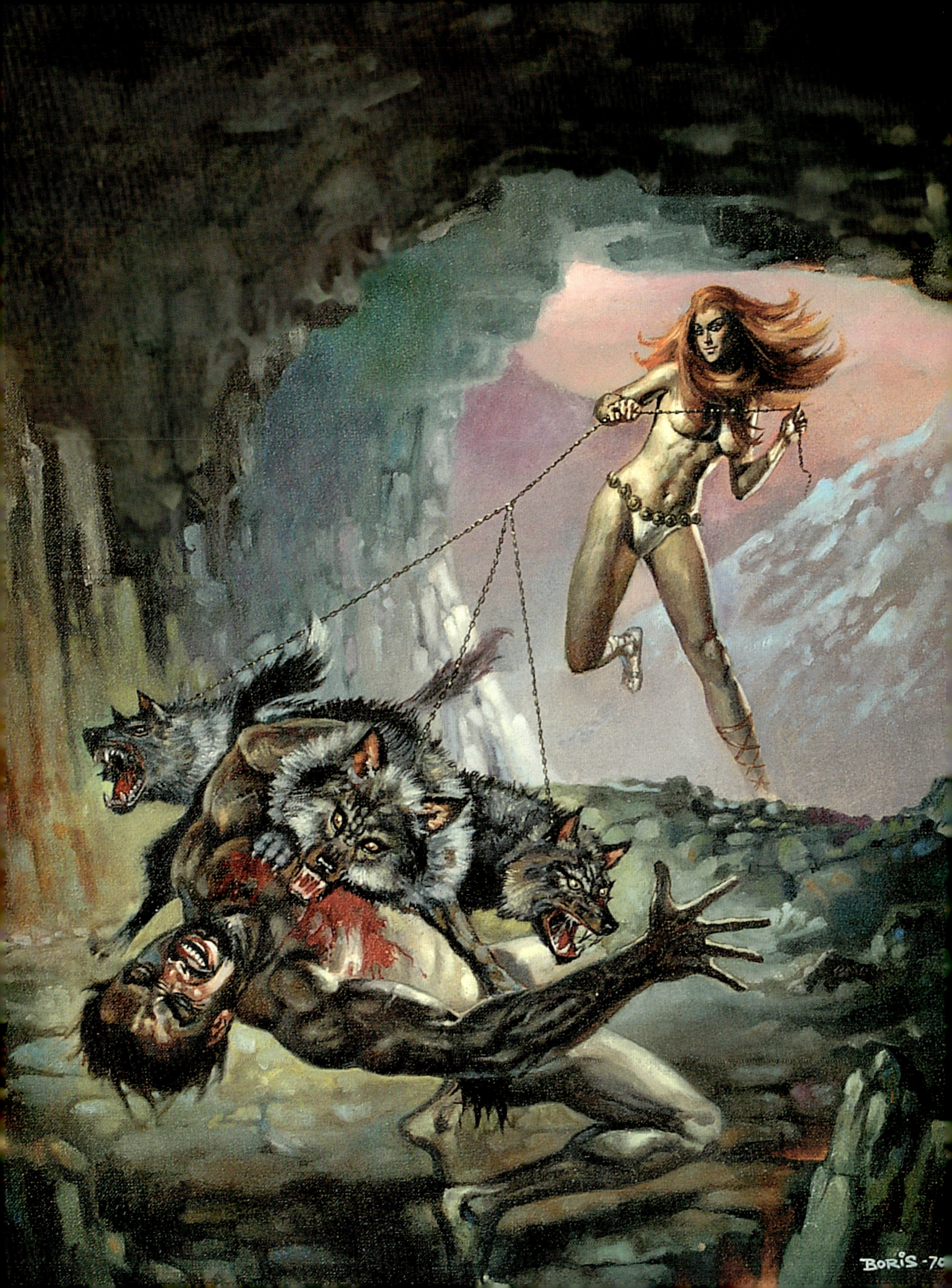
BORIS -70

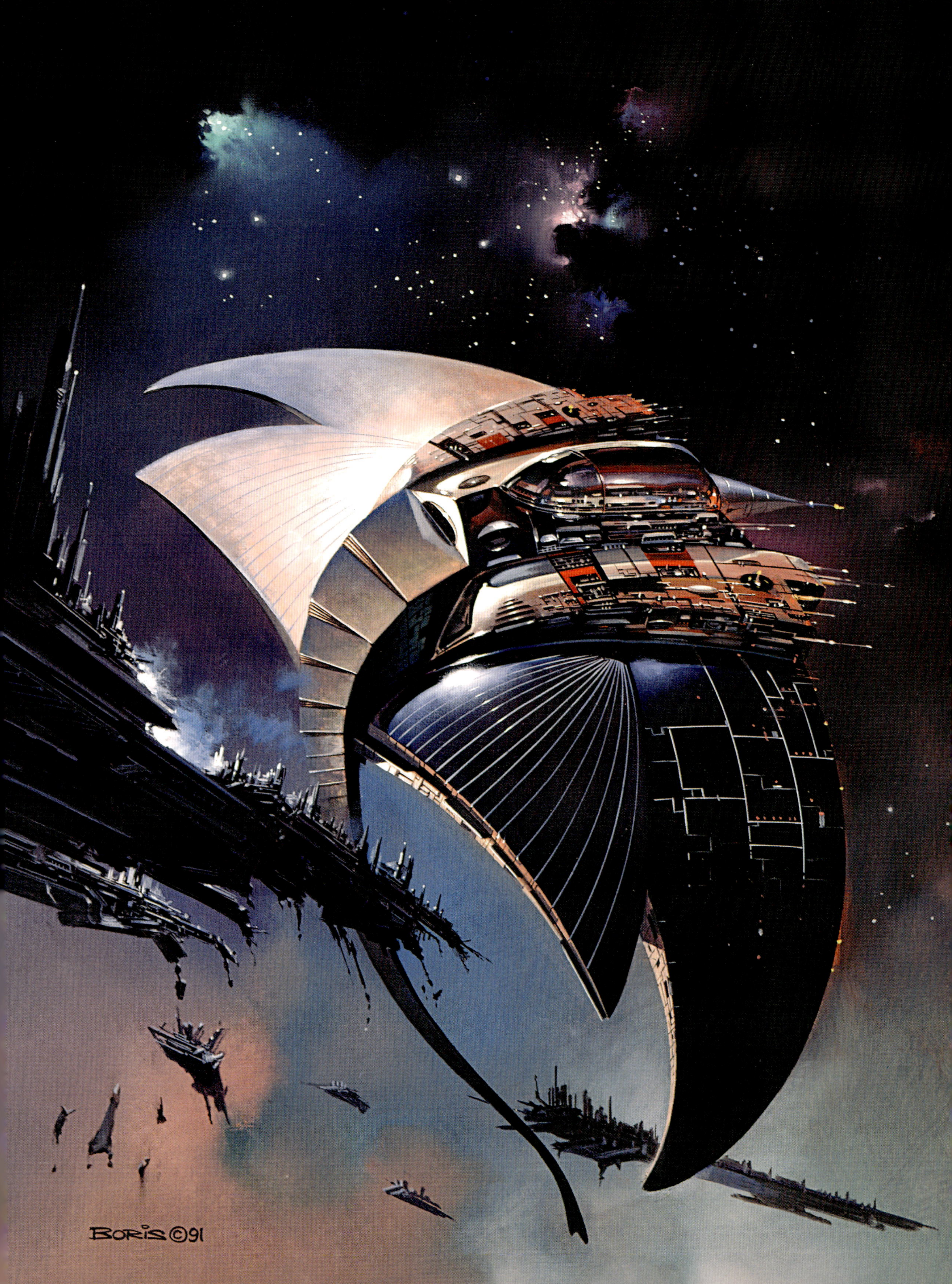
BORIS ©91

chapter 5

Space hardware is not what usually comes first to people's minds in relation to Boris and Julie, but they turn their hands to it as readily as any other kind of fantasy. Boris actually has some grounding in technical illustration because as a student in Peru he had a job for a while painting cars and motorbikes for an advertising agency. Julie just kind of picked it up as she went along. They say their spaceships and other hardware are much more improvized than they appear. They aren't planned out in great detail beforehand but pretty much worked up on the board with paint until they just look right.

Further on in this chapter we have a variety of pictures that don't quite fit any of the usual categories, including some straight nature paintings and portraits by Julie. These were mainly done for simple pleasure but also as samples to show publishers and possibly open up new areas of work. Both artists do this from time to time because despite their reputations and body of work they are still always keen to find fresh fields of art to conquer. Sculpture designs are just one of the current possibilities. They have already done a few but possibly will be doing many more in future, depending on the demand.

For the future in general there seems no sign of Boris and Julie easing up on their astonishingly prolific output. In fact as we were talking through this book they had an efficiency expert in to organize their lives so the chances are that they will in future be doing even more, rather than using the extra time to put their feet up.

As ever it has been a great pleasure for me to be involved in this small way of providing a bit of text for their book and helping organize the pictures. It's always refreshing to be in the presence of such enormous energy and enthusiasm for art, and a treat to be able to feast on so many new pictures all at once. Roll on the next project!

SPACE MANTA
1991, Boris

Boris enjoys tackling space hardware from time to time. He particularly enjoys combining organic and 'hard tech' forms. For the technical side he has a background of training in technical illustration in his youth followed by a spell of merchandising illustration for a variety of machines. It was not terribly exciting at the time but gave him the patience needed for gradually building up machines like this spaceship.

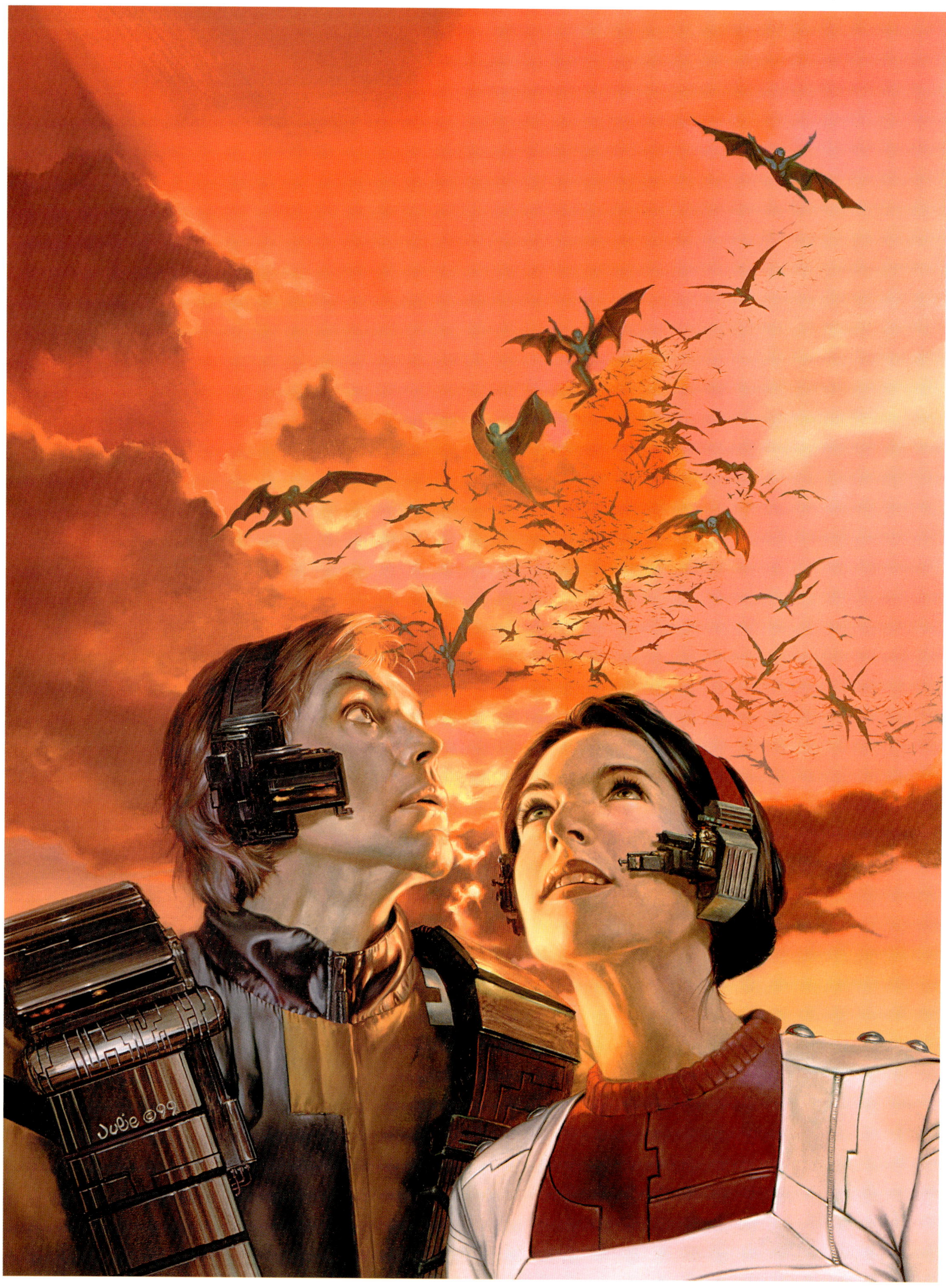
Julie ©99

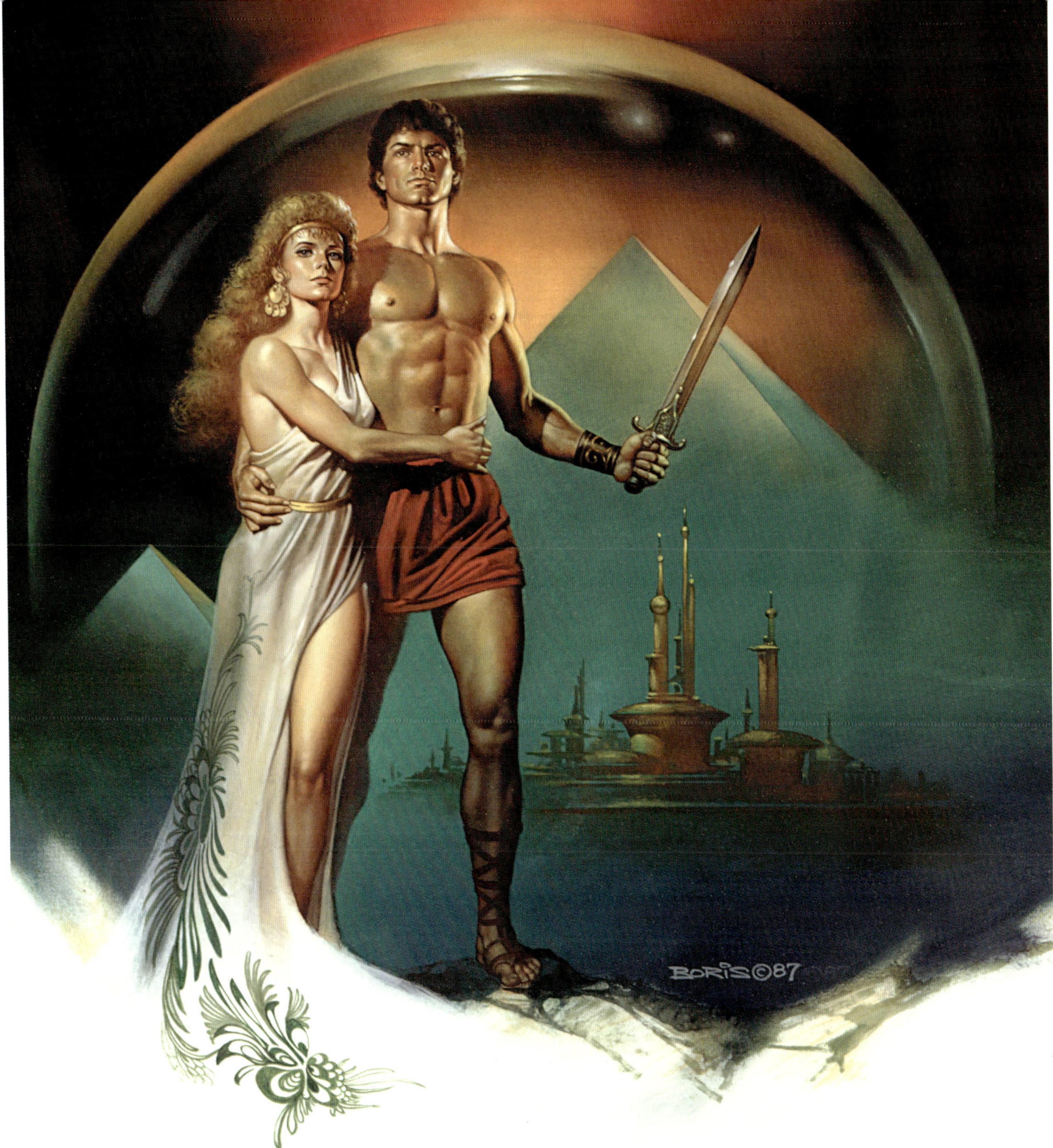

SEARCHING THE SKY

1999, Julie *(left)*

For this book cover Julie wanted to capture a feeling of the love and wonder these scientists feel for what they are studying, which is the breed of winged humanoids flying above. Their awe and bliss is reflected in the colour of the sky – which was suggested by the Art Director. Boris and Julie themselves posed for the main figures, as they often do in their paintings. Julie says that when using family and close friends this way it takes half the usual time because they are so familiar: 'It almost feels like just tracing over something that's etched into the mind'.

PYRAMID

1987, Boris *(above)*

This stars Boris's son Dorian as a young man. He is also a professional artist.

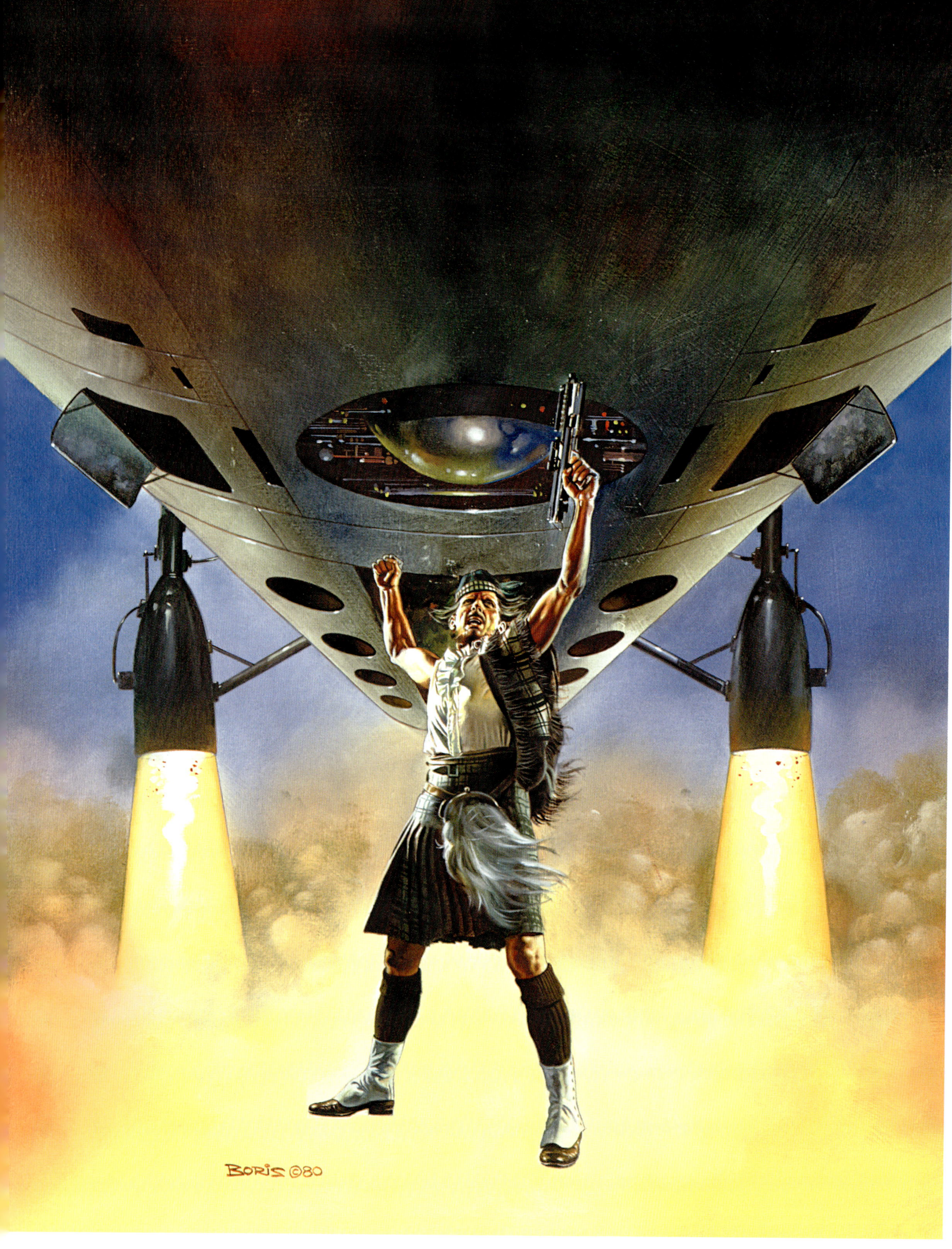
BORIS ©80

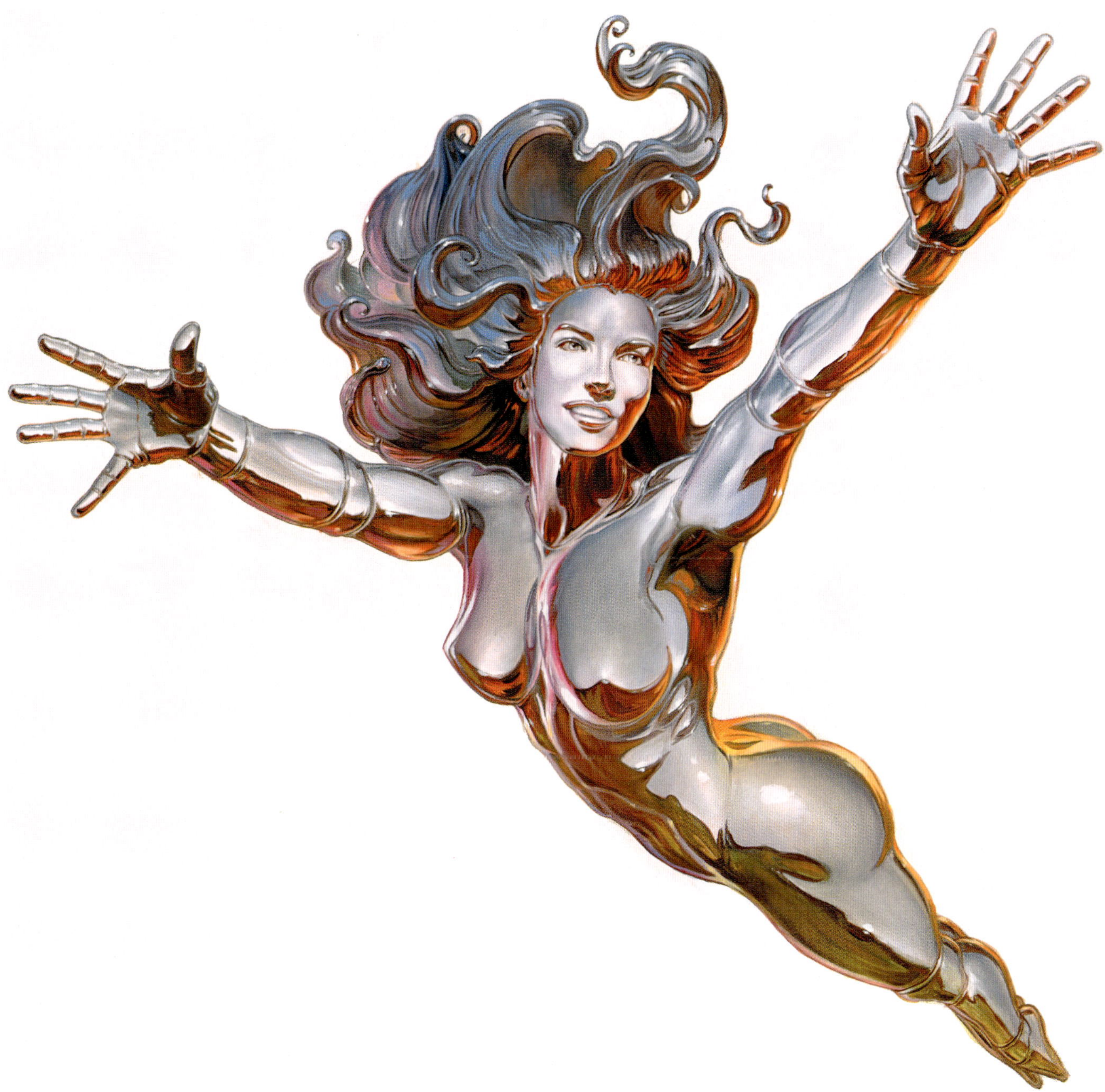

SPACESHIP FOR A KING

1980, Boris *(left)*

There was a nice contrast to be drawn here between the Scotsman in full traditional regalia and the spaceship.

LADY OF THE FUTURE

1999, Julie *(above)*

This is one of the figures dropped into the Pyramids background on page 36 but Julie feels it looks quite neat on its own.

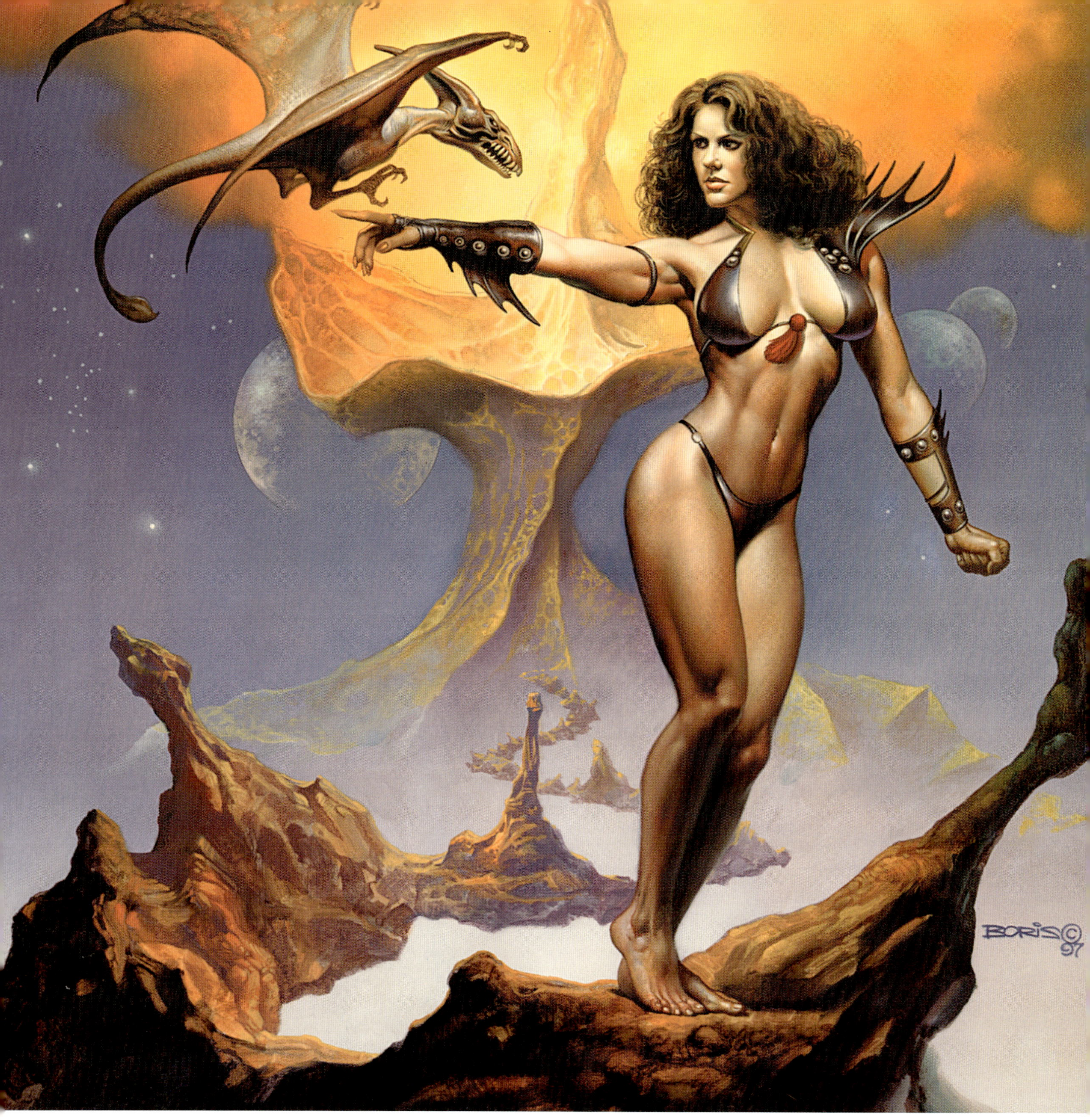

FALCON TAMER

1997, Boris *(above)*

Just as Boris's trees possess an almost animal vitality, so his rocks often seem organically alive, while still looking like stone. You'd have to look hard to find anything like them in the real world but nevertheless they always feel right.

SUPERHERO MAN

1995, Boris *(right)*

This is another rare example of a painting that Boris has gone back to and reworked. It was originally a T-shirt design but when that venture never materialized Boris added a background and used the picture in a calendar.

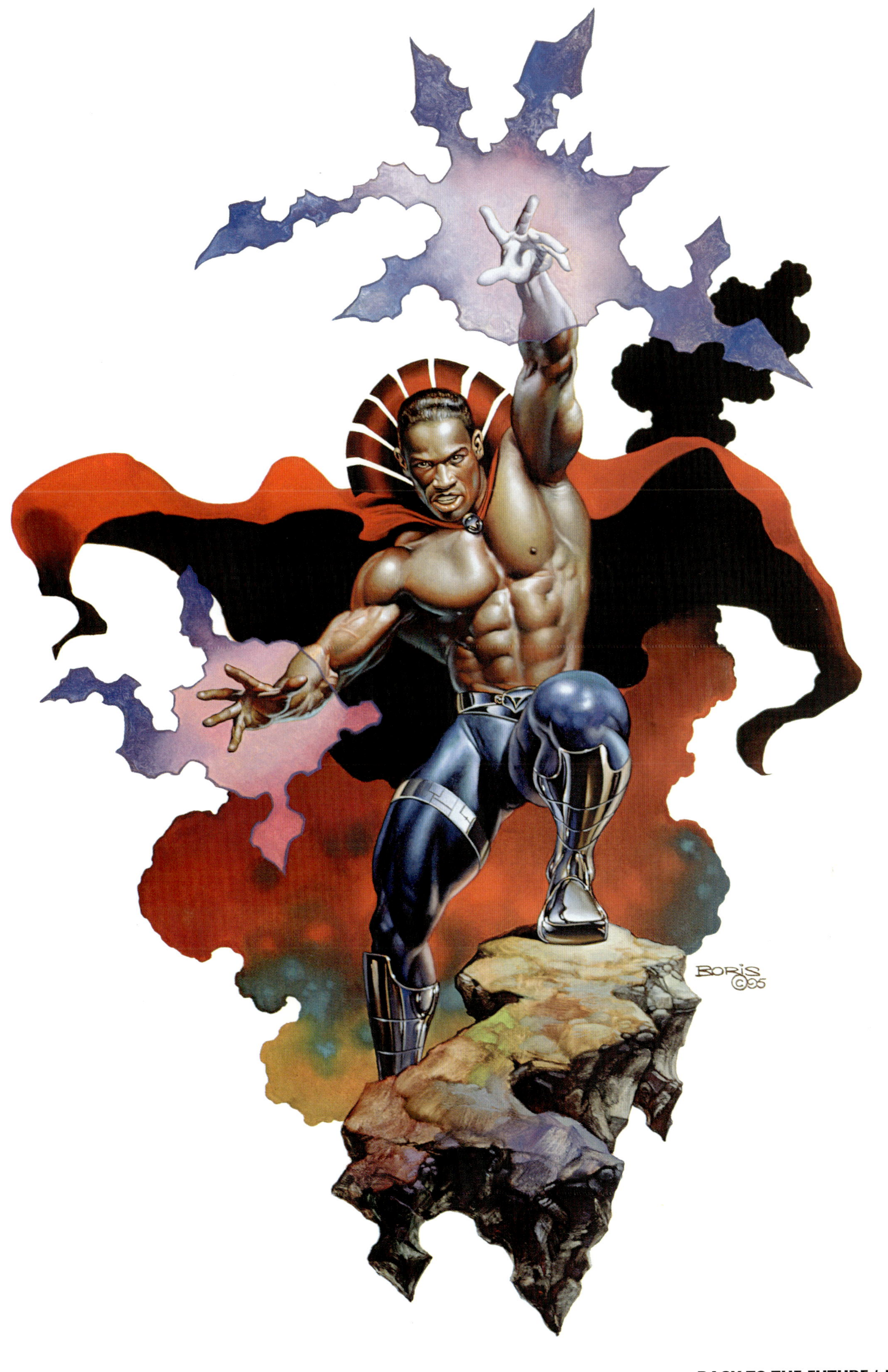
BORIS
©95

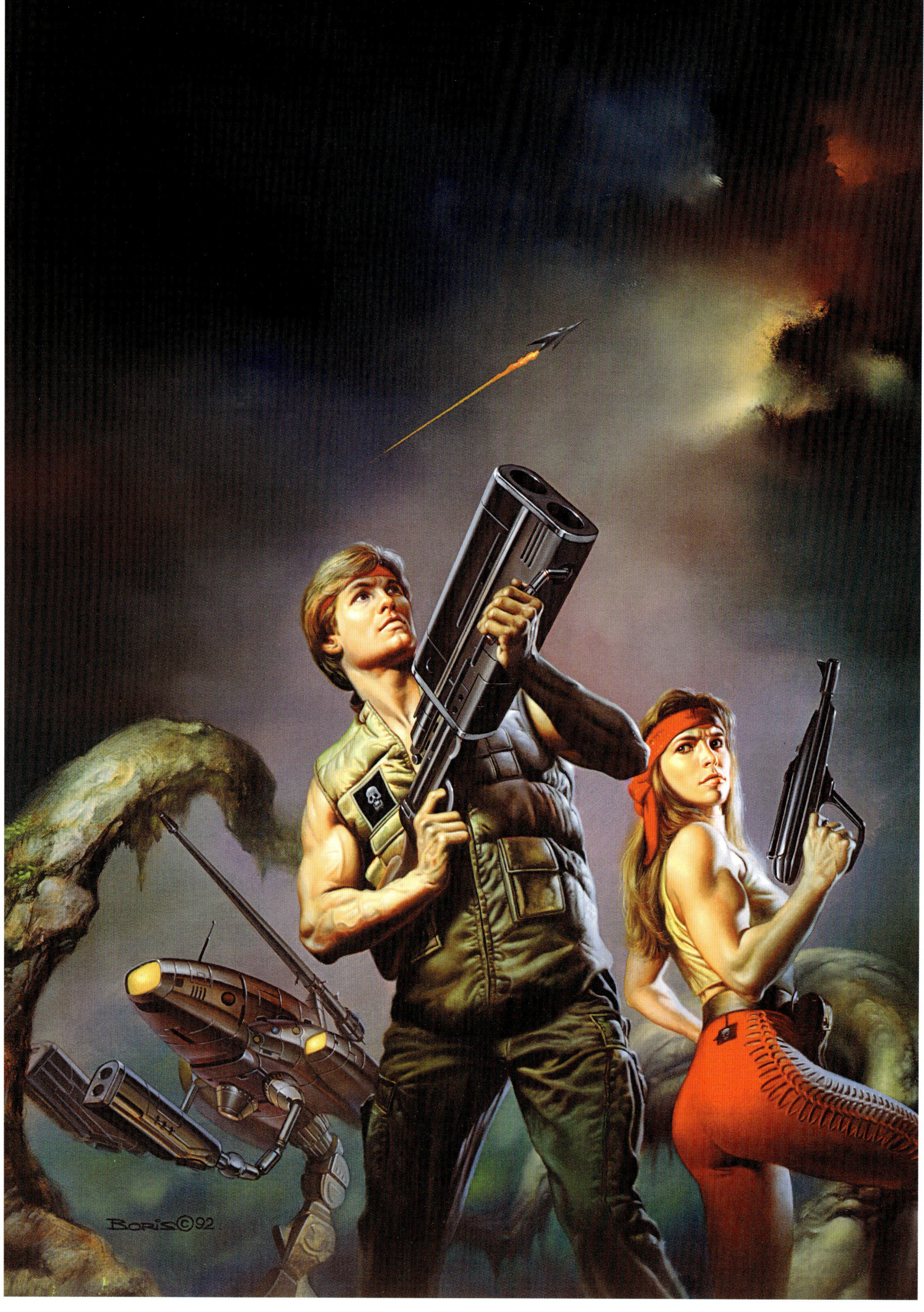
BORIS©92

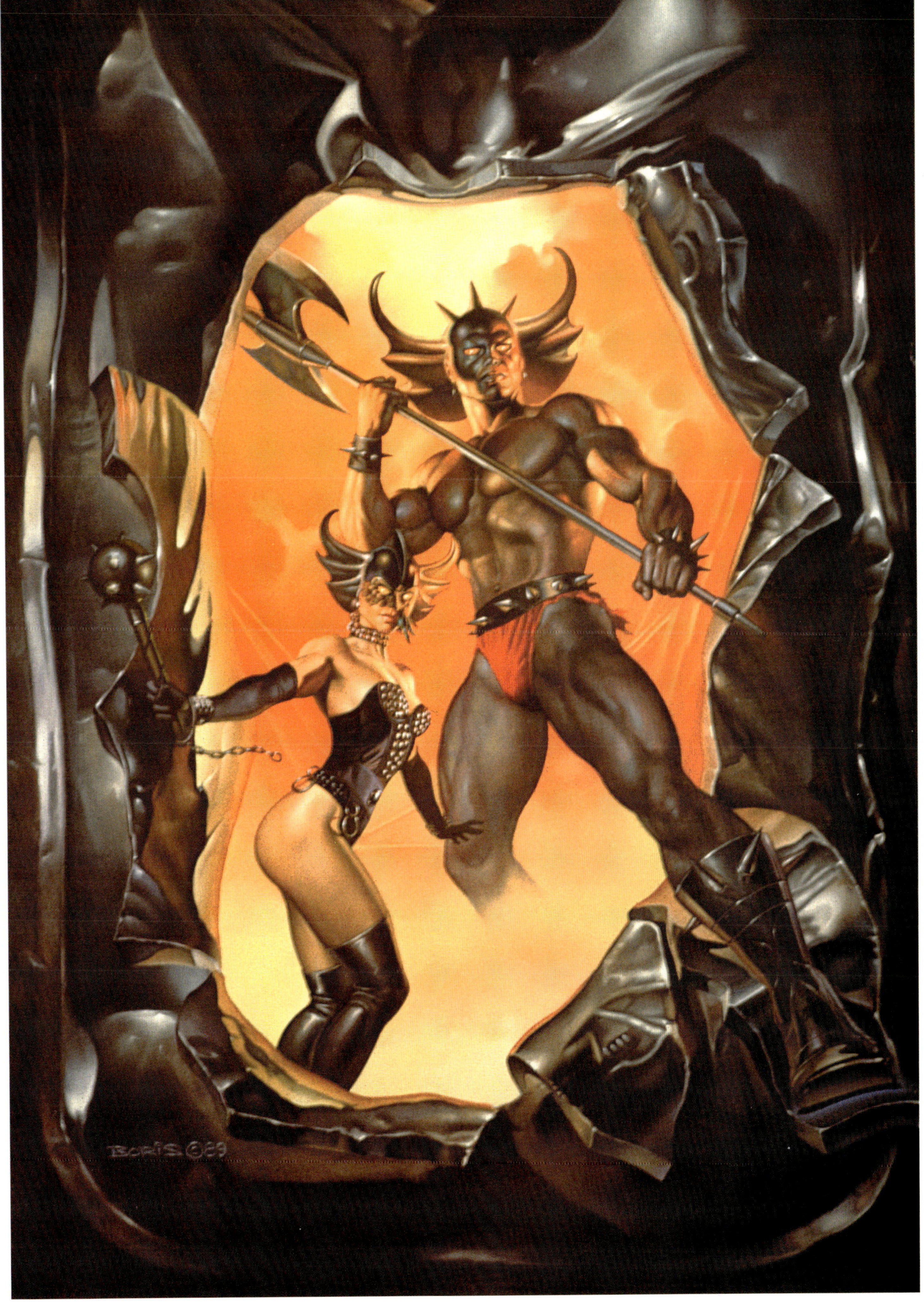
BORIS ©89

TECH WAR

1992, Boris *(page 112)*

One of Boris's favourite things when asked to do a book jacket is also being asked to paint prominent figures with a sketchy background, so he 'totally enjoyed' this painting.

STRONGER THAN STEEL

1989, Boris *(page 113)*

This was the cover of a video game that never quite made it to the marketplace, but it was a useful exercise anyway in painting metal that looks really strong despite having been bent and twisted like paper.

SUPRISE ENCOUNTER

1993, Boris *(right)*

The BattleTech role-playing game has generated a whole subculture and a library of books, for two of which these pictures were covers.

THE AX OF THE ROBOT

1992, Boris *(far right)*

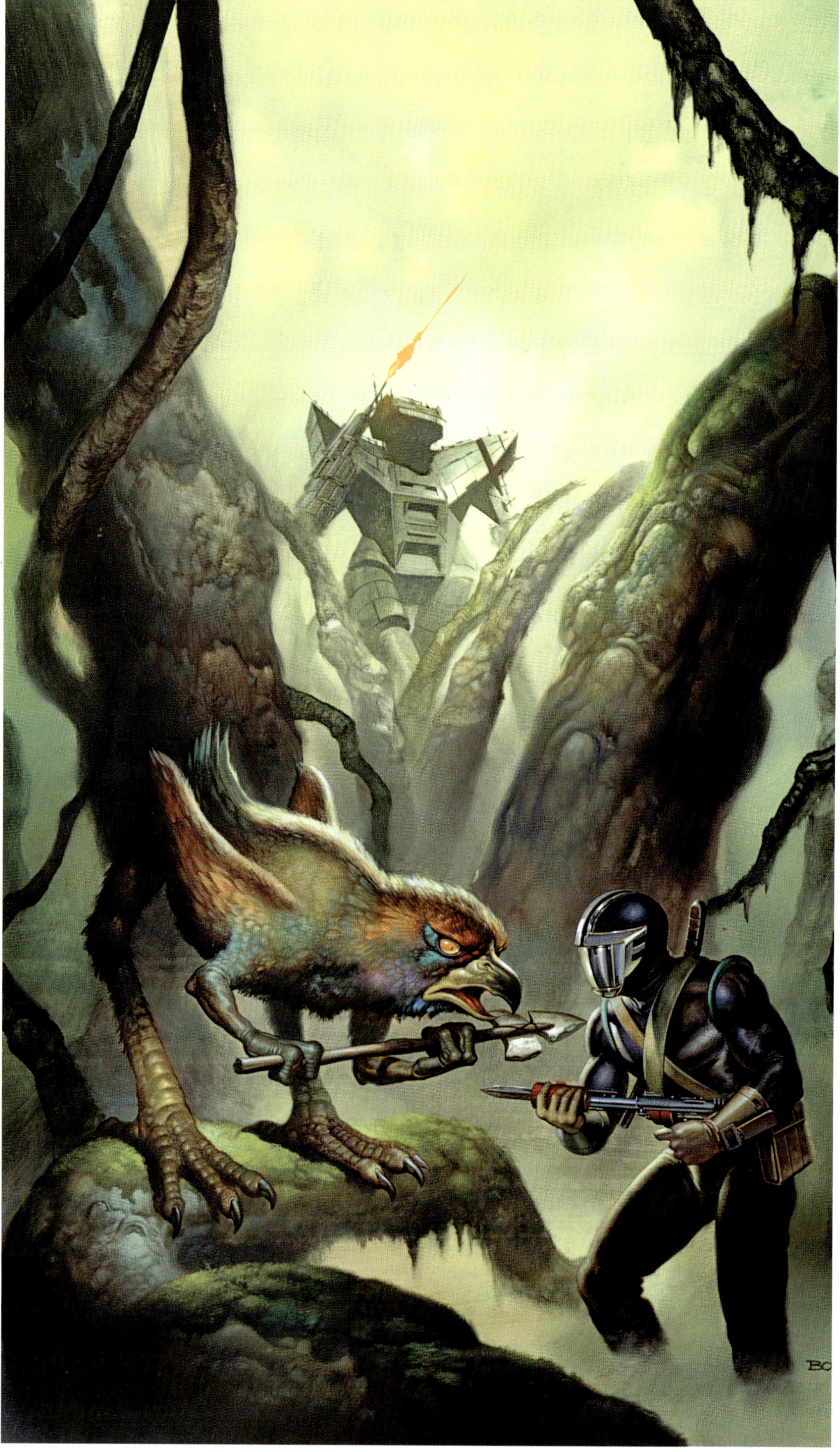

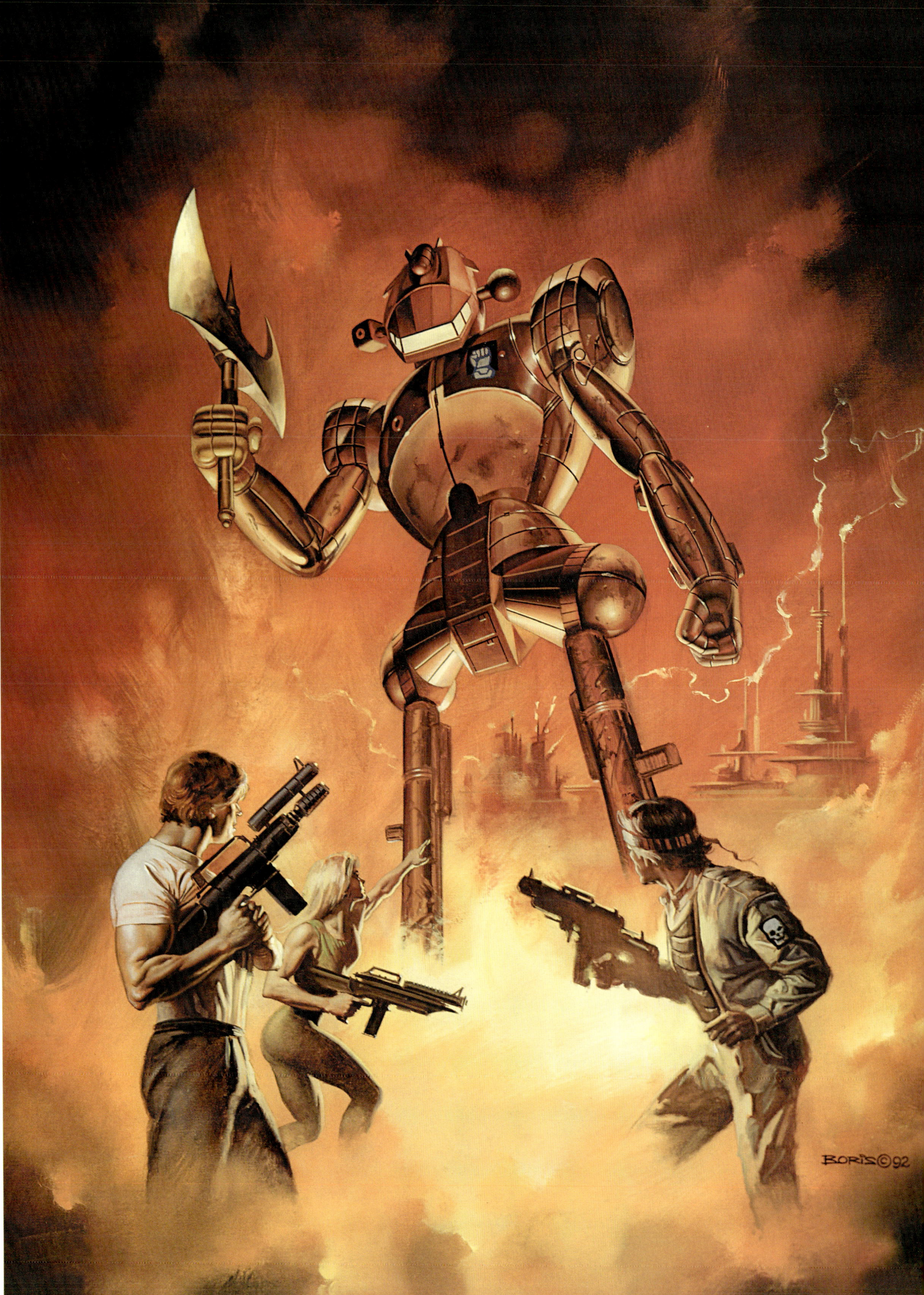
BORIS©92

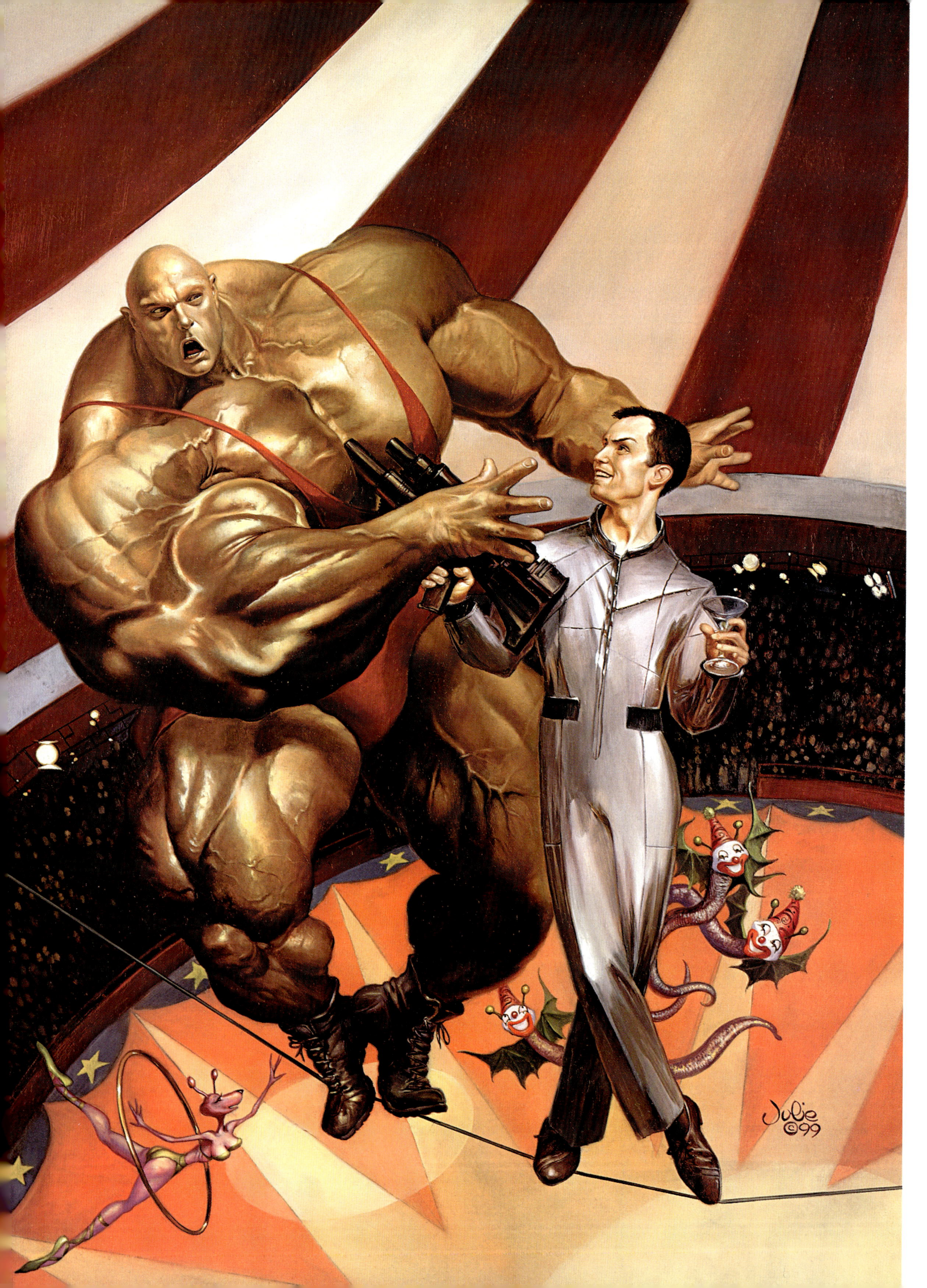
Julie
©99

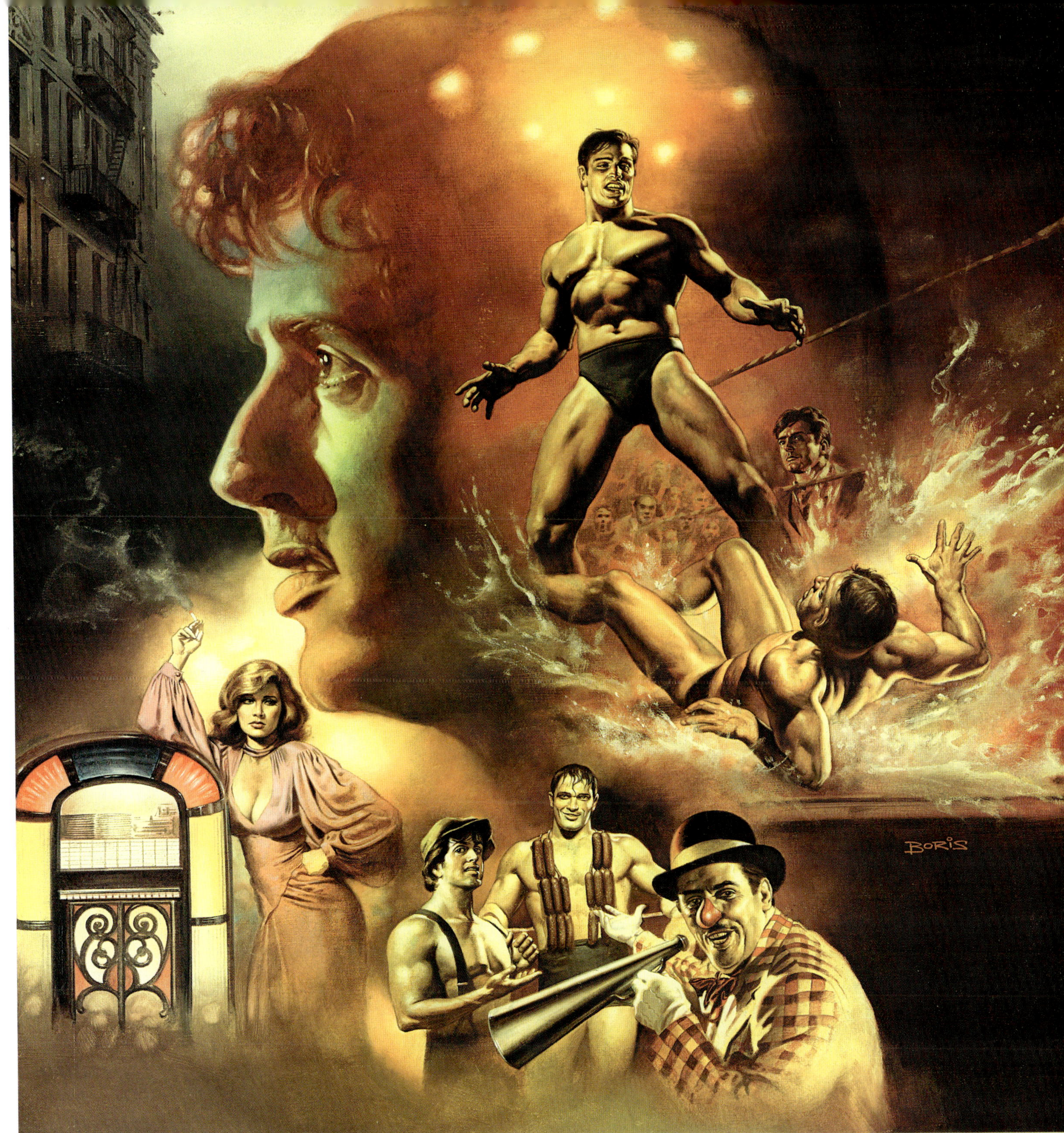

STAINLESS STEEL RAT

1999, Julie *(left)*

Cover for *The Stainless Steel Rat Joins the Circus*, one of the comic series of futuristic novels by Harry Harrison starring a hero who makes James Bond seem flustered. Julie enjoyed the chance of humour and had fun with the tightrope-walking bodybuilder.

PARADISE ALLEY

1979, Boris *(above)*

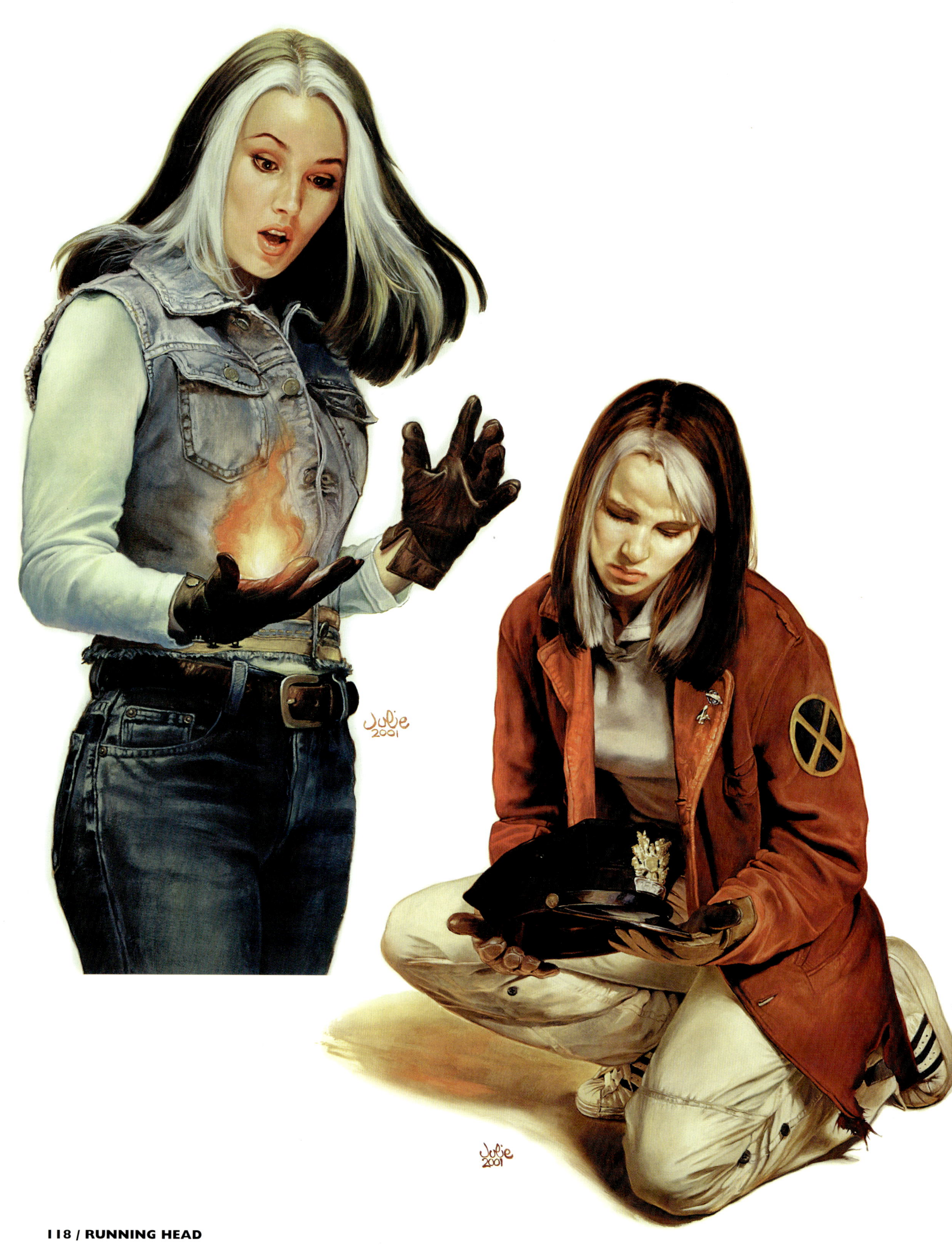
Julie
2001
Julie
2001

ROGUE 2

2001, Julie *(left below)*

ROGUE 3

2001, Julie *(left above)*

These three pictures were a set of covers for some Marvel books about the X-Man Rogue. The aim was for very natural, un-comic book portrayals of her as a teenager against a white background to give the covers a kind of *Saturday Evening Post* feel. A friend of the family posed for the part and suited it perfectly.

ROGUE 4

2001, Julie *(right)*

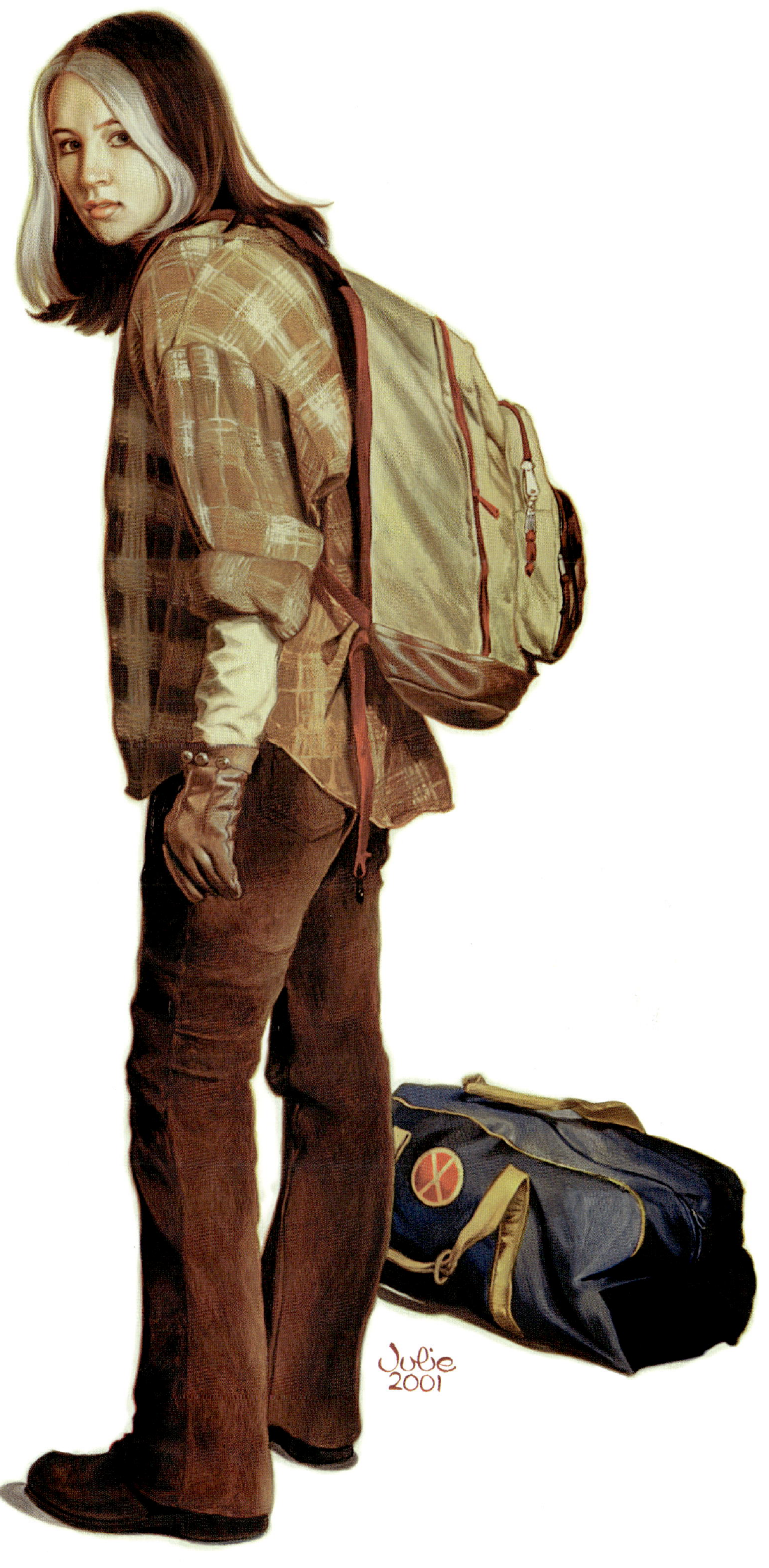

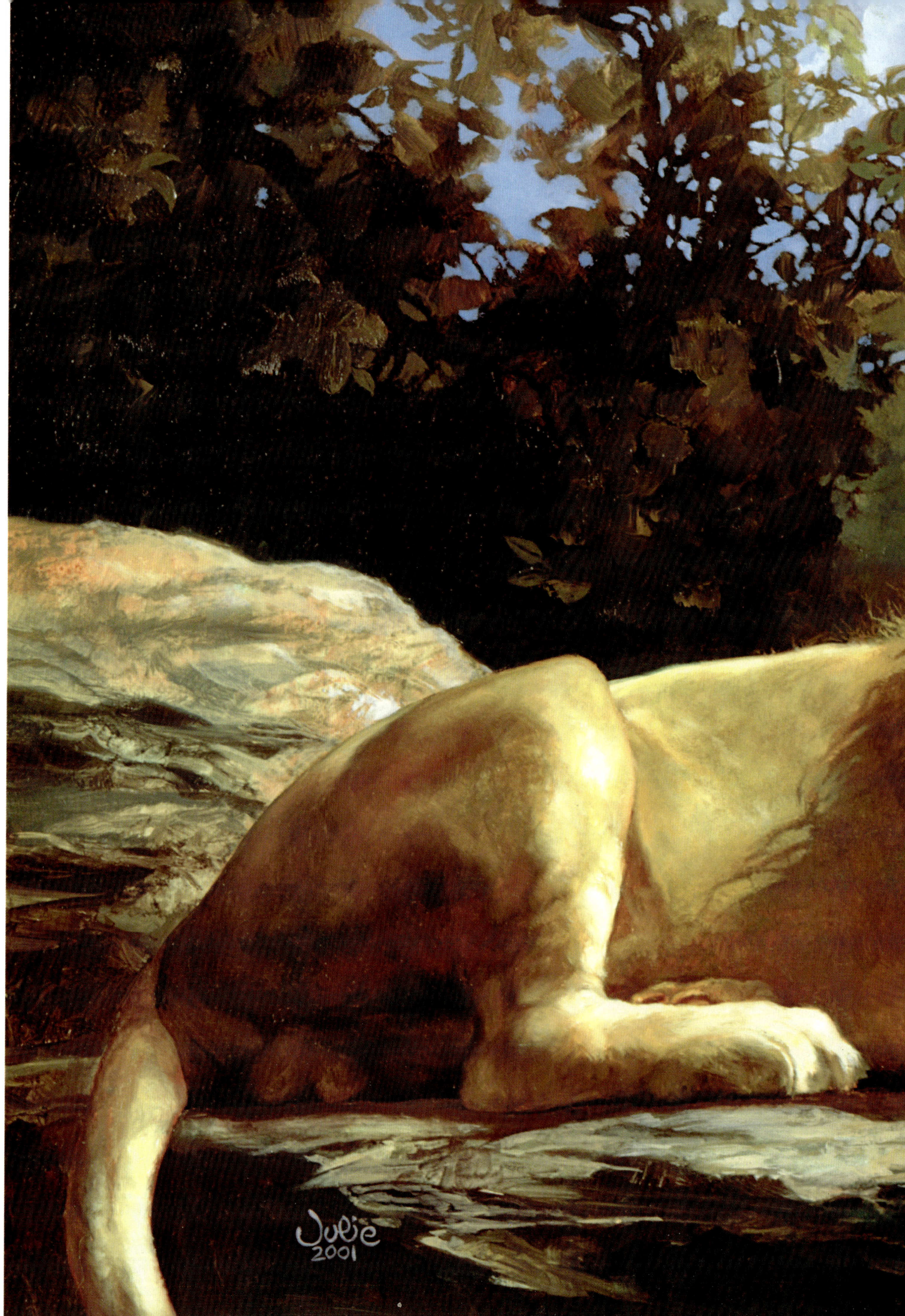
Julie
2001

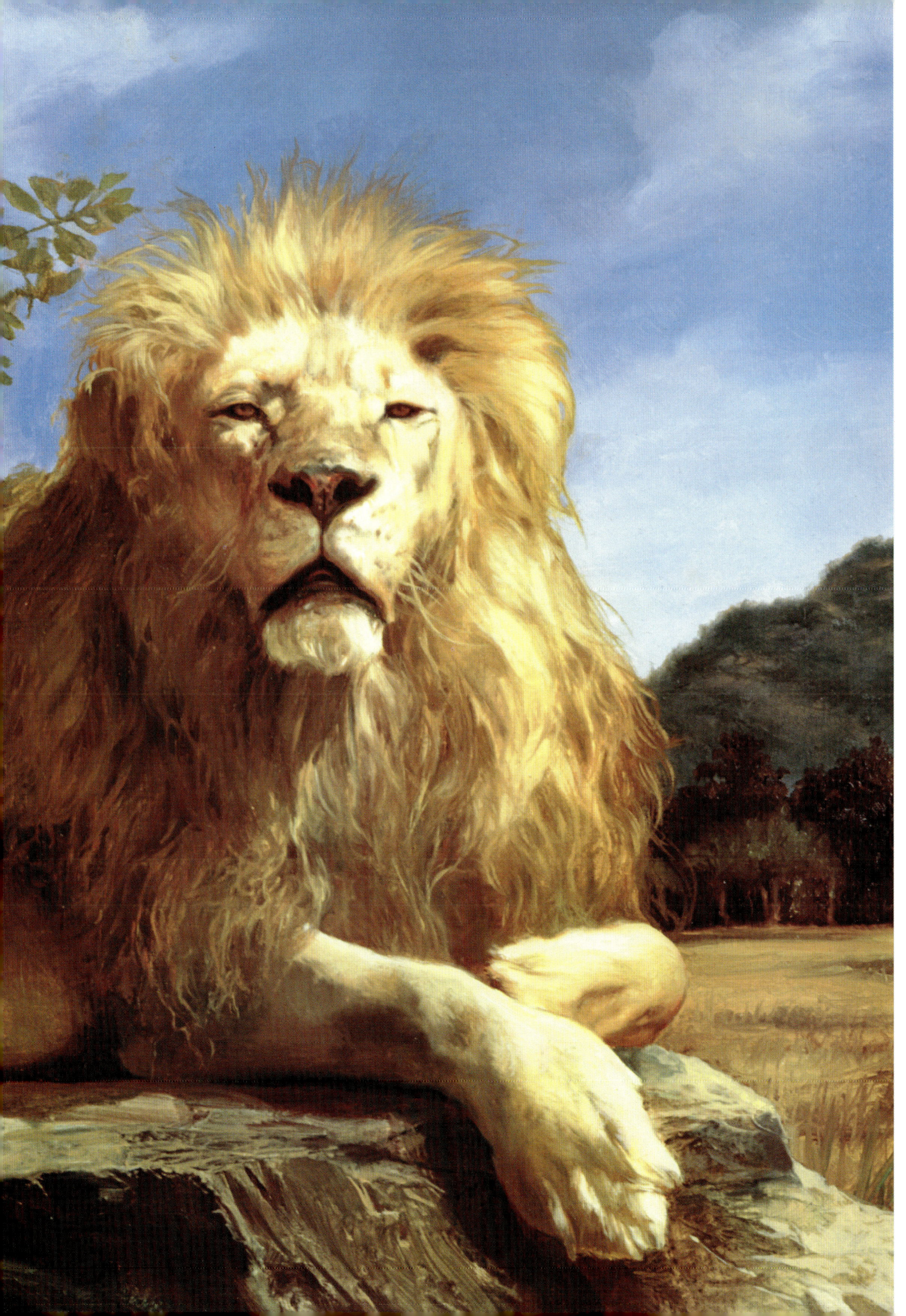

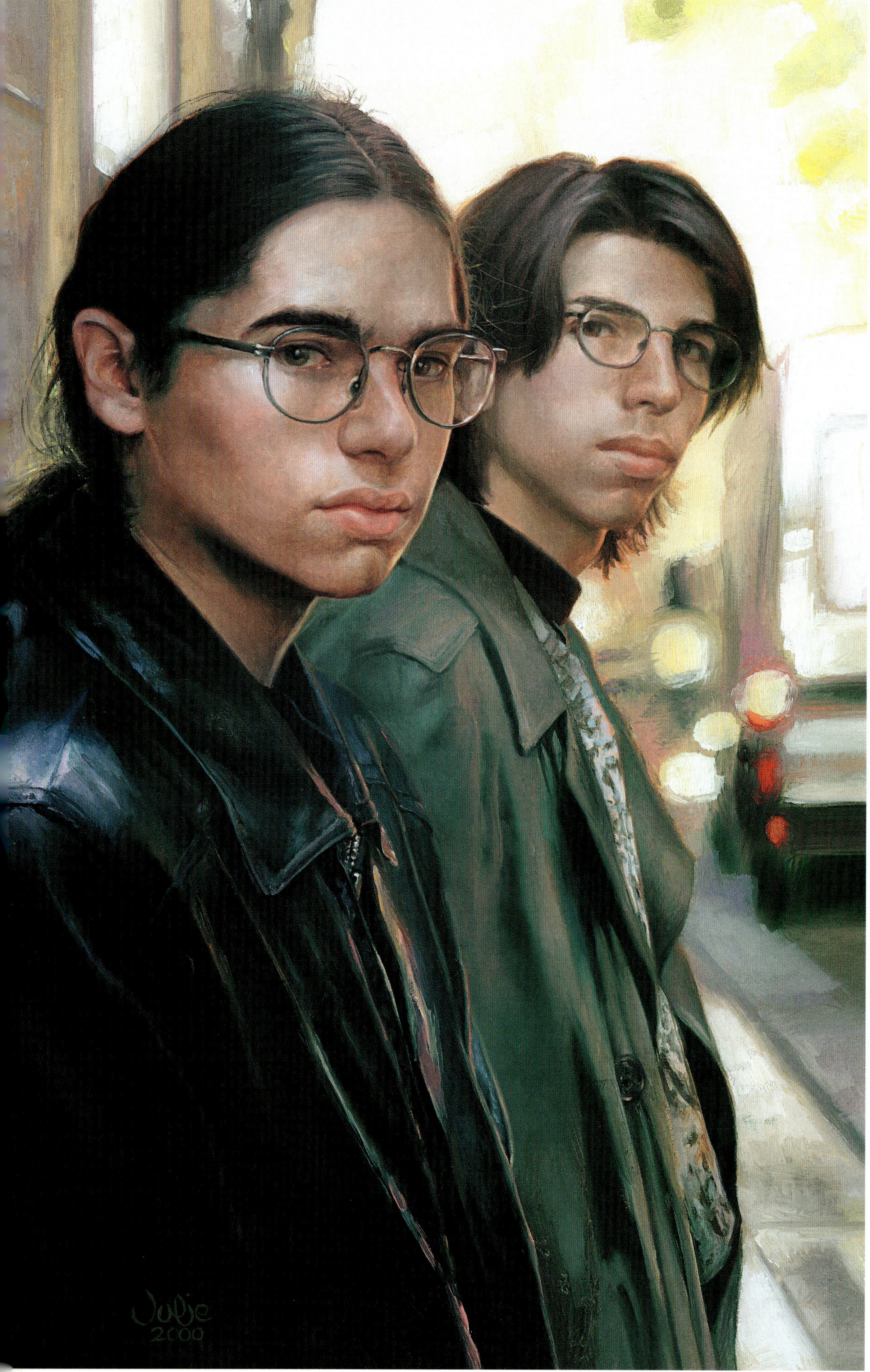

LION

2001, Julie *(pages 120,121)*

A painting that was 'just for the heck of it'. This lion in the Philadelphia Zoo posed so well that Julie felt obliged to do it justice. She had originally thought of adding a few fantasy touches to the lion but this seemed unnecessary.

BARCELONA

2000, Julie *(left)*

A portrait of Julie's sons one beautiful midwinter morning in Barcelona.

DEER

1998, Julie *(right)*

Straight wildlife painting is something Julie would happily do much more of, although not to the exclusion of her usual work. She came across this deer in a local wildlife reserve.

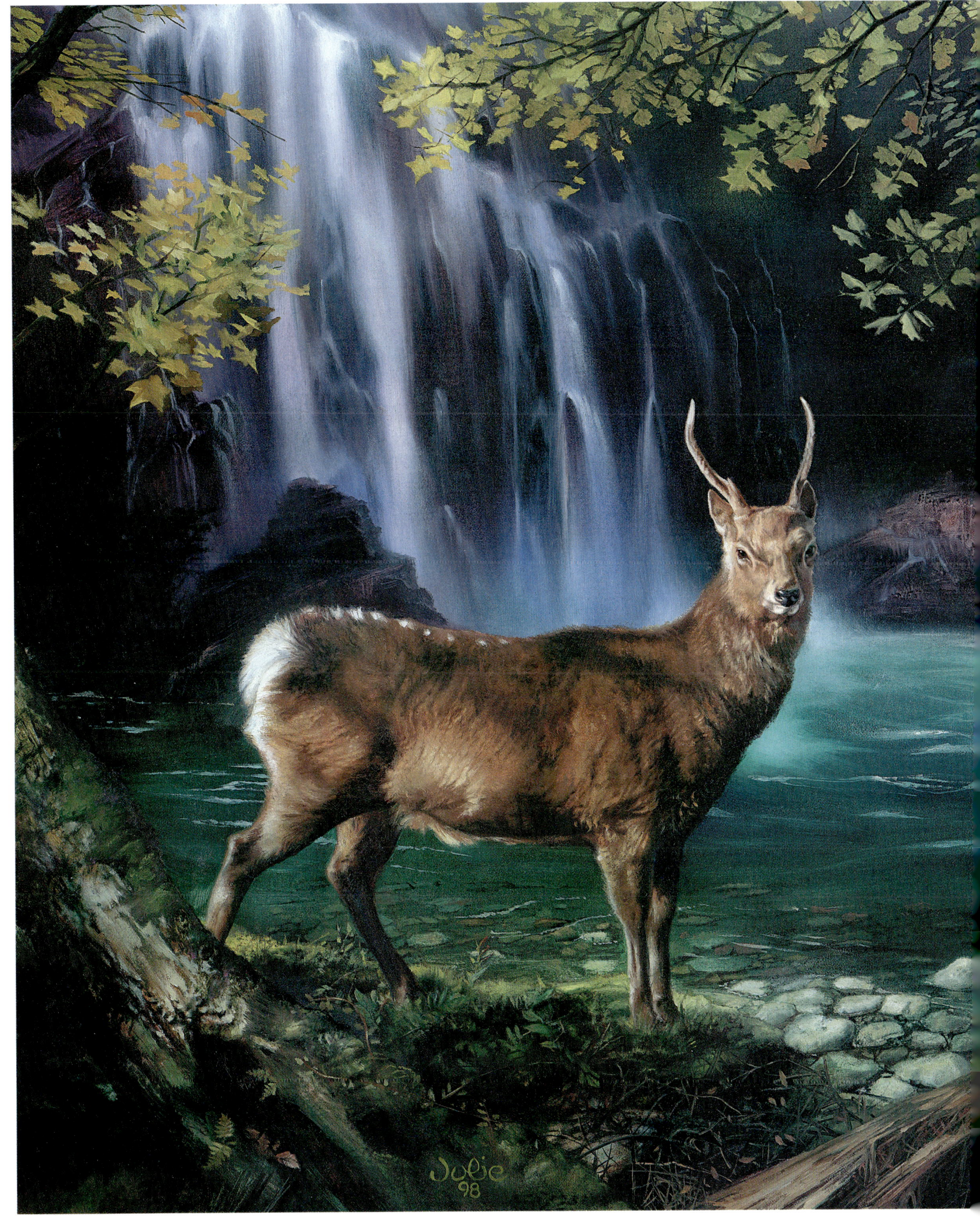
Julie
98

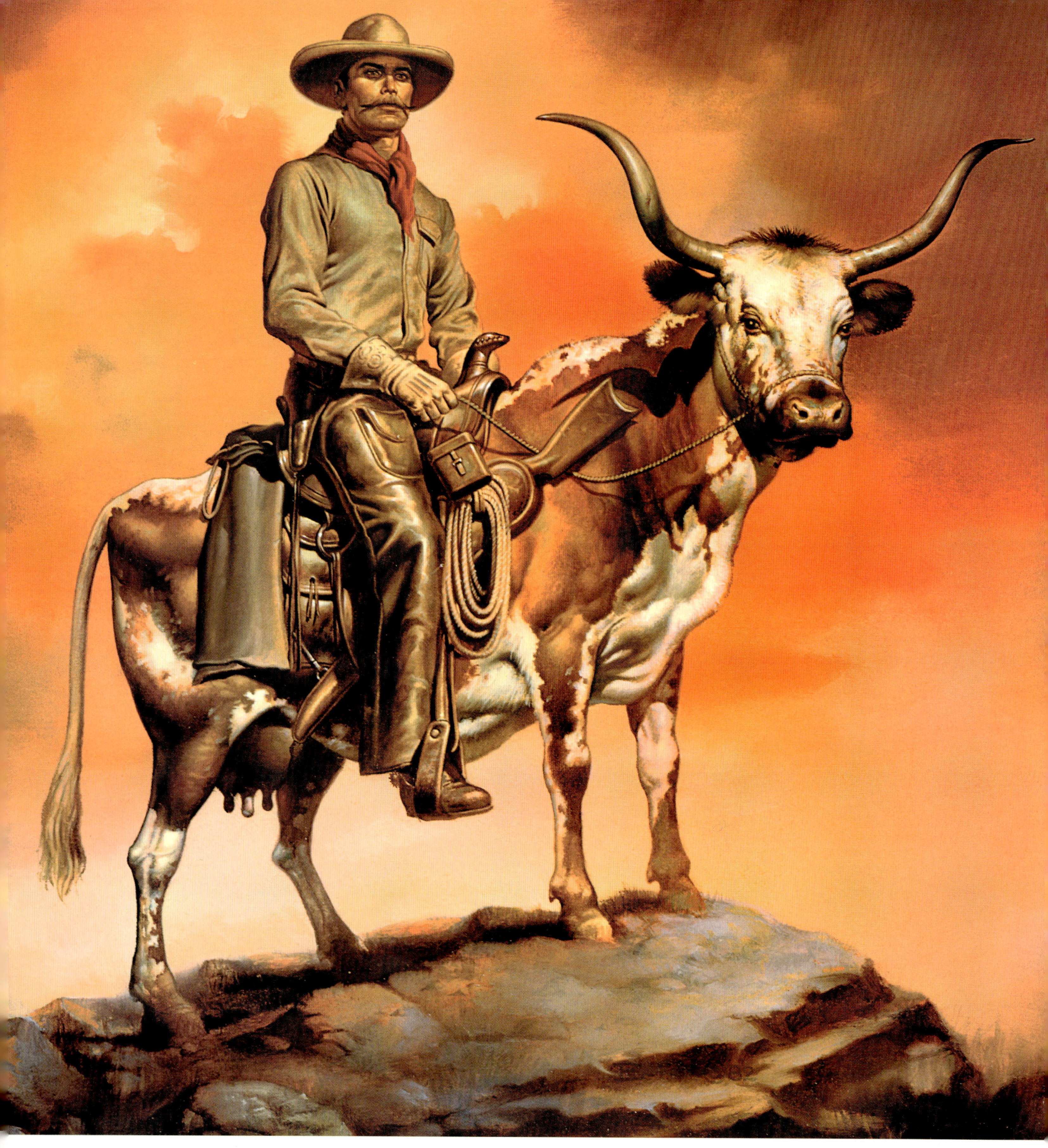

LONGHORN

1988, Boris *(above)*

A jokey album cover. Boris: 'It was a bit absurd having a cowboy riding a cow instead of a horse, but done with a sense of humour it works'.

BACKSTAGE

1987, Boris *(right)*

A book jacket that spoofs some SF and Fantasy themes. Boris himself was one of the models.

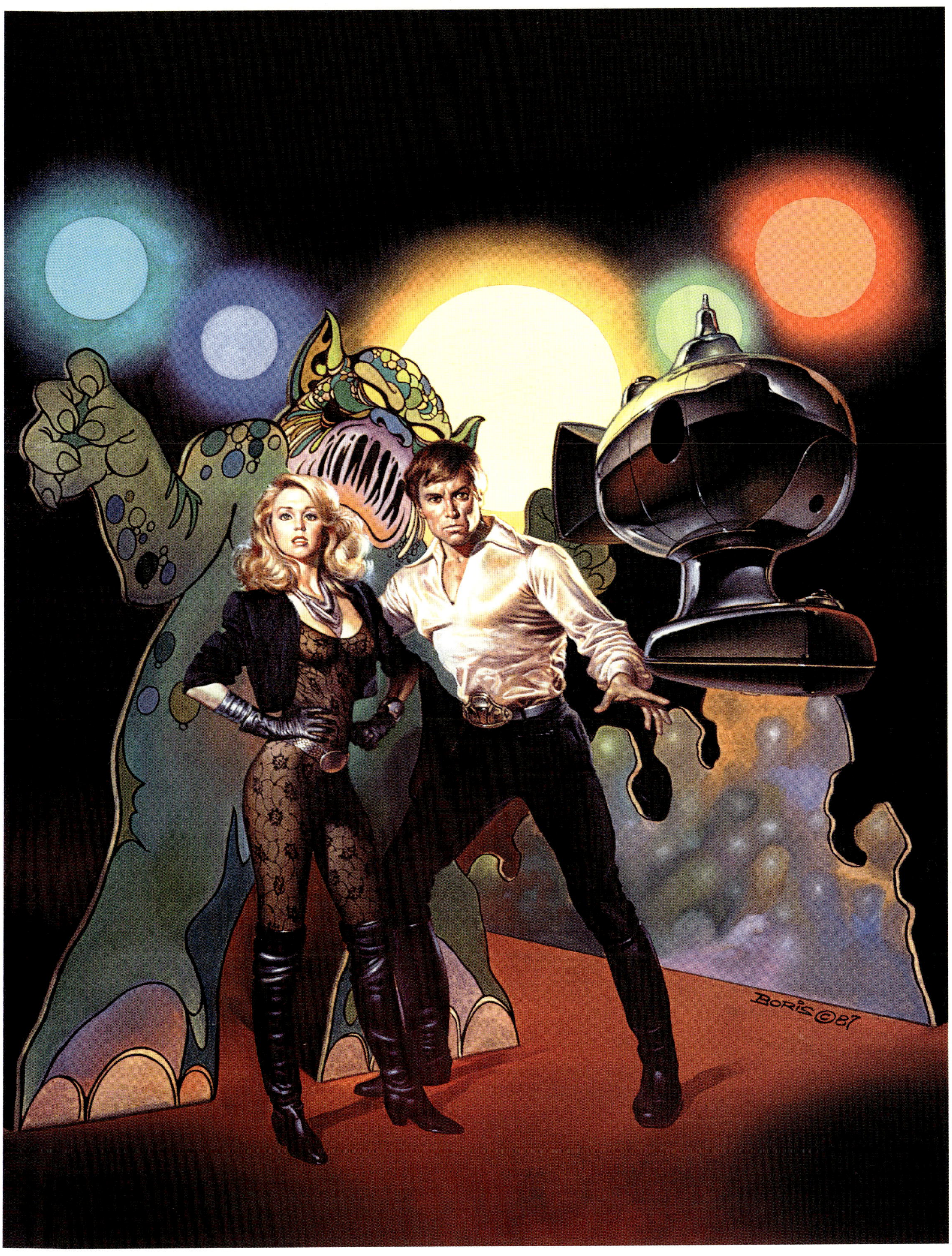
BORIS ©87

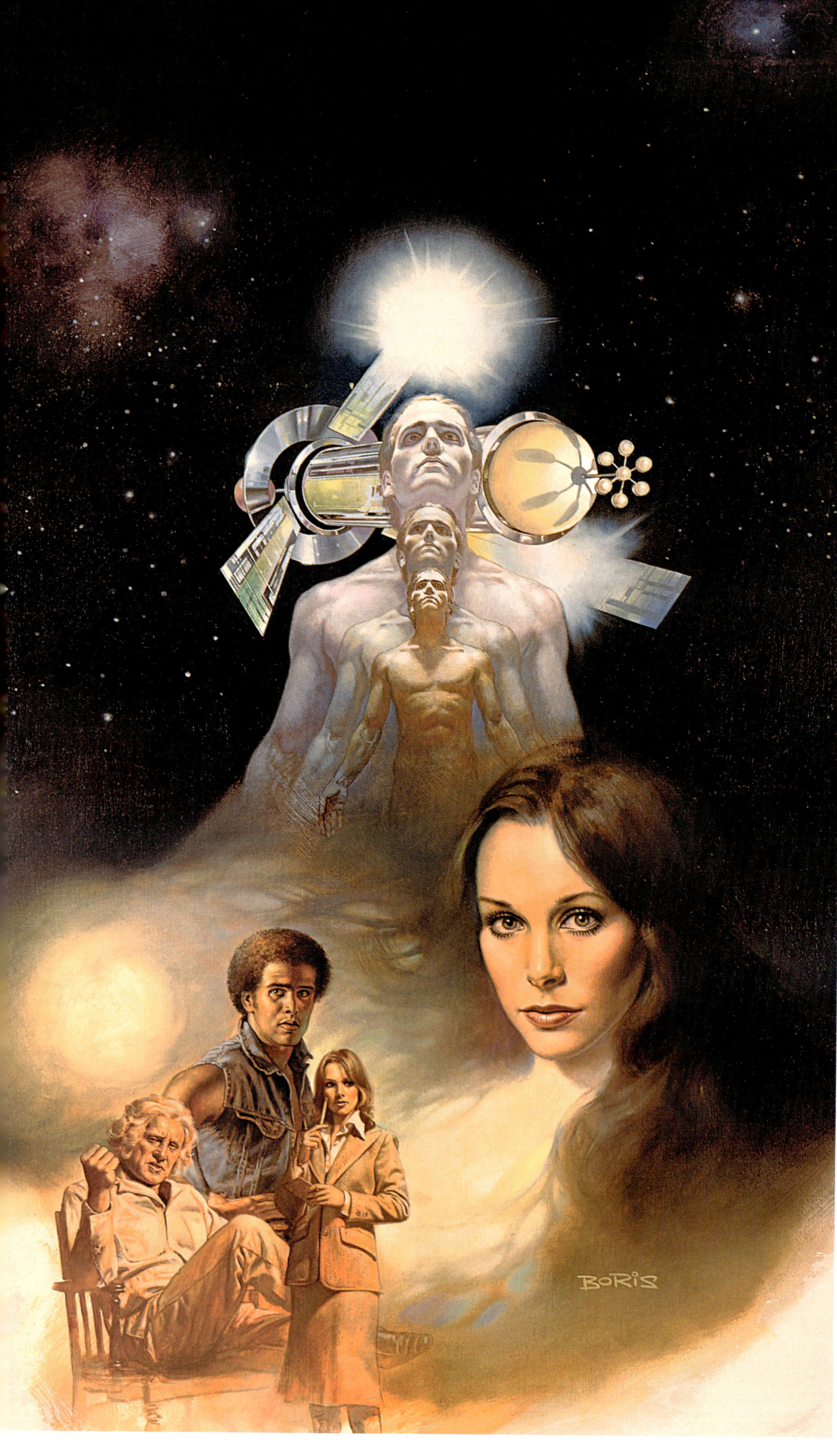

COLONY IN SPACE

1979, Boris *(left)*

An early book jacket that required five different models, far more than Boris would consider now. In fact this design generally looks too cluttered to him now, though he's still pleased with the picture.

MOVIE POSTER

1979, Boris *(right)*

At this time it was the custom of advertising agencies to commission up to twenty different artists to design posters for the same film and then choose just one. Sometimes agencies did this even when they were just bidding for the contract of promoting a film. This put a lot of quite enjoyable work Boris's way though most of it, including these three pictures, was not used for its original purpose.

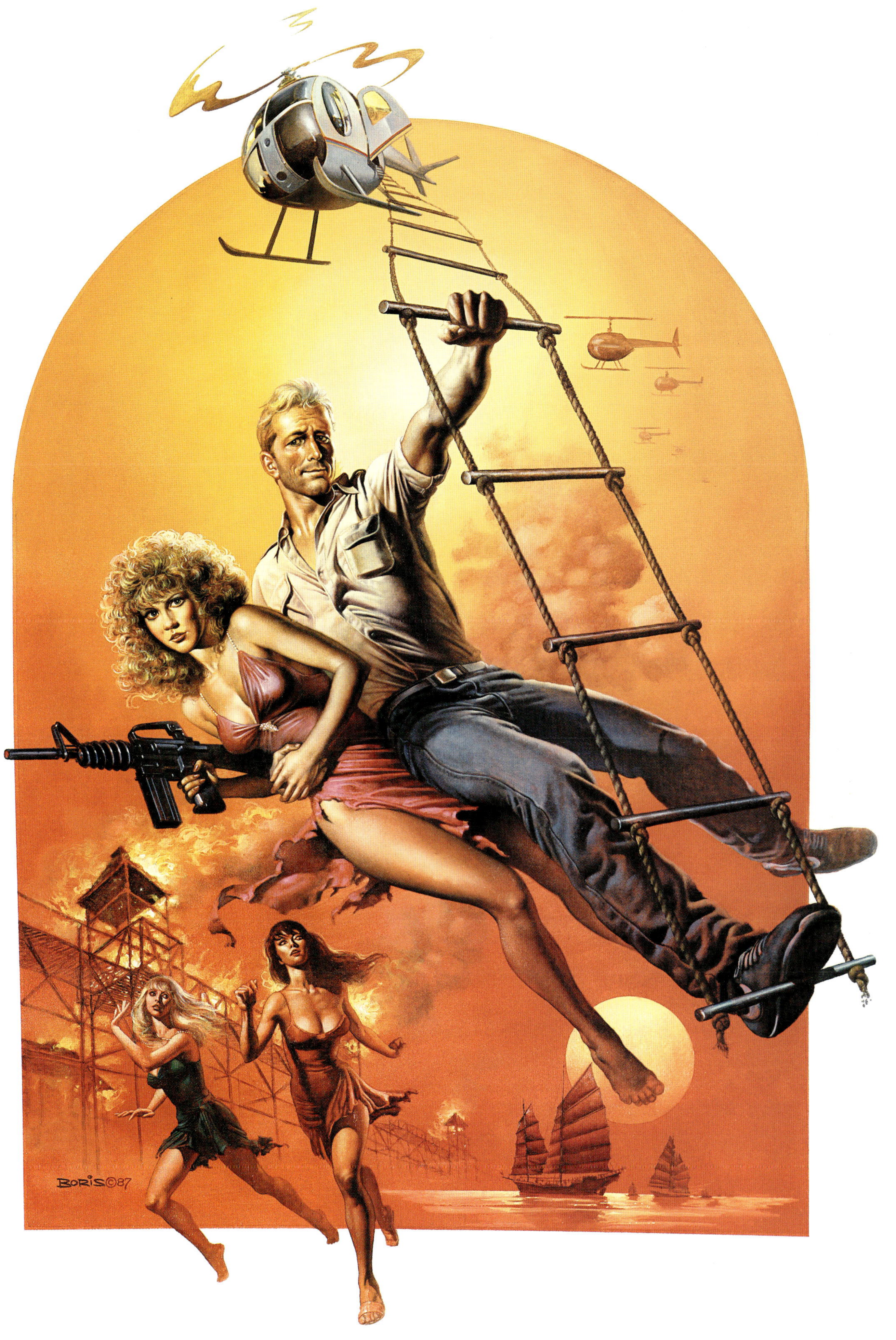
BORIS©87

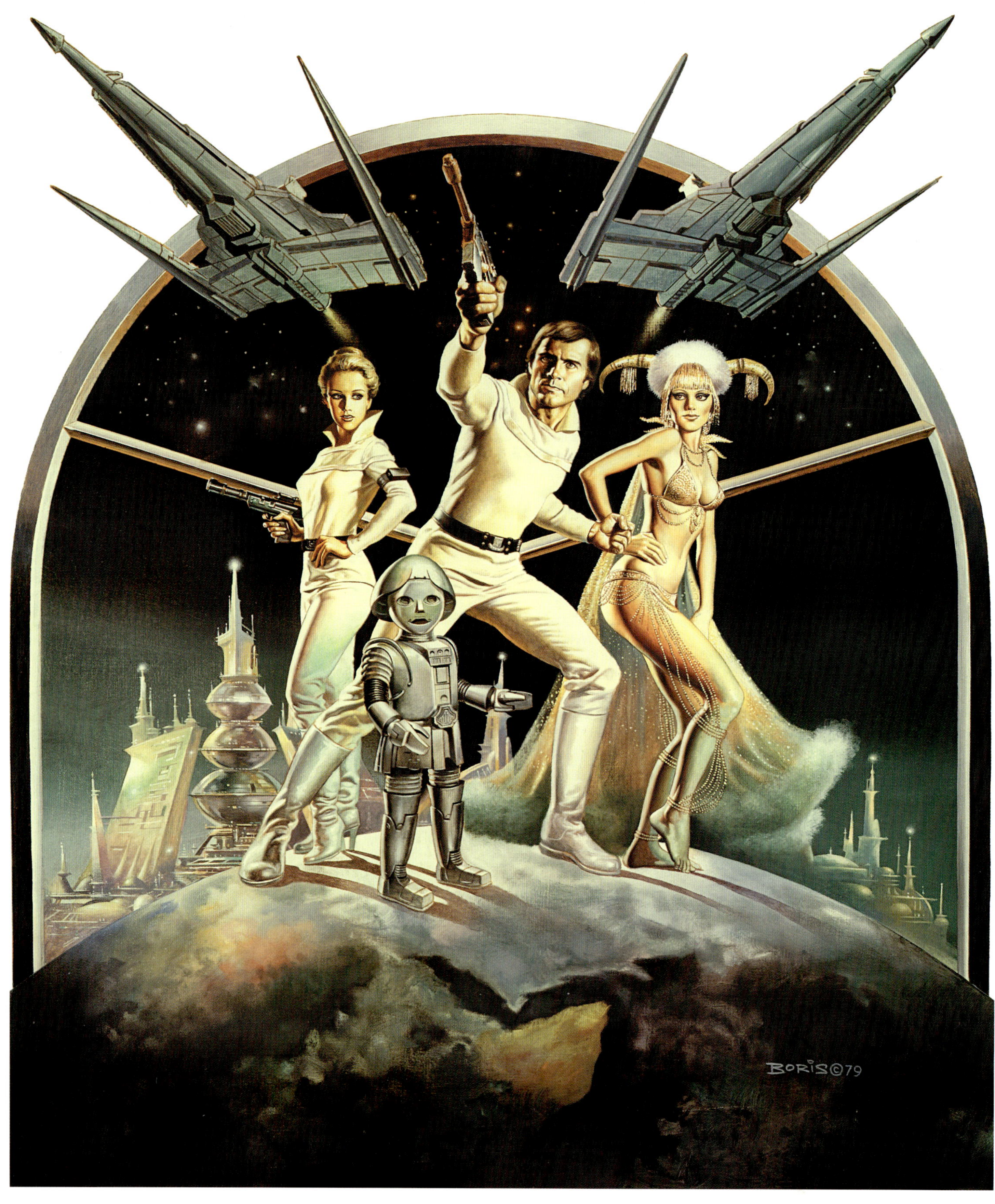

BUCK ROGERS
1979, Boris